Regional Policy
and Planning for Europe

edited by
MORGAN SANT

with a foreword by
LORD ZUCKERMAN

SAXON **S** HOUSE LEXINGTON BOOKS

Published by

SAXON HOUSE, D. C. Heath Ltd.
Westmead, Farnborough, Hants., England.

Jointly with

LEXINGTON BOOKS, D. C. Heath & Co.
Lexington, Mass. U.S.A.

C.C

ISBN 0 347 01045 8
Library of Congress Catalog Card Number 74–3918
Printed in Great Britain
by Unwin Brothers Limited
The Gresham Press, Old Woking, Surrey

REGIONAL POLICY AND PLANNING FOR EUROPE

Contents

14 DISCUSSION AND EPILOGUE

List of figures

List of tables

Foreword

Central government has an immediate interest in what happens in the regions, and the broad lines of regional policy necessarily have to be agreed at a national level. It could hardly be otherwise, since the objectives of regional policy — whether the relief of localised pockets of high unemployment, or limiting the expansion of congested conurbations, or achieving a balance between population and environmental resources — essentially relate to the better management of our national resources. A coherent national development plan implies wise policies for the regions.

These therefore have to be relevant, rational and realistic. Their design can undoubtedly be aided by the kind of theoretical analysis which pays attention not only to objectives, but also to local institutions, to technological change and, not least, to the actual process of social change as it occurs. The contributions in this volume represent an important attempt to meet the requirement for a more informed debate on regional policy, made all the more necessary following Britain's accession to the European Economic Community.

It is clear that we need 'rolling' policies. Regional plans cannot be rigid. There is not just the problem of obsolescence; we also have to deal with the unpredictable. I would say that over the past twenty years our lives have been as much, if not more, conditioned by such practical developments as nuclear and solid-state physics, or antibiotics and pesticides, as by any single set of social decisions. These things represent one class of the unpredictable; they came about because of a few very clever people who, at the time, had no possible vision of the social consequences of their discoveries.

Planning and policy-making will therefore always remain immensely difficult, not only because of the unpredictable and because so many variables have to be taken into account, but also because of inevitable conflicts of interest. The fact that progress is made at all is largely a result of the willingness and ability of individuals, such as the contributors to this volume, to explore and analyse the problems which beset regional policy and to agree about methods by which they can be solved — or at least ameliorated.

Zuckerman
Professor at Large
University of East Anglia

Preface

> ... a Commission should forthwith issue to inquire into the causes which have influenced the present geographical distribution of the industrial population of Great Britain and the probable direction of any change in that distribution in the future; to consider what social, economic or strategical disadvantages arise from the concentration of industries or of the industrial population in large towns or in particular areas of the country; and to report what remedial measures if any should be taken in the national interest. (From the Royal Warrant to the Commission on the Distribution of the Industrial Population, 1937)

In the four decades since they were posed, the questions placed before the Barlow Commission have become no less relevant. They might have lost their importance if, in the intervening years, adequate solutions, which could be seen to have removed the causes for concern, could have been found for regional problems or to be in the process of quickly doing so. But this has not been the case. Although the policies emanating from Barlow, and subsequent reports, have been effective in shifting a large volume of industry and employment from richer regions to poorer ones, disparities still remain. Indeed regional policy has been described as a 'holding operation', preventing the gulf from growing wider but not materially reducing it either.

If this description is true, as most of the evidence seems to show, then a number of questions are raised. To start with the most basic: why has regional policy been no more than a holding operation? Is it because insufficient resources have been diverted to the problem regions? How much more could be diverted? Is it possible, in any case, to divert *enough* resources to reduce disparities to zero, or even to acceptable levels in a relatively short time? Perhaps, to be realistic, we should not expect more than a 'holding operation'. That, by itself, might be a worthwhile objective and its achievement a mark of success.

But human nature is rarely satisfied with the *status quo* and, no matter how successful past policies might be regarded, there are good reasons for continuing to discuss problems of regional policy and planning. Not the least of these reasons is that regionally based grievances continue to be voiced. A contemporary example lies in the demand by Scottish Nationalists for Scottish control over the revenues from oil brought ashore from the North Sea fields. Whatever one's view of the rationality of such a proposal, it is one that is seriously made, and requires serious attention. Whatever decision one makes on this, and similar, issues, one is bound to enter a discussion on regional policy.

Other, equally valid, reasons also exist. Social goals are rarely constant except under the broadest, almost meaningless, definitions. If, with limited resources, it is impossible to achieve them all then a list of priorities must be drawn up. This list (which in fact never exists, though we shall assume it does) may, from time to time, change its form, with some goals being promoted and others relegated. The cause of changes might be the achievement of one objective, the loss of relevance of another, or the emergence of a third. Thus, for example, in explaining patterns of industrial movement since 1945, it is necessary to balance the requirement of New Towns against those of the problem regions. In the 1950s the relief of metropolitan congestion held a greater priority than the demands of the peripheral regions and absorbed a disproportionate volume of industrial movement. Not until the 1960s did the objectives turn again in favour of the peripheral regions and industrial movement diverted accordingly, through the more rigorous control of industrial development certificates and more generous inducements to locate in the assisted areas.

But, if society can change its goals in relation to a static set of problems, consider how much more complex and demanding the situation becomes when the problems themselves are subject to change. No sooner may something be done to ameliorate conditions in one area than another issue arises elsewhere. Often these are linked, as the Hunt Committee on the Intermediate Areas discovered. Aid to the least viable regions can exacerbate the problems of their marginally more viable neighbours. With growing awareness of regional and sectoral interdependencies, forecasting such effects as this ought to be — but rarely is — fairly simple. Much less tractable is the forecasting of technological innovations and their impact on regional economies, or the exogenously determined decline of localised industries.

Another dimension of change is institutional. Until 1973 the United Kingdom enjoyed the relative simplicity of being a unitary state seeking to solve its own problems, by itself. Entry to the enlarged European Economic Community created a new dimension in policy and planning. Now one needs an awareness of regional interdependencies on a continental scale and has an extra, supra-national organisation, charged with the duty of balancing different demands and formalising a common policy to cover a range of problems far wider than those of a single country.

But, on a more mundane level, institutional modifications also occur within countries through the alteration of policy instruments. For example, without changing the overall policy (moving industry to peripheral regions), the institutional framework in Britain was exceptionally volatile, at least until 1972. Different areas have been designated for assistance and the type and volume of aid has been changed, with a rapidity bewildering to industrial decision-makers. The principle of stability has now come to be accepted, with the government intending to maintain the system of incentives introduced under the 1972 Industry Act until at least 1978. Even so, this does not prevent discussion about whether the incentives are the best ones, and how the system could be improved.

The catalogue of reasons for continuing to investigate the role and nature of regional policy need not be carried further. To summarise, regional development takes place against a minutely varied and dynamic backcloth. The social, political and economic environments are continually modified; goals and objectives may be altered; different policies may serve a single objective; and a single policy can employ different instruments.

The collection of essays which follows reflects this profusion. But, more importantly, the essays also bring order to it and succeed in projecting the discussion forwards in search of new ways of dealing with regional issues. All of them accept the need for public intervention in economic and social life; their concern is with the quality of that intervention. All of them are inspired by the changing conditions which affect policy and planning, not least the new requirements which result from Britain's membership of the EEC.

The papers fall broadly into five groups. Firstly, there is a set dealing with regional economic policies. Cameron leads with a critical review of British problems and responses. Outlining the causes of the problems he goes on to examine the major alternative strategies: unconstrained expansion in, and migration to, the southern regions of Britain, decentralisation of industry and raising the level of demand for the resources of the problem regions 'at source'. These are related, towards the end of the paper, to the future scale of regional problems.

Rhodes and Moore provide a more specialised and, possibly, more controversial contribution in which they argue that, in combination with the national policy of demand management which aims at maintaining full employment and a satisfactory balance of payments, British regional policy in the 1960s led to increased output, employment and real income. The benefits in terms of real disposable income, moreover, were shared by *all* regions. Included among these benefits is a reduction in levels of taxation. In making this case, Rhodes and Moore have obviously moved radically away from the view that the justification for regional policy is simply political and social.

Stabenow's paper[1] on regional policy in the European Economic Community takes us into a wider context. Noting the wide disparities which still exist and the stress which these impose, he asks how the EEC can move on towards full economic and monetary union in 1980 without first having a successful regional policy. The short answer, of course, is that it cannot and this was recognised in the Paris Summit Conference of 1972, which gave a high priority to correcting structural and regional imbalances. This, in turn, led to the preparation of the report on regional problems in the enlarged Community (the Thomson Report) in May 1973. Stabenow concentrates on the two main proposals — the Regional Development Committee and the Regional Development Fund — and describes the role and manner of operation of these instruments.

An overwhelming impression from Stabenow's paper is of the sense of urgency that exists in Brussels. No one can deny that there is virtue in this but it must be asked whether the targets and resources of the EEC are realistic, bearing in mind the size and diversity of the problems and the short time lapse between the Paris Conference (1972) and the intended implementation of economic and monetary union (1980). Allen's paper, which first examines the policies of individual members and then goes on to discuss policy at the community level, urges a more measured approach.

The second group of papers transfers attention away from the strictly economic side of regional policy towards the fabric of regional development. Goddard foresees an increasing convergence of urban and regional policies. In effect, this involves a continued shift from the particular to the general, culminating in the formulation of national settlement strategies rather than plans for individual cities or regions.

The same theme is developed by Boudeville. Taking as his starting point the growing interdependence of the regions in the EEC, he asks what role the development of urban systems can have in furthering the social and economic goals of the Community. Two types of systems co-exist within Europe: the classical hierarchy of central places found within less densely populated zones, and a set of burgeoning urban regions. Together they form a megalopolis circumscribed, at its extreme points, by Liverpool, Hamburg, the Swiss Plateau, Le Havre and Southampton and contain about 53 per cent of the population of the enlarged Community. Each type of system requires a different response from planners, both at the national and supra-national levels.

In the next group, which contains papers by Powell and Jay, attention is transferred to the regional dimension. The redistribution of resources ensuing from regional policies has to be accommodated within regional strategies and, on a more local scale, sub-regional structure plans. Two contrasting regions which have been the subject of strategic plans, the South East (1970) and the North West (1974) are discussed by Powell. Strategic plans clearly have an important role, as their terms of reference show. They have on the one hand to take account of past and present policies and decisions of local and central government and at the same time provide a framework plan to guide local authorities in their planning and preparation of structure plans and central government in its public expenditure and economic and social policies relating to a region's development. When one considers the size of the task facing strategic planning teams and the speed with which they must operate (the North West team was given two years to produce its study), one is forced to draw a parallel with the work of the Regional Policy Directorate General of the EEC and cannot be surprised that the strategic plans have evoked criticism.

Jay, writing against the background of the Strategic Plan for the South East, examines the basis for some of these criticisms. Confusion exists because of local government reorganisation, lack of experience in strategic and structure planning and uncertainty over national and European institutions. More specifically, in the South East the strategic plan barely considered Greater London (that was left to a separate plan) which, if nothing else, provides the motor for the region as a whole.

The fourth group focuses on institutional aspects of regional policies and policy-making. Donnison, after asking what regional policy is trying to achieve, moves on to assert a need for a better forum for debate at the regional level. However, the form this should take is not easily identifiable, for while Scotland, Wales and Northern Ireland all have a degree of autonomy and a local patriotism, the regions of England lack both. Furthermore, Donnison questions whether there are in England many decisions which are too big for local authorities to handle yet small enough for action at the regional level without intervention by central government. There is also the question of whether democratically elected institutions are necessarily the best bodies to pursue vigorous development policies, especially in those regions which most need such an approach.

This theme is continued by Gaskin in his exploration of the centre–region relationship, in which he asks what the regional input to policy is and what it should be. Accepting the case that central government could not tolerate the unpredictability of pressure on resources which wholesale devolution might bring about, he sees virtue in giving regions the power to exercise some selectivity in the encouragement of economic development. Regions vary in their possibilities, in their economic structures and in the kinds of new or revitalised activities that can be appropriately promoted within them. To a degree these are recognised in the 1972 Industry Act, but it is questionable whether this encourages sufficient local involvement.

Stewart introduces another view: that of industry. Looking first at the factors which influence industrial decision-makers, he then goes on to examine industry's reactions to the objectives and methods of regional policy in Britain. Since at least the time of Adam Smith it has been known that businessmen try to minimise risk usually, we might add, by quite laudable methods. To some extent government assists in this by diminishing the risks of operating in marginal locations. But prior to 1972 this was accompanied by uncertainty concerning both the overall objectives of government and the frequent changes in the instruments of policy, which tended to counteract the risk-diminishing assistance given to industry. Greater clarity of objectives, policies and instruments is an essential ingredient for success and, in turn, requires greater stability.

The same requirement is put forward by Diamond, though in a broader context. In particular, he stresses the need to make the *rate* of structural change the central focus of regional policy. A major part of the present shortcoming is that emphasis is put on the broad long-term perspective of the *direction* of change which, while essential, cannot be fulfilled without devising short-run aims which incorporate more specific statements about rates of change.

Lastly, Townroe examines a quite separate issue, the priorities for research in regional policy and planning. After examining the sources of pressure he provides a personal view of the fields of research which are likely to be most urgent in the foreseeable future. He then discusses some of the institutional problems and conventional wisdoms that need to be overcome, such as the current predilection for 'interdisciplinary studies' and the tendency to derive concepts, techniques and comparisons from North America rather than from Europe.

Of course, in thirteen papers it is not possible to represent every shade of opinion or to cover every question relevant to regional policy and planning. But all of them deal with urgent problems and although the majority are concerned with regional disparities there is an awareness in them that policies must be applied and that this, in turn, requires plans for the allocation of resources and improvement of opportunities within regions. No regional policy can be fully successful unless it is related to a positive restructuring of the economic and social landscape and, perhaps, also the physical environment. Much more could have been written about this side of the developmental equation but space and time placed their inevitable constraints on the programme of the original seminar.

Acknowledgements

We are grateful to the Ford Foundation for providing the support to bring together the contributors to this volume in a seminar at the University of East Anglia in September 1973. We hope that the appearance of the volume will justify their generosity.

Following that meeting we had to work speedily to prepare the manuscript for publication and we are grateful to the authors for their help in meeting editorial deadlines. We also received valuable assistance from Mr L.W. Bear, who transcribed the discussions, Miss Scott Glover, who typed the manuscript, and Miss Barbara Satchell who redrew the maps.

Finally, we owe a debt of gratitude to Lord Zuckerman, who not only provides the Foreword to the volume but also was chairman of the seminar.

Morgan Sant

Note

[1] Stabenow's paper was written in the autumn of 1973 — before the energy crisis following the Arab—Israeli war. Final agreement of the terms of the Community's regional policy was delayed by the need for emergency debates on energy policy and other issues. As a result the events expected in December 1973 had still not occurred when this book went to press. However, this does not affect the basic text of his paper and no editorial alterations have been made.

In passing, it might be noted that the delay was accompanied by vigorous 'horse-trading' in the December debates, in which energy policy, foreign policy and regional policy were regarded by the participants as pawns to be manipulated until a consensus could be achieved.

One might reflect that the patron saint of European unity is St Willibrord, to whom the inhabitants of Echternach, in Luxemburg, have, over the centuries, dedicated a peculiar dance which consists of taking five steps forward and three back (Fritz Wirth, *The Times*, 8 January 1974).

1 Regional Economic Policy in the United Kingdom[1]

G. C. Cameron

Introduction

For forty years British governments of all political hues have sought to narrow inter-regional differences in employment opportunities, personal incomes, social service provision and environmental quality. To be sure, there have been ebbs and flows in their concern. Indeed, the Churchill government in the 1950s considered that the regional problem had been solved and took steps to reduce central government activity. By the late 1950s, however, another Conservative government, that of Macmillan, was once again active at the regional level, this time in response to massive employment reductions in several basic sectors, such as coalmining, railway workshops and textiles. Many of these sectors were heavily concentrated in the older industrial and largely peripheral areas of the North of England, Scotland and Wales. The passing of the latest regional measure, the Industry Act of 1972, confirms that all three major political parties continue to accept that the problems of restructuring these older industrial areas have not been solved and all are committed to powerful measures and large expenditures to improve their economic performance. Furthermore, all of these parties — though with varying degrees of enthusiasm — accept the need to control the rate of development of the relatively prosperous core (or central) regions of the South and the West Midlands of England with the overall objective of steering some of the new growth to the areas of employment lag. As a result of this continuous and continuing concern, the UK has developed a battery of inducements, controls and government investments, which, without any shadow of a doubt, have affected the spatial incidence of the demand for labour and consequently the level of employment in, and the rate of out-migration from, these peripheral areas.

It would be quite erroneous to detect a pursuit of *national efficiency* as the major justification for national measures to aid the peripheral regions. Whether in the form of curbing London's stranglehold over decision-making, the acceptance of a work-to-the-workers programme, or in the blatant exercise of political influence over the siting of government facilities, *equity* arguments are constantly to the fore. On this level the regional problem consists of grievances, often ill-defined but acutely felt, which are laid at the door of government and couched in terms of the right to work, the right to a secure future, or the right not to have to migrate — and so on. Typically the response to such claims, which is greatly affected by the disparity between the peripheral regional rate of unemployment and that of the nation, is directly political and very often *ad hoc*.

And yet, although political pressures and political responses give regional policy its main justification and ever-changing vitality, *efficiency* arguments are never far away. In this context, efficiency could have two meanings. The first is concerned with the maximisation of the growth in the real GNP, probably with a long-run perspective in mind. The second concerns the use of public resources in such a way that the goals of regional policy are achieved efficiently. This might imply a criterion such as the minimum of social costs for the achievement of a given quantum of regional goals. It is with both kinds of efficiency arguments that this chapter is concerned.

The causes of the regional problem

From an economic point of view, the starting point is a persistent tendency towards disequilibrium in the inter-regional labour market, with some regions operating at a level of unemployment significantly short of the full-employment position — despite continuous outflows of labour — and other regions suffering persistent labour shortages — despite continuous labour in-migration both from within the country and from overseas. The consensus is that the basic cause of this problem is found in inter-regional differences in the structure of industry and the differing increase in the *demand* for labour, region by region, which derives from this differential structure of activity. A secondary cause is the relatively high rates of natural increase of labour supply in precisely those regions in which the economic structure does not generate a rapid increase in job opportunities. In the peripheral regions, the reduction of employment in major industries and their inadequate replacement by new fast-growing sectors causes a slower growth in the demand for labour than in the supply of labour. Surpluses of labour grow and persist. In contrast, the central or core regions, which capture the bulk of the fast-growing manufacturing and service sectors, experience a growth in demand for labour which exceeds the available sources of local labour supply.

In these circumstances labour, and inactive population, tend to flow out of the peripheral regions and into the fast-growing regions. A reverse process, that of capital flowing to the regions of labour surplus and away from the regions of labour scarcity, is also set in motion. However, even in conditions of a high aggregate level of demand, these equilibrating mechanisms are never powerful enough to prevent persistent regional imbalance. This occurs largely because there are frictions which prevent adequate inter-regional flows of labour and capital. With regard to labour, the major constraint is the broad degree of regional uniformity in wages for given skills achieved by nationally organised trade unions. Thus, regardless of differences in productivity, cost of living or demand and supply conditions, wage rates within the lagging regions tend to follow the pattern set by bargains made in national negotiations or in the core regions. This effectively restrains the outflow of labour from the lagging regions and removes an obvious inducement which could attract large flows of capital to such regions. In terms of capital mobility, moreover, the possibilities of achieving an *adequate* rate of return within a lagging region may be clouded by personal prejudice or insufficiently obvious when set against personal preferences for the known locale. In any event, capital may not flow into the problem regions on a scale sufficient to restore equilibrium. Thus, in the absence of any mechanism for adjusting regional factor prices, the structure of economic activity changes all too slowly and labour-market disequilibrium persists (McCrone, 1973).

In some circumstances — and apart from the social and political problems associated with marked disparities in employment conditions — this kind of intra-regional disequilibrium would not present a serious *economic* problem if (a) the volume of unemployment and underemployment in the peripheral regions was small; (b) the natural growth in labour supply within the core regions was large; (c) there were large reservoirs of low-productivity agricultural labour which could be drawn into higher-productivity activities within the core regions.

None of these conditions apply to the UK. As we shall see, the peripheral regions contain large reservoirs of unemployed labour, the growth in labour supply in the economy as a whole is expected to be only 3 per cent between 1967 and 1981, whereas population is expected to grow by 8 per cent[2] and there are now no substantial reservoirs of agricultural labour available for transfer to urban-based activities. It follows that the reserves of labour which exist in the peripheral regions represent a valuable resource which, if drawn into employment, could make a substantial contribution to national employment and national output.

There are three alternative strategies by which this spare labour capacity could be absorbed into national production. The first is to permit

3

unconstrained output expansion in the areas of labour shortage so that earnings for given skills are raised and migrants from the problem regions are sucked into these fast-growing regions. This movement could be stimulated by information, cash allowances or other inducements to the migrants. A second alternative is to force activities to decentralise from major centres within the core regions, either by physical controls of one kind or another, or through a use of taxes, fees for development and so on. The third alternative is to devise policies which directly raise the level of demand for the resources of the problem regions at 'source' so that unemployment is reduced, out-migration curbed and the structure of economic activity adapted.

Post-war governments' almost total preference for the second and third courses of action have been buttressed by a number of critical tenets of economic wisdom. The first argument concerns the generation of inflation. If the demand for labour within the core regions is expanded rapidly, then migration from the labour surplus areas would not increase markedly in the short run. In conditions of a relatively inelastic supply curve of labour, large wage-rate and earnings increases would be inevitable. These increases would then be spread quickly by nationally organised trade unions to all other regions of the country, including the labour-surplus areas. The obvious result would be that the marginal increment to national output could only be achieved with a very large marginal increase in labour costs. In contrast a similar expansion of demand for labour in the surplus areas would not be inflationary, since there would be a far greater elasticity of labour supply at existing wage rates.[3] This argument has frequently been used to justify control of industrial development in the inflation-generating regions.

A second set of arguments concerns the long-run effects of encouraging increased migration out of the labour-surplus areas and into the core regions. Whilst it is reasonable to expect that most migrants would be economically better off as a result of their move, their improvement in welfare would have to be set against losses incurred by others. For example, net out-migration would cause a reduction in expenditure upon local goods and services (i.e. non-basic production) and these negative multiplier effects could depress factor incomes and possibly employment levels. Moreover out-migration may result in an under-utilisation of social and economic overhead capital within the population-losing areas and a duplication of capital in the migrant-receiving areas. Over the long run too, persistent net out-migration may be discriminant in that it creams off the most talented and vigorous sections of the labour force. Obviously, given the size of the 'standard regions',[4] the flows in and out are liable to be on

4

a large scale. However, the assumption here is that the population-losing regions are liable to lose more from out-movement than they gain from in-movement of the highly productive sectors of the labour force. If this is indeed the case, then the labour-surplus areas are liable to have a diminished capacity for entrepreneurship and, *ceteris paribus*, a diminished appeal to mobile enterprises seeking reserves of proficient labour. Viewed from the fast-growing regions on the other hand, any further in-migration is liable to increase the unwanted externalities of growth, such as traffic congestion, noise, air and water pollution and possibly environmental decay. More specifically, migration into London and Birmingham, which are assumed to have reached an excessive population size, could complicate the problems of dispersing population to planned overspill and new town settlements in the respective outer metropolitan areas.

The final and most critical assertion is that every major surplus region is urbanised, industrialised and accessible to every region, has a labour force of broadly equal productivity (after training) for any given skill and is open to the flow of general technological information and, more particularly, to knowledge on the 'best practice'. Accordingly, since the heart of the regional problem is how to adjust out-dated industrial structures, each problem region possesses the necessary attributes to make this reconstruction possible and successful. This means that over the long run the bulk of British manufacturing capacity can operate just as profitably within the labour-surplus regions as in the core regions. It follows that the use of government subsidies to encourage an inflow of capital to the problem regions need only cover the short run. Such subsidies are assumed to be needed partly to overcome ill-informed business prejudices or lack of information, partly to cover the real short-run costs of settling in and partly to compensate for the short-run costs of an environment weak on specific or industry-external economies. However, as these new industries expand and internal and external economies of scale are reaped, continuing state support will become unnecessary. Of course, there is every reason to use subsidies to stimulate increments of expansion of the efficient firm once it is well established within the problem region. The objective here is simply to improve the rate of return from producing within the labour-surplus areas, relative to other unassisted areas, with the hope that this will result in a bigger share of expansion projects being undertaken in areas of labour surplus than would have occurred without the subsidies.

Therefore on all these grounds — the more elastic supply of labour at existing wage rates, the relatively greater supplies of social and economic-overhead capital, the possibilities of output expansion without unwanted externalities and the underlying conditions for competitively efficient pro-

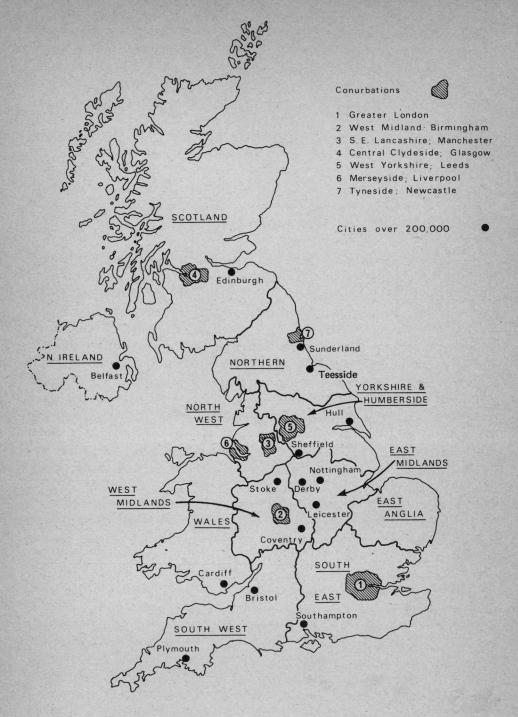

Fig. 1.1   Economic planning regions in the UK, 1971

duction — the assertion is that a given increment to national output can be achieved at a lower social cost by expanding the demand for labour within the labour-surplus regions rather than within the core regions. Similarly, over the long run, such a policy can avoid the process of cumulative decline which is assumed to accompany persistent out-migration of the most talented.

In a later section we will attempt to evaluate the validity of these assertions but first we must provide some measures of the extent of the regional problem.

The dimensions of the regional problem

Despite thirty years at, or close to, national full employment during which the annual unemployment rate has ranged from a low of 1·1 per cent in 1955 to a high of 3·8 per cent in 1972, certain of the peripheral regions (called development areas officially) have suffered persistently high unemployment, low female-activity rates, relatively low per capita incomes, persistent net losses of population from out-migration and severe environmental decay. All of Northern Ireland, and the bulk of the two other Celtic regions, Scotland and Wales, together with parts of the north, north west and south west of England tend to display all or many of these symptoms of economic distress. Taken together, these areas contain more than 20 per cent of the UK's $55\frac{1}{2}$ million population, a roughly equal proportion of its 24 million labour force and 40 per cent of its land area.

Another type of problem area — often referred to as an intermediate area, since it is neither prosperous nor in deep economic distress — shows all the signs of incipient economic difficulties. Here the symptoms are relatively low income growth, out-migration and environmental decay and a general economic climate which does not seem conducive to new investment and a broadening of narrow economic structures. If these areas — which are largely concentrated in parts of Lancashire and the mining areas of south Yorkshire and north Derbyshire — are included in the problem category, then no less than 44 per cent of the UK's population is covered.[5]

In the development areas, unemployment rates typically run 50 per cent to 100 per cent above the national rate (Table 1.1). In contrast the South East has unemployment rates persistently and substantially below the national average. There is nothing ephemeral in this situation. Indeed the persistency of the problem is shown by the fact that the regional rank order of unemployment rates has remained unaltered during the last fifty years (Brown, 1968).

7

Table 1.1

Unemployment rates in the regions
(averages of monthly figures, per cent)

	1960	1961	1962	1963	1964	1965	1966	1967	1968	1969	1970	1971*
South East	1·0	1·0	1·3	1·6	1·0	0·9	1·0	1·7	1·6	1·6	1·6	1·7
East Anglia						1·3	1·4	2·1	2·0	1·9	2·2	2·7
South West	1·7	1·4	1·7	2·1	1·5	1·6	1·8	2·5	2·5	2·7	2·9	3·0
East Midlands	1·0	1·1	1·6	2·0	1·0	0·9	1·1	1·8	1·9	2·0	2·3	2·5
West Midlands						0·9	1·3	2·5	2·2	2·0	2·3	2·4
Yorkshire and Humberside						1·1	1·2	2·1	2·6	2·6	2·9	3·1
North West	1·9	1·6	2·5	3·1	2·1	1·6	1·5	2·5	2·5	2·5	2·7	3·1
North	2·9	2·5	3·7	5·0	3·3	2·6	2·6	4·0	4·7	4·8	4·8	4·9
Wales	2·7	2·6	3·1	3·6	2·6	2·6	2·9	4·1	4·0	4·1	4·0	4·1
Scotland	3·6	3·1	3·8	4·8	3·6	3·0	2·9	3·9	3·8	3·7	4·3	5·0
Northern Ireland	6·7	7·5	7·5	7·9	6·6	6·1	6·1	7·7	7·2	7·3	7·0	7·0
UNITED KINGDOM	1·7	1·6	2·1	2·6	1·7	1·5	1·6	2·5	2·5	2·5	2·7	2·9

* First four months only, seasonally adjusted.

Source: Department of Employment, *Gazette.*

The principal cause of this relatively high unemployment is not to be found in seasonal factors, labour-market imperfections or the incidence of unemployables. In large measure differences in unemployment levels, region by region, can be attributed to differences in the pressure of demand for labour. As a result the growth in the employed labour force in the last 50 years has varied markedly region by region. For example, Table 1.2 shows the marked disparity between the growth performance of Northern Ireland, the northern group of regions and Wales between 1921 and 1961 as contrasted to the southern and midlands group of regions. In Northern Ireland, Wales, Scotland and the north west of England, there was either an absolute decline or a stationary condition, whereas all of the midlands and southern group expanded their employed labour force markedly. Though these disparities in employment growth have been somewhat more muted in recent years, they still persist, as Table 1.3 shows quite clearly.

Estimates of the number of unemployed workers actively seeking work who would require to be employed before every region contained only

Table 1.2

Percentage increases in the occupied population at work, 1921—61*

Region	Percentage change
Northern Ireland	− 4·6 †
Wales	+ 0·3
Scotland	+ 1·0
North West	+ 1·3
Yorks and Humberside	+ 7·9
North	+ 10·8
East Anglia	+ 20·4
East Midlands	+ 26·5
South West	+ 29·3
West Midlands	+ 39·9
South East	+ 41·3

*   As percentages of total employment in 1921.
†   Period 1926—61.

Source: Lee, C. H., 1971.

Table 1.3

Percentage increases in employees in employment, 1953—66

Region	Percentage change
Scotland	+ 3·0
North West	+ 4·0
Wales	+ 6·6
North	+ 6·9
Yorks and Humberside	+ 9·1
East Midlands	+ 15·3
South East	+ 18·6
South West	+ 18·6
West Midlands	+ 18·9 †

Source: Brown, A. J., 1972.

unemployables, or those affected by seasonal or frictional factors, have varied enormously. However, as a minimum, 100,000 jobs would have been required in the late 1960s to achieve this goal.

Accompanying high unemployment in many regions is a low regional activity rate, especially for females. With a national activity rate of just under 40 per cent in June 1968, for example, only 30 per cent of the females aged 15 and above were in the labour force in Wales whereas no less than 43 per cent were economically active in London and the South East (Table 1.4). Given this degree of variation, one estimate has indicated that if every region had its age-specific activity rate raised to that of the highest attained anywhere within the nation then nearly 900,000 women would be added to the 8·8 million women in the 23 million labour force (Brown, 1972, p. 214).

Generally speaking the development areas not only suffer from a persistent under-utilisation of their human resources, they are also the poorest regions. Certainly the differences in real consumption per head are not great and, if we exclude Northern Ireland, only range from a high of 7 per

Table 1.4

Activity rates, standard regions, June 1968* (per cent)

New standard regions	Male and female	Male	Female
South East	59·7	77·9	43·4
East Anglia	48·5	64·6	33·1
South West	47·0	63·5	32·2
West Midlands	60·2	78·4	42·6
East Midlands	56·3	74·1	39·3
Yorks and Humberside	56·1	74·7	38·8
North West	58·1	75·9	40·1
North	51·8	70·0	34·8
Wales	47·1	65·6	30·1
Scotland	56·4	74·5	40·4
Northern Ireland	48·9	64·0	35·2
United Kingdom	56·2	74·1	39·8

* Employees as a percentage of the home population aged 15 years and over. See *Abstract of Regional Statistics*, 1969, no. 5.

cent above the national norm in the South East to 10 per cent below in northern England and the North West (Table 1.5).

This narrow range is largely due to a high degree of uniformity in regional gross product per head. Although this tends to have a wider range than that of real consumption with a low in 1961 of 85 per cent of the national figure in Wales and a high of 115 per cent in the South East, this range is further narrowed by progressive taxation, central financing of the social services and a relatively low cost of living in many of the development areas as compared to London.

Apart from the effects on the environment of dereliction and industrial obsolescence, of major concentrations of slum dwellings, which once housed the artisans of the burgeoning Victorian cities, and the limited range of services appropriate to relatively low incomes, the final indicator of development-area malaise is found in the net migration trend. Three powerful processes are at work shaping the spatial distribution of British population. Of longest standing is the transfer of rural population to cities

Table 1.5

Inter-regional price indices and real consumption, 1964

	N	Y&H	NW	EM	WM	SE	SW	Wa.	Sc.
Price indices (GB = 100)									
Food	99	101	98	100	102	99	99	104	105
Housing*	82	85	92	79	89	129	88	80	89
Fuel & light	95	96	98	93	96	109	112	102	101
Travel to work	80	89	96	90	92	119	78	104	89
All goods & services	96	97	99	97	98	106	97	98	99
Consumers' expenditure (UK = 100)	86	91	95	91	105	114	92	90	93
Consumers' expenditure valued at GB prices	90	94	96	94	107	108	95	92	94
Consumers' expenditure plus beneficial current public expenditure[†]	90	94	97	94	105	107	95	94	95

*　Including maintenance
†　On goods and services

Source: A. J. Brown (op. cit., 1972). The figures are based on Central Statistical Office, *National Income and Expenditure 1964*, HMSO 1964; Ministry of Labour, *Family Expenditure Survey 1966*, HMSO 1967; Ministry of Agriculture, *Household Food Consumption and Expenditure 1964*, HMSO 1965; Ministry of Power, *Statistical Digest 1966*, HMSO 1967; Government Social Survey, *Labour Mobility in Great Britain 1953–63*.

and small towns. This has occurred and continues to occur throughout every region but quantitatively it is largely a spent force. The UK now has one of the smallest agricultural and natural-resource-based populations in the world: only 3 per cent of the labour force is now classified as engaged in agriculture and forestry. The second major process is the dispersal of population out of the central cities of the major conurbations and into the outer conurbation areas. In part this reflects the scarcity of land within the central cities and the consequent spread of suburbs across central-city boundaries, in part the necessity for new and expanding population settlements to occur outside the green belts, many of which have been given statutory enforcement. However, in addition to these largely private movements, there are also large movements of population and of industry under planned over-spill schemes typically to 'close-in' new towns and expanded towns though sometimes, as in the case of London, to centres as much as a hundred miles away from the origin of the migrants.

The final and, from our point of view, the most interesting process is the migration from the north to the south of the country. Between 1961 and 1966 more than 2 million people moved across regional boundaries and changed residence. In terms of net flow, the figure was 200,000. Approximately half of these net flows consisted of gains made by the South West and East Anglia at the expense of the South East. In contrast, the South East gained almost 28,000 from Scotland. As Brown has noted,

> Scotland shows net emigration to every other British region, the North to every one except Scotland. There is a general tendency for each region to receive from those to the north of it and to give to the south as if they formed a cascade, until at the bottom, the South-East's outflow surges into its westerly and north-easterly neighbours and even splashes into the East Midlands. (Brown, 1972, p. 258)

Taking internal and external migration together, the four regions north of the Trent[6] tended to lose 50,000 people per annum over the period 1961—66 whereas the rest of Britain was gaining over 75,000.

A number of points should be noted about this north-to-south migration pattern. It is clearly of long standing since it has occurred during periods of mass national unemployment as well as in the period of post-war full employment. Nevertheless, since the war no region has actually had a declining population. Apart from Scotland, where the net migration losses are very severe and almost equivalent to the natural increase, the internal growth in population in every other peripheral area has been approximately three times greater than the net migration loss (Table 1.6). Indeed, the actual gross movement of population across regional bounda-

Table 1.6

Change in population by region, 1951—69

Region	Net migration (thousands)	Natural increase (thousands)	Actual increase as per cent of natural increase
Scotland	− 579	+ 632	8·4
Northern	− 133	+ 344	61·3
North West	− 197	+ 523	62·3
Yorks and Humberside	− 142	+ 414	65·7
Wales	− 48	+ 169	71·6
West Midlands	+ 102	+ 604	116·9
East Midlands	+ 96	+ 342	128·1
South East	+ 515	+ 1,510	134·1
East Anglia	+ 135	+ 133	201·5

Source: Great Britain, Department of the Environment, *Long Term Population Distribution in Great Britain — A Study*, HMSO, 1971.

ries is, by the standards of most other countries, on a very limited scale — approximately $1\frac{1}{2}$ per cent of the population cross regional boundaries in any one year.

As a result of this relatively limited amount of inter-regional migration and the above-average rates of natural increase in the two regions with the most serious losses of population from migration — Scotland and northern England — the actual share of each region in total national population has changed very little in the last fifty years. Recent official projections (Department of the Environment, 1971) point to a continuation of this relatively slow process of regional population adjustment, for even Scotland, the region with the most sizeable proportionate drop in population, is expected to have three-quarters of a million more people residing in it by 2001 than the five million it had in 1951 (Table 1.7).

In sum, the differences in welfare across the British regions are small. Rural depopulation has already occurred to a very great extent. The domination of the primate city has declined — at least if measured in terms of population. Despite the inter-regional migration processes which constantly

Table 1.7

The changing regional distribution of population, 1921–69, and projected distribution to 2001

Region	Population 1921 (thousands)	Percentage distribution					Population 1969 (thousands)	Projected home population 2001 (thousands)	Percentage distribution 2001
		1921	1931	1951	1961	1969			
England									
Northern	3,019	7·06	6·78	6·39	6·32	6·19	3,346	3,634	5·64
Yorks and Humberside	4,095	9·57	9·61	9·22	9·01	8·90	4,810	5,435	8·44
North West	6,022	14·09	13·83	13·12	12·73	12·53	6,770	7,431	12·31
East Midlands	2,337	5·46	5·61	5·92	6·05	6·20	3,349	4,472	6·94
West Midlands	3,504	8·19	8·36	9·05	9·27	9·52	5,145	6,235	9·68
East Anglia	1,211	2·83	2·75	2·84	2·90	3·07	1,657	2,261	3·51
South East	12,317	28·80	30·22	31·10	31·81	32·02	17,295	20,762	32·22
South West	2,725	6·37	6·24	6·64	6·69	6·91	3,730	4,714	7·32
Wales	2,656	6·21	5·79	5·29	5·13	5·04	2,724	3,096	4·80
Scotland	4,882	11·42	10·81	10·43	10·09	9·62	5,195	5,891	9·14
Great Britain	42,769	100·00	100·00	100·00	100·00	100·00	54,022	64,431	100·00

Source: Great Britain, Department of the Environment, *Long Term Population Distribution in Great Britain*, HMSO, 1971.

shape the balance of population in favour of the South East, the South West, East Anglia and the West and East Midlands, the overall regional changes in population distribution, both historically and forecast, are on a modest scale. However, a high level of unemployment, low activity rates and often appalling environmental conditions create a continuing need for active measures to improve regional economic performance and the regional physical environment.

National goals for regional growth

For reasons which are largely related to a desire to leave policy objectives as fluid as possible in the face of Britain's seemingly endless struggles with balance of payment deficits, rampant cost inflation and puny private investment, both Labour and Conservative governments have resolutely shunned giving precise specification to the goals of regional policy and neither have shown any willingness to set quantified targets. Thus vague terms, such as the prevention of regional imbalance, the regeneration of the regions and so on are in common parlance. Nonetheless a careful reading of legislation, parliamentary debates and government statements on regional development shows quite clearly that the implicit goals are a reduction in the unemployment levels and an increase in the activity rates of the peripheral regions. The slowing-up of the drift of population out of the northern regions and into the South East appears to be a complementary goal. Per capita income convergence is never specified as a goal, presumably because it is assumed that employment growth in the peripheral regions will occur in growing industries and that this by itself will mould the income-generating characteristics of these areas to correspond to that of the nation as a whole.

It is crucial to stress the totally unquantified nature of these goals. In forty years of regional policy, no central government has publicly announced targets for the number of jobs to be created in all the problem regions over a specified future period. Similarly, although there are annual regional population projections[7] which necessitate inter-departmental agreement on inter-regional migration assumptions, a Cabinet unit which reports to the Chief Scientific Adviser to the Government on the social and economic implications of population growth and population distribution,[8] and a never-ending stream of official plans — which include population assumptions — for regions, sub-regions and metropolitan areas,[9] there are no regional population targets laid down by central government. This philosophy of non-quantified goals can best be captured through the

15

words of Anthony Crosland, then Secretary of State for Regional Planning in the last Labour government.

> I do not believe that ... a case has been made out for precise regional population targets although all governments have formed the view that we want to stop the drift to the south-east. I believe we have not got the quantifiable factors which would lead us to set targets. We do not want to stop inter-regional migration. We live in a democratic society ... where people are free to move from the places where they live ... and there is no region which cannot cope with a very considerable increase in population.[9]

Clearly this suggests that central governments tend to see no insoluble *physical* difficulties in accommodating the expected natural population increase of each and every region within regional boundaries. Moreover, although central governments have shown a preference for reducing the drift of the population from north to south, this is not seen as requiring precise migration and population targets for every region.

This desire by central governments to retain open-ended targets has been reinforced by the weakness of planning institutions at the regional level. In 1965, the newly elected Labour government created a nationwide set of economic planning councils and economic planning boards within the eight planning regions of England and within Scotland and Wales. The councils are not elected by the 'local' population but appointed by central government and tend to be composed of private citizens, public officials, trade-union representatives and leaders of industry, all of whom are supposed to represent the key sectors of regional society. The boards, on the other hand, consist of the senior government officials who direct a ministry's activities at the regional level.

When they were first established it was expected that these councils, with the assistance of the boards, would formulate long-term regional-development strategies which could inform and help mould the medium- and long-term plans of the central government for each and every region. Over the longer run it was anticipated that these institutions would be the first building blocks in the creation of elected regional governments which would remove much of the planning and decision-making from London.

The development of these institutions (which still exist) has been fitful. Their early strategies varied enormously in style, content and sophistication and there is no unequivocal evidence that the central government took particular notice of their conclusions. Certainly, as their sophistication has grown, the councils have played a useful role in evaluating government proposals for given regions and the boards have provided a needed regional forum for the exchange of information across ministry frontiers. But these are minor achievements. The reality is that the Labour government lost interest in the idea of powerful regional institutions. The Conservative government decided to follow this attitude. Thus the councils remain purely advisory bodies, have limited financial resources, lack legitimacy in that their members are not elected and have no rights to *openly* question central-government decisions affecting a given region. [10] The result is that the real power over resource allocation, spatial planning and inducements still rests at the centre and especially in the Treasury, the Department of Trade and Industry and the Department of the Environment.

The nature of government measures

Area designation

Ever since the Town and Country Planning Act of 1947 successive central governments have used a 'carrot and stick' approach to encourage private enterprise to help solve the problems of the peripheral regions. The carrots consist of a whole range of incentives backed up by a huge range of government actions, which seek to raise the level of investment and the demand for labour within the lagging regions. The stick consists of controls over new industrial and office buildings in some of the full-employment regions with the explicit objective of diverting some capital and enterprise to the problem regions.

Given this system of *positive* encouragements to growth and *negative* controls upon growth, the designation of areas into an assisted or controlled category is a crucial first step in a process which ultimately affects the spatial disposition of government resources, the spatial incidence of private investment and the level of consumption, employment and growth in the different regions.

The spatial building blocks are the ten economic planning regions — first designated in 1965 — which are used as the basis for all regional administrative machinery, for regional economic planning and for the subnational evaluation of government strategies which may affect the regions. Eight of these regions are in England, and Scotland and Wales make up the two other regions. Northern Ireland retains a large degree of planning and expenditure autonomy and is, to all intents and purposes, a separate entity (Figure 1.1). Of these ten economic-planning regions, only the south east of England and East Anglia do not have any areas in which some

17

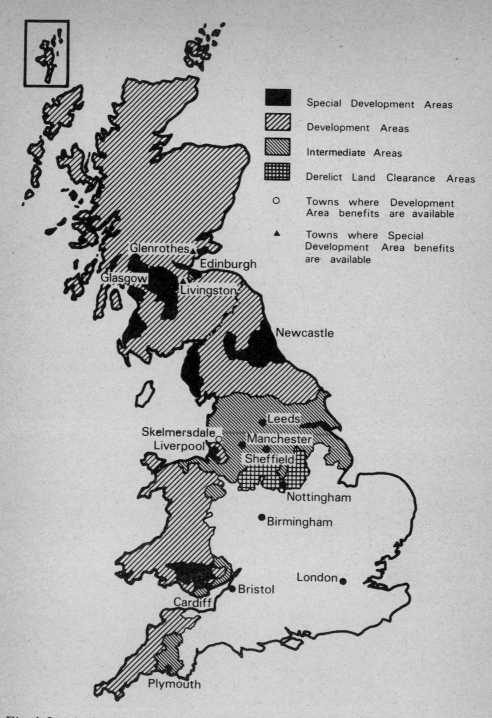

Fig. 1.2   Assisted areas in Great Britain, 1972

18

form of special government development assistance is available. In parts
— or in some instances the whole — of the other regions, varying types and
levels of assistance are on offer. Four different gradations of assisted area
are currently used and these are listed in ascending order of available
assistance and, more generally, of severity of economic distress (Figure 1.2).

(i) Derelict land clearance areas

In areas where severe despoliation of the environment from mining or
industrial working is currently creating difficulties in attracting and developing new sources of employment, the central government covers the bulk
(75 per cent) of the costs incurred in approved clearance schemes. The
northern parts of both the West Midlands and East Midlands are specifically covered by this designation.

(ii) Intermediate areas

Large parts of the north of England show many signs of incipient economic distress. Typically their economic structure is narrow, their physical
environment is poor, income growth is lagging and out-migration is a
constant drain on population growth. The limited range of inducements
and assistance presently on offer in these areas (which cover most of the
North West, all of Yorkshire and Humberside, and parts of the South West,
Wales and Scotland) are designed to encourage new industrial building,
training and retraining of labour and derelict land clearance.

(iii) Development areas

These represent the hard core of the regional problem and are primarily
designated because of their level of unemployment. Here the full range of
incentives and assistance is on offer. Currently, the whole of Scotland,
apart from Edinburgh, the whole of Northern England, Merseyside, the
bulk of Wales and a large part of the South West are development areas.

(iv) Special development areas

Within parts of the most northerly development areas (Northern England
and Scotland) and in the valleys of Wales, the expectation is that severe
unemployment will persist. In these special development areas, which originally embraced worked-out mining areas but now take in two major

industrial areas in Scotland (Clydeside and Dundee) and in the north east of England (around Newcastle and Sunderland) the highest rate of development grant is paid.

Taken together, these areas embrace almost half (48·2 per cent) of the British population of more than 54 million. Thus, in mid-1972, 4 per cent of the population was in derelict land clearance areas, 21·7 per cent in intermediate areas, 14·1 per cent in development areas, and 8·4 per cent in the special development areas.

Government controls and assistance

(i)   Controls
Outside development areas and special development areas, all new industrial building or extensions to existing industrial buildings of more than 10,000 square feet in the South East and 15,000 square feet elsewhere,. are subject to administrative scrutiny both by the Department of Trade and Industry and by the local planning authority. Before such developments are approved an *industrial development certificate* (IDC) is required and this can be refused if the production company 'could reasonably be expected to set up in an assisted area ... and/or ... is likely to add appreciably to existing pressure on resources principally on labour, in an area of labour shortages'.[11]

In this system of control the onus of proof rests upon the company (whether British-owned or foreign-owned), which must show that its long-run efficiency and/or, its export competitiveness, would suffer if it was diverted to a development or intermediate area. This proof must be based on calculations which allow for all the likely government inducements associated with development in the assisted area.

Office developments in London are also subject to control through an *office development permit* system. Proposals to erect offices are scrutinised against the criteria of whether the development 'would enhance London's prospects as an international financial and commercial centre'.

(ii)   Government assistance
The central government seeks to favour the development of the assisted areas in four ways. The most obvious is the host of financial inducements aimed at encouraging private investment and an expansion of the demand for labour within these areas. A second method is through the disposition of spatially discriminant government expenditures on both capital and current account. The third and fourth methods use the location of government offices and the nationalised industries to favour the assisted areas.

(a) Assistance to private enterprise

In the post-war period the British method of encouraging private enterprises to help meet the government's objectives for the assisted areas has never included direct tax reliefs or tax holidays. Instead, varying combinations of subsidies for the use of new capital and of labour have operated. On capital investments, the initial allowance for depreciation purposes to be set against tax has also been used in a variety of ways. In addition government grants to cover the costs of labour training or retraining are on offer and low-interest loans may be obtained in special circumstances.

Three broad categories of assistance apply, the first being the assistance given to particular industrial sectors. For example, in circumstances where a key privately-owned industry within the development areas has shown signs of imminent collapse, central governments frequently have stepped in, either with direct assistance for the industry as a whole or for particular companies. The classic case is the shipbuilding industry, which has received substantial grants and reduced-interest loans over a number of years.

The other principal method of encouraging private enterprise to aid in the achievement of the central government's regional goals is through a complex set of financial incentives. As we have already noted, post-war British governments have never used 'tax holidays' but instead a varying combination of financial incentives to encourage investment in fixed capital and in the employment of labour. Currently the key inducements consist of:

1 A development grant of 20 per cent of the cost of new plant and machinery and of new industrial building, with free depreciation on the plant and machinery and an initial depreciation allowance of 40 per cent on buildings. This contrasts with a no-grant situation in non-development areas but with free depreciation allowed on plant and machinery and a 15 per cent initial allowance on buildings. It is important to stress that the value of the grant can be offset against tax when depreciation is being calculated so that the real value of the grant for the company earning profits is approximately 30 per cent. Secondly, grants are not conditional upon employment creation.

2 A regional employment premium, an *ad hominem* subsidy, paid to manufacturing concerns which employ labour in the development areas. It was introduced in 1967 with an initial life of seven years and is due to be phased out after September 1974. When first introduced it represented a subsidy of approximately 7 per cent of the average earnings of male manual workers. Its value early in 1973 was probably less than 4 per cent.

21

3   Selective assistance, normally in the form of low-interest loans but also by interest relief and removal grants may also be paid to companies moving to a development area or already operating there. The criteria for allocation is wide-ranging: from unemployment creation to employment stabilisation.

4   Training grants to offset the cost of training or retraining labour in the development areas can be paid in authorised schemes.

Taken together, the magnitude of these grants and loans is substantial. The official estimate is that, excluding REP, £250 million will be required in the financial year 1973/74 though this largely depends upon the volume of new private investment. In fact, approximately £200 million will be available for development grants, £75 million for selective assistance and a very small amount, £2 million to £5 million, for training grants. If this is measured in terms of total manufacturing costs, Wilson (1973) has calculated that the development grant on its own will give development area producers a cost advantage of between 1 and $2\frac{1}{2}$ per cent — or, approximately, $2\frac{1}{2}$ to 5 per cent of net value added.

(b)   Government expenditure

In very simple terms this can be broken down into expenditures on real assets such as roads, advance factories, industrial estates, schools, ports, current expenditure from the government sector for specific goods and services, and equalisation payments to supplement local authority resources. On the first two of these items, regional criteria enter quite explicitly. For example, additional real expenditures for the development areas are typically allocated as a counter-cyclical device or, more normally, as an inducement to capital, for population redistribution purposes, or as a general method of improving the real standard of living. The government also favours the development areas through its own buying policy, giving special status to contractors in such areas, who are equally competitive with non-development area bidders.[12]

Once again the magnitudes involved are very large. The government tends to spend more than £10 million each year on building factories which are let at non-competitive rates and in its general spending on infrastructure clearly favours the DAs. For example, in 1968/69 total public investment in new construction was £2,340 million, and if the DAs had received their per capita share, then £826 million would have come to them. In fact the figure invested was over £100 million more than this.

(c)   Government offices

The government has dispersed its own offices, particularly out of central

London, and increasingly the claims of the DAs have been answered. Between 1963 and 1970, 22,000 office jobs were dispersed — 38 per cent of them going to DA locations. This proportion is expected to increase. Between 1965 and 1975 the dispersed flow will number approximately 30,000, over 50 per cent of which is promised for the development areas. Given that they have approximately one-fifth of UK employment the degree of favourable treatment is considerable.

(d) Nationalised industries

It is extremely difficult to be categorical about the extent to which nationalised industries are used to achieve regional employment and development goals. Certainly all nationalised sectors operate under profitability targets devised by central government. Accordingly, where specific loss-making activities are imposed upon an industry by the government, then it is the government which agrees the nature of the service and assumes the subsequent losses. Apart from a few limited loss-making activities, such as the air and steamer links to the Scottish islands, there are very few explicit services which are exclusively or largely regional in their impact. However, the level of employment in the problem regions may enter into nationalised-industry decisions in a way which is difficult to quantify but is none the less real. The most obvious example is the run-down of employment during the 1960s in the coal industry. Both the relatively slow rate of run-down and the personal subsidies which were used to induce early retirements, transfer to other coalfields and retraining, together with the provision of advance factories and the highest level of development assistance within the areas of closure, largely reflected an awareness of the acute unemployment problems which the problem regions would face if the industry and the government had sought to achieve a fast run-down.

Examples of where nationalised industries increase the growth of employment for explicitly regional reasons are harder to find, though the decision of the Conservative government not to allow consideration of a south east site (Maplin Sands) by the British Steel Corporation for a new steel-producing complex and the subsequent choice of a development area (Teesside) can be seen as an example of deliberate regional bias.

The effects of policy

It is obvious that the identification of the effects of policy is a particularly tricky exercise when policies have changed so frequently. Companies may have made decisions which favour development in the assisted areas without government aid, and some of the objectives of government investment are geared to long-run development goals.

Given these complexities we are fortunate in having two skilful and valuable exercises in measuring regional policy effects. Brown (1972), in comparing the performance of the four major development areas, Scotland, Wales, Northern England and the North West, over the years when policy was weak, 1953–59, and strong, 1961–66, concluded that something other than structure and changes in the characteristic performance of industries as such improved their relative performance by about 70,000 jobs per annum. This he ascribes to increases in mobile jobs (15,000 p.a.), increases in new jobs associated with IDC approvals within the four regions (30,000 p.a.) and multiplier effects in the service sectors (20,000 p.a.). He concludes:

> It seems likely from our previous discussion that most of the change in patterns of moves and approvals was due to the strengthening of policy. If this is granted, it is very hard to suppose that the improvement in the relative performance of the assisted areas (after eliminating structural factors) was not largely the result of strengthened policy also. (p. 318)

Brown has also concluded that, if policy had not been strengthened, the GNP would have been reduced by the order of £150–£200 million per annum. This, of course, assumes that workers remain unemployed in the problem regions and do not migrate to the regions of labour shortage. However, the real economic question, as already pointed out, is how much GNP, for a given social cost, would be increased by raising the demand for labour in the problem regions as opposed to raising the demand in the labour-shortage regions. No one, including Brown, has provided a definitive estimate of this kind.

The other careful estimate of regional policy effects has been made by Moore and Rhodes (1973). Using a modified shift-share technique, they concluded that over the years 1963–70, employment in manufacturing within the DAs was 12 per cent higher than it would have been if regional policies had been as 'passive' as in the 1950s and early 1960s. In quantitative terms, and allowing for multiplier effects, they estimated that over 200,000 extra jobs were generated by the active regional policies in force over these years. As far as private manufacturing investment was concerned, the policy effect was an extra £90 million per annum or a 30 per cent increase over the anticipated investment level.

Measured in more general terms, regional policy has contributed to an improvement in the relative unemployment level, has underpinned a rate

24

of per capita income growth which in most development areas has mirror-ed that of the nation and has probably increased the flow into the DAs of talented personnel. At least then, these measures can be regarded as a major holding operation, pending the structural reform which is essential to the more rapid growth of the development areas. There are, however, more fundamental questions which must be asked of regional policy, and these are discussed in the next section.

The validity of the regional arguments

In a country with as poor a post-war growth performance as the UK's it is patently obvious that if policies which improve the economic performance of specified regions only do so by retarding the overall growth of GNP, then this should be clearly perceived and justified. It has already been stressed that the economic case for raising the demand for labour in the high-unemployment regions is that this is the most efficient method of raising GNP *and* employment. The alternative method, it was argued, of allowing workers to migrate to the fast-growing regions could only generate additional economic costs and therefore was less efficient. It is not difficult to develop an entirely different case which would substan-tiate Samuelson's verdict (1969) that regional aid typically results in a 'sentimental distortion of the national production pattern'. Here the real fear is that some quantum of new development is either being stifled alto-gether or forced to occur in locations which are not the best of the alternatives available. Both effects would reduce the rate of growth in the British GNP. This section tries to reach some conclusion as to which of these views is more consistent with reality.

It is clear that some of the arguments which have been used against the movement of people from the problem regions have been rather poorly founded. The notion that out-migration results in severe negative multi-plier effects in the population-losing regions has probably been over-stressed. In terms of *primary* effects upon employment Brown (op. cit. p. 275) argued that in conditions of slack demand these effects are mini-mal.

> Unemployed outgoers obviously do not ... [affect employment] ... while employed outgoers bequeath their jobs, in effect, to local unemployed. Incomers either stay unemployed or, more probably, get jobs that would otherwise have gone to local people. In these conditions the primary effect of migration is simply that the number

of unemployed is reduced by the number of migrants in the region of origin, increased equally in that of destination. There are no primary effects on production in either region.

However, Brown concludes that there will be secondary effects as the spending power of the unemployed out-migrants (from unemployment benefit, supplementary benefit and personal savings) is transferred to the region of destination. His calculation is based on the realistic assumptions that the average unemployed person spends between 40 per cent and 60 per cent of the average employed person's expenditure and that 40 per cent of this goes into factor incomes within the region of the unemployed. Thus, for every unemployed out-migrant, 18–30 per cent of an average job might be lost. This means that for every 100 unemployed out-movers, perhaps 18–30 jobs in the region of origin might be lost. This figure, of course, relates only to the short run. The migrant's spending power in the new region will be subject to normal leakages and this, in time, will have positive factor income and employment effects in the migrant's origin region.

Thus, although the loss of any jobs in labour-surplus region is unwelcome, the highly integrated nature of the British spatial economy and the correspondingly large inter-regional leaks from any given regional expenditure mean that reductions in employment, following the migration of unemployed workers, tend to be relatively limited.

A similar conclusion applies to the argument that out-migration results in the under-utilisation or even the redundancy of social capital in the migrant-losing area and its duplication in the migrant-receiving area. We know that the *physical* life of most forms of infrastructure — such as roads, schools, hospitals, libraries and ports — is in excess of 50 years. Allowing for technological obsolescence and changing consumer preferences, perhaps an average of 2 per cent of social and economic overhead capital falls due for replacement each year. In broad terms this means that unless population as a whole is falling by more than 2 per cent, or alternatively there is a greater than 2 per cent reduction in the numbers of specific age or social groups which use particular types of infrastructure, then problems of redundancy and duplication do not apply. In fact, as we have already noted, no standard region has actually suffered a population decline in the last decade and, even in those sub-regions where population has declined, the percentage losses have typically been significantly less than 2 per cent (DOE, 1971). We can therefore discount this argument as a major justification for preventing out-migration from the problem regions.

One other alleged cost of out-migration was that the migrants would crowd into congested centres and increase the unwanted externalities of noise, air and water pollution, traffic congestion and perhaps environmental overcrowding. There is simply no evidence on the magnitude of these effects but two general points should be borne in mind. It is obvious that the migrants, in leaving their home environment may, by this action, reduce the unwanted externalities there. Thus before we could reach any definite conclusion on the net costs of migrant moves (that is unwanted externalities created in the new location minus unwanted externalities diminished in the old location) we would require a substantial amount of information on the characteristics of both locations. A second point is equally obvious but has often been forgotten in British population analysis. The popular fallacy is that all migrants from the problem regions crowd into the most densely populated areas of the biggest cities of southern England. Inner Birmingham and inner London, on this reckoning, must be bristling with newly-arrived Scotsmen, Tynesiders and Merseysiders. The reality is more complex. If we take, as an example, the census of population figures on migration flows between England and Wales and Scotland over the years 1961—66, we can readily dispose of the fallacy. Between these dates, Scotland lost 59,000 population from net migration flows. Over a third (35 per cent) of these net losses were to the south east of England and six other regions shared the bulk of the remaining net losses. The crucial point, however, is that, relative to the population size of the receiving areas, the biggest net loss was not to the South East but to the East Midlands, which picked up 15 per cent of the net losses, although it only had 7 per cent of the population of England and Wales in 1966. The bulk of these net losses was concentrated in Corby New Town, where steel-making has continuously attracted Scottish migrants ever since the 1930s. Even in the net losses to the South East, Greater London only picked up a 13 per cent share. The bulk of the net losses went to the fast-expanding outer metropolitan area and to the counties between London and Birmingham. A similar picture emerges in the West Midlands, with the conurbation only receiving $1\frac{1}{2}$ per cent of the net losses with the remaining share, $9\frac{1}{2}$ per cent, being concentrated in the outer conurbation area, especially around Coventry.

There is one further point to add. Even if peripheral-region migrants crowd into the central parts of London or Birmingham, it does not follow that unwanted externalities will increase. London, in particular, has been losing population rapidly for several years as people move to suburban areas, new towns and outer metropolitan areas. Thus between 1961 and 1966, Greater London gained from in-migration, as a percentage of population, 4·1 per cent but lost an equivalent of no less than 10·1 per cent of its population from out-migration.

If none of these arguments carry weight, three other factors in favour of raising the level of demand for peripheral region labour have greater intrinsic merit. Though the evidence is by no means unequivocal, it does appear that wage inflation tends to be initiated in the South East, and perhaps the West Midlands, and thereafter spreads to the other regions regardless of their factor market conditions. This has been corroborated in a general kind of way in a recent study which found that 'unemployment dispersion (over the standard region) exerted an upward pressure on aggregate rates of wage change of more than two percentage points in the post-war period'. (Thomas and Storey, 1971)

If this finding is valid, then a reduction in the demand for factors in those fast-growing areas already at the margin of full capacity and a transfer of that demand to the areas of labour surplus, would tend to slow the pace of wage inflation. The reasoning here is that the bargains struck in the surplus areas would result in lower wage rates than would have occurred in the areas of labour shortage and, secondly, that the bargains struck in the shortage areas would ultimately reflect the relative diminution of the pressure of demand. To quote Brown (1972, p. 331) once again, '... there seems to be a reasonable presumption that a more even spreading of the pressure of demand between regions would do something to reduce the speed of wage inflation, though it is difficult to quantify this effect.'

Other crucial points relate to the nature and magnitude of migration flows. If out-migration from the problem regions is officially encouraged there is a real possibility that this process will cream off the most vigorous and talented members of the losing region. Once again the census figures for Scotland between 1961 and 1966 provide some justification for this argument. Scotland's *net* loss of people was largely made up of economically active persons (60·4 per cent) who form only half of the overall population. Of these net losses, more than 60 per cent were in the socio-economic groups normally regarded as the most productive. These figures, of course, do not provide conclusive evidence that net out-migration has harmful long-run effects on Scotland's developmental capacity. At most, they indicate that there are some detectable differences in the socio-economic characteristics of the out-migrants as compared to the in-migrants. Indeed the whole subject of the effects of different degrees of out-migration on the losing region's economic structure and performance requires much more thorough research.

A second, more obvious, possibility is that the scale of unemployment — and even more especially of disguised unemployment as measured by exceptionally low activity rates for females — is such that only very large increases in out-migration would begin to bring the problem regions into demand/supply equilibrium. Thus subsidised emigration is unlikely to solve either the immediate problem of surplus labour or the longer-term problem of how to re-create the economic base.

It is precisely at this point that the ground becomes particularly treacherous because what is at stake is whether:

(a) the costs, in terms of growth forgone in controlling development in privately chosen locations, are of a large magnitude; and
(b) the real resource costs of manufacturing plants producing and distributing from lagging-area locations are substantially different, over the long run, from the costs of producing and distributing in a preferred non-peripheral-area locale.

If the first type of cost is of a large magnitude then the GNP will be affected markedly. If the second type of situation applies, then central governments may be forced to provide long-run operating subsidies — simply to keep businesses competitive — rather than subsidies to cover short-run settling-in costs or subsidies to increase the share of national production occurring in the peripheral areas.

On the first question, the evidence is by no means clear cut but it does seem likely that the loss of growth caused by IDC controls is not large. Data from the controlling ministry, the Department of Trade and Industry (DTI), show that in the two regions where controls have been most rigidly applied (the South East and West Midlands) an average of 20–30 per cent of all employment associated with applications tends to be refused. Moreover the IDC system has been loosened considerably since 1971. In any event the bulk of those refused projects go ahead in other parts of the non-assisted areas and only about 5 per cent of all projects are abandoned or take place outside the UK (Brown, 1972, p. 303). However, it is arguable that some projects are lost because manufacturers do not approach the DTI for permission to expand.

The Confederation of British Industry (the principal British employers' association) looked into this point carefully. In reviewing their evidence Brown came to the conclusion that this kind of potential loss of growth was of a very small magnitude indeed. Thus we can probably discount the IDC control system as a major restraint on potential growth.

A verdict on the other possible undesirable effect, a mal-location of economic activity, cannot be given with such confidence. The critical question is whether the long-run costs of the new branch, the new division or the transferred operation are higher than the costs associated with development in a non-assisted area which is almost certainly more central to major centres of population and of economic activity and to international trade routes.

Some general points are worth bearing in mind. First, a proportion of mobile industry actually moves to the development areas to serve the local market there. Sometimes this is a general market coverage and sometimes it is production for a specific producer or producers within the development area. Evidence from a study by the author suggests that in the case of Scotland approximately 10 per cent of the moves arose from this kind of motive (Cameron and Clark, 1966). The second fact is that industries in which transport and communication costs form a relatively high proportion of total costs tend to avoid settling in the distant peripheral areas (Logan, 1972). To whatever extent this is due to the skilful administration of the IDC system or the lack of growth in these industries so that new buildings are not required, the end result is that industries which might be particularly sensitive to distance from major markets and inputs tend not to settle in distant regions. A. J. Brown, in a fascinating analysis (1972, pp. 323–4) has also found no strong tendency for activities which are clustered together with others of the same industry to have a significantly higher net output than activities which are not clustered. Indeed,

> ... an extra 10 per cent of a trade's national employment in a particular region seems to go with a raising of its net output per head in that region by about a seventh of one per cent ... [thus] so far as manufacturing industry is concerned ... a move towards a new pattern of regional specialisation at all comparable to that of the nineteenth century is not visible. Dispersion and diversification rather are the rule.

It is also clear that mobile companies have shown a marked preference for the development areas most accessible to the core regions (Keeble, 1972) and from this one could conclude that what is happening is a natural extension or widening, rather than a forced attenuation of these regions.

Apart from these factors it does appear that the extra costs of operating a distant development-area plant as compared to an *in situ* extension, or a more localised development, mainly consist of greater settling-in costs and perhaps some longer-run costs associated with duplication of staff and buildings, extra transport and communication costs and extra training costs. The most comprehensive evaluation of these extra costs has been made in a study by Luttrell (1962). Unfortunately, his study is now rather out of date, since it dealt with moves in the immediate post-war period. Certainly Luttrell's findings were reassuring in that most mobile industries appeared able to operate, after the running-in stage, at a level of costs not markedly different from a potential location in a prosperous region and this 'favourable' conclusion could be backed by a number of other more recent findings. There is no doubt that transport costs are falling in most industries as a proportion of net output (op. cit., Logan). Moreover many British companies use average-cost delivery charges so that for inputs the development area producers may not be at a disadvantage. Executive communication factors may present more serious problems but once again these typically tend to represent a very small proportion of resource costs. Furthermore, if the development areas are marginal locations, then we could expect relatively high closure rates and a tendency to treat development area plants as the point of first redundancies during business downturns. A study of industry-specific closure rates in plants which migrated to the development areas suggested that these were not particularly high as compared with the closure rates at the national level (Sant, 1974). The DTI has also studied the decline in employment in branch plants within Scotland over a cyclical downturn and compared this with the decline at the headquarters plants of the parent companies located outside DAs. This comparison showed that the Scottish plants declined by considerably *less* than the headquarters plants. Finally, studies by Hart and Macbean (1961) and by Mulvey (1973) suggest for Scotland, at least, that comparison of profitability with similar manufacturing sectors in England gives results which are not significantly different in the two countries.

In contrast to these studies, which all seem to point to the conclusion that the costs of developing in an assisted area are not significantly different from operating in a prosperous core region, there is a growing body of literature which claims that the UK cannot afford to have major companies suffer *any* degree of cost disadvantage (West, 1973). Memoranda to the Expenditure Committee of the House of Commons (1972–73) from several leading manufacturers who had experience of operation in the development areas often concluded that, even after allowing for government inducements, they had incurred sizeable cost disadvantages and these were normally caused by higher transport bills. When faced with these criticisms, the DTI could only stress that no company was forced to select a DA location, that there were a number of DAs which were highly accessible to the core regions and that private manufacturers were not likely to pay attention to the inflationary effects on the labour market of expanding in the labour-shortage regions.

Given this range of conflicting evidence, we must agree with Foster's (1973) conclusion that regional policy cannot be securely based unless some of the crucial efficiency magnitudes are known. Thus whilst the 'credit' side of regional policy is fairly clear — unemployed and under-employed resources have been put to work, the pace of wage inflation probably has been reduced and some of the undesirable economic effects of out-migration have been avoided — the 'debit' side is not so clear cut. Certainly, although the evidence suggests that the development control system has not caused a large volume of growth to be lost to the UK, it is not conclusive enough to permit any convincing statement on the degree of the private cost penalties suffered by companies which have been 'invited' to develop in the problem areas. Indeed, until additional research has been undertaken, the economic justification for (or the case against) regional policy will remain tantalisingly in a state of being 'not proven'.

The future scale of the problem

Despite the obvious effects of powerful regional measures, as indicated by the studies of Brown and also Moore and Rhodes, it is obvious that the regional problem has by no means been solved. The magnitude of the problem still seems enormous. One recent estimate has suggested that for the major problem regions, that is Scotland, Wales, Northern England, Yorkshire and Humberside and the North West, a job-creation target of more than 1 million may be required over the next ten years (Ridley, 1972). It is important to note how this target was derived. The first assumption was that the full-employment rate for the nation is reached when unemployment falls to 1·5 per cent. Assuming no regional policy, the estimate was that, even if this rate was reached nationally, these five regions would continue to have surplus labour. If the unemployment rates in these regions were to be equalised with the national rate, then 120,000 jobs would be required.[13] The second component of the target is made up of 250,000 extra jobs required to increase female activity rates. This, in fact, represents a half-way stage in a raising of regional activity rates to the highest level obtained anywhere. The third elements were the expected growth in labour supply and the expected change in labour demand. Even if net migration continues at current rates (an average loss of 50,000 in the 1960s) labour supply is expected to increase by 350,000 in the decade. In the absence of regional policy, the assumption was that aggregate demand for labour would be static but that 300,000 redundancies in the coal, steel, textile, shipbuilding and engineering industries would have to be filled to meet this static-employment assumption.

It would be easy to quibble with some of these magnitudes. For example, the activity-rate reduction could be regarded as an optional target.

Clearly there is no compelling reason to assume that the same proportion of females in every region necessarily wish to be economically active. On the other side, a job reduction of only 300,000 over ten years may seem a ludicrously small estimate, when seen against a reduction in the total number employed in these regions of 176,000 in the two years between 1969 and 1971. Thus it seems reasonable to conclude that the overall magnitude of the problem has not been overstated and a target of 100,000 jobs per annum seems a reasonable working assumption. To meet this target there are several obvious sources of employment growth:

1 Manufacturing activities moving from the non-development areas of the UK.
2 International manufacturing companies being steered to the development areas.
3 Indigenous job creation from within the development areas themselves in the form of new manufacturing firms starting up and expansion of existing activities.
4 Public-sector dispersion, particularly of central government office functions.
5 Private service sector dispersion.
6 Indigenous growth in service employment.

Before we embark on a scrutiny of these possible sources of employment growth, one factor should be borne in mind. Like most other economically advanced nations, the balance of UK employment is constantly shifting towards the services sector. The last authoritative unofficial projection suggested that, between 1968 and 1975, the number employed in services would rise by 900,000 but the numbers in goods-producing activities would fall by 300,000 (Department of Applied Economics, 1972).

Manufacturing employment

(i) Mobile enterprise
With the economy expanding relatively rapidly, the development areas tend to pick up approximately 30,000 jobs per annum from mobile British enterprises — both transfer and branch-type developments. Allowing for job multiplier effects within the receiving areas,[14] a total increase of approximately 35,000 jobs per annum might seem a reasonable expectation. This, of course, could be too optimistic. We have already noted that IDCs are one of the influences in encouraging expanding companies to move to the development areas but also that the system has been considerably relaxed in recent years. Indeed, in its 1973 report on the UK econo-

my, the OECD warned of the weakening of regional policy if this course of action was pursued. Moreover, even when the system is applied, companies refused an IDC to expand in, say, the South East may increasingly bluff the government into a favourable decision by threatening to open a plant on the Continent. It is also possible that a general rise in unemployment levels in the non-assisted areas, and the growing capital intensity of most manufacturing activities, may diminish businessmen's interest in the *relatively* more abundant supplies of labour in the development areas. Finally, the considerable improvement in communications brought about by the establishment of the main parts of the motorway network may mean that companies do not have the same incentive to establish branches in the development areas to service local customers. All of these factors would tend to reduce the magnitude of the mobile flow.

The other obvious source of mobile enterprise is from foreign companies setting up in the UK. British governments have been particularly successful in steering foreign companies to development areas and, of the regions, Scotland and Northern Ireland have gained most. Indeed, Scotland now has 20 per cent of its manufacturing employment in US-owned firms (Forsyth, 1972). Great faith is being pinned on attracting European capital. It would, however, be too optimistic to expect a large job flow from this source, if the past few years are a valid guide. US capital, some of it associated with North Sea oil and gas developments, and Japanese companies seeking an offset to their country's embarrassingly high balance of payment surpluses by establishing production bases within the EEC, should provide some new jobs — but even here the magnitudes will probably be small. Overall it is unlikely that more than 3—5,000 jobs per annum will result from foreign investment.[15] Obviously we are still a long way short of the target.

(ii) Indigenous growth in manufacturing

This has two components — the creation and growth of new companies 'from within', and the diversification and development of existing companies. The evidence on the first is scanty and unsystematic but work by Firn (forthcoming) on the Clydeside conurbation over the years 1958—68 suggests that the flow of new enterprises has been minimal and most of the new companies appear to be in local supply activities rather than *basic* activities (Table 1.8).

Data generated by the DTI also suggest that the assisted areas were particularly deficient in generating applications for IDC approval from the small-firm sector. This, of course, embraces both new firms and expansion projects, but it does suggest that the small-firm sector has tended to be

Table 1.8

Components of employment change in manufacturing industry
in the central Clydeside conurbation, 1958–68

		Scottish controlled plants	External controlled plants	All plants
1	Employment growth	+ 32,192	+ 50,518	+ 82,710
1.1	In existing plants	+ 19,908	+ 29,350	+ 49,258
1.2	In new plants	+ 12,284	+ 21,168	+ 33,452
2	Employment decline	− 46,938	− 57,842	− 104,780
2.1	In existing plants	− 18,900	− 30,260	− 49,160
2.2	In plant closures	− 28,038	− 27,582	− 55,620
3	Net employment change	− 14,746	− 7,324	− 22,070
3.1	In existing plants	+ 1,008	− 910	+ 98
3.2	Stock changes (1.2−2.2)	− 15,754	− 6,414	− 22,168

Source: J. R. Firn, *The Sources of Regional Economic Growth* (forth-coming).

weak in the development areas.

There are, of course, a great number of explanations of why this has occurred. The traditional answer is that the DAs simply do not generate sufficient new projects which could be profitable over the long run. Possible reasons for this are: a diminution in the flow of entrepreneurial skill as a result of persistent out-migration; the desire by individuals for security and the quiet life in regions prone to calamitous collapses of their leading industries; the difficulties of access to fast-expanding markets elsewhere within the country; or the relative paucity of sub-contracting opportunities. The real problem here is seen as how to create an atmosphere in which enterprise and risk-taking flourish. The alternative explanation is that there are market imperfections and, perhaps, policy barriers which prevent the flow of new ideas from taking shape in the form of new companies and vigorous expansion. Not surprisingly some critics have detected the root of the problem in the conservative local lending institutions, which demand a higher rate of return from DA borrowers for a given degree of risk. Similarly some critics have seen the problem as the obvious outcome of administrators concentrating too much upon mobile capital to the neglect of locally initiated enterprise.

Whichever of these explanations is more accurate — and on balance it would appear that the first set of arguments 'holds more water' — there is a real need for policy to take greater notice of the requirements of the new small-firm sector within the DAs. Whether this will require a separate regional institutional framework is clearly a point yet to be decided, though the apparent success of a Northern Ireland agency specifically created for such a purpose perhaps indicates that the answer should be 'Yes' (Simpson, forthcoming).

When we come to the question of all other activity, apart from new mobile companies and newly created indigenous companies, we begin to enter no-man's-land. Here the critical questions are how to encourage diversification, rationalisation, greater competitiveness — and a host of other laudable objectives. Nonetheless two general points are worthy of notice. First, it is a mistake to assume that all manufacturing enterprise in the development areas is collapsing dramatically. Apart from for the half a million jobs in the more than a thousand companies which have moved to the development areas under post-war industrial mobility policy, many old-established manufacturing sectors continue to thrive.[16] The second point is that government aid in encouraging greater competitiveness and growth by indigenous (and other) activity must somehow avoid paying out subsidies for companies which would have taken such actions without this aid. Thus the stress ought to be upon marginal cases whenever possible. This of course is easier said than done. The current approach — and indeed that favoured by the last Labour government — relies heavily upon standard grants for all investment-creating projects, regardless of employment created. REP is also a standard, 'no strings attached' kind of grant, since it is paid *ad hominem*. The advantages of this type of approach are obvious. The schemes are easily understood, simple to administer and the benefits to the recipients are fairly clear cut. Moreover such an approach is sophisticated enough to recognise that economic growth may come about without a growth in employment. It also avoids equity questions since everyone is 'equal before the law'. However, this type of approach inevitably provides blanket benefits and favours those companies which may require no assistance. Standard grants may become an expensive system of 'overkill' — and this may, in time, bring regional policy into disrepute.

Now it is true that, under section 7 of the 1972 Industry Act, loans and interest relief on especially favourable terms may be made available to companies expanding their employment. This indeed represents a type of discrimination but it may not go far enough.[17] This is not to argue the case for providing discriminatory assistance in growth centres. The structure of the lagging regions is so diversified, the trading inter-relations between the regions so complex, and the spatial incidence of wanted externalities so changeable, that no one could predict with any confidence where growth will be maximised, or where the spread and backwash effects will be greatest or where the creation of external economies will be largest (Cameron, 1970). Equally there is no great interest in providing special subsidies for companies which are part of an integrated industrial complex. The administrative complexities alone seem to overwhelm any alleged advantages of faster regional growth for a given subsidy. However, Wilson (1973) has provided cogent arguments for a basic standard invest-ment-grant system, topped up by regionally administered discretionary grants, for those companies which increase employment markedly and for those which set up research and development divisions. The first kind of discretionary assistance might appropriately allow for direct and expected induced employment created by a given project. The latter is clearly aim-ed at stimulating the growth of those companies which provide opportuni-ties for able people who might otherwise emigrate.

Services growth
Here the most obvious possibility is the dispersal of government offices, particularly of the standard decision-making type. Currently some 14,000 jobs are awaiting dispersal to the development areas, and the Hardman Com-mittee, looking at the further dispersal of headquarters staff, has recom-mended that the DAs and intermediate areas should receive a further 17,000 jobs (Cmnd 5322, 1973). However, even if the government increases the latter figure, it is unlikely that the problem areas will gain more than 4,000 jobs per annum and clearly this cannot be a large contributor to regional equilibrium. This suggests that there should be much greater effort to encourage private-service activities to grow from within the DAs and to decentralise from the south east of England – especially from London. Certainly the success to date in achieving dispersal to the DAs has been minimal. This is regrettable, because a major study by Rhodes and Kan (1970) has suggested that the subsidy cost of dispersing private-sector office work could be much smaller than in the case of manufacturing. Until mid-1973 the Heath government still appeared to think that services only supplied local needs and tended to argue that any aid, particularly to locally established services, would automatically result in local closures which offset the benefits of the subsidy. Belatedly measures were intro-duced in 1973[18] which would increase the flow of service activities out of the South East; but until there is far greater effort made to understand how service industries operate and, in particular, which services are 'basic' sectors, government promotional efforts are liable to remain puny and almost certainly inappropriate.

Conclusions

The new measures of the Industry Act of March 1972, and the general support given to them by all major political parties, represents a consensus view that the regional problem has not been solved and must now be tackled with increased resources. Thus, whilst there is no doubt that policy did have substantial successes during the 1960s — especially if measured in terms of extra employment created in the development areas — the task which still remains seems dauntingly large. Certainly the well-tried component of private industrial dispersal from the core regions will continue to provide a useful method of raising the demand for labour in the lagging regions, though the extent to which this affects private efficiency will have to be scrutinised much more closely. Moreover government office dispersal will continue to provide some stable work. But these components are clearly not sufficient and the first is especially sensitive to success or failure in maintaining a high rate of national growth and a system of industrial development controls. Considerable imagination will therefore be required if the base of the regional effort is to be successfully broadened. In particular, there must be far greater effort to encourage that part of the private service sector not tied to local consumption requirements to locate or expand in the DAs. There is also a clear need for greater discrimination in the use of financial subsidies if regional policy is not to fall into the evil company of other large programmes which deliver the goods at a very high cost. Finally, the whole question of how to stimulate new growth from within the problem economies and especially of how to encourage small new enterprises should be given high priority.

Notes

[1] The author is grateful for the penetrating comments of A. J. Brown, C. D. Foster, R. Crum, J. Sundqvist and K. Allen. None of the above, of course, bears any responsibility for remaining errors.

[2] The Department of Employment provides working population forecasts every few years. This data relates to the 1969 forecasts.

[3] This greater elasticity arises from higher unemployment and lower activity rates.

[4] The regions with their 1971 population (millions) are as follows: Northern Ireland (1·53), Wales (2·73), Scotland (5·23); and, in England, the North (3·29), North West (6·73), Yorkshire and Humberside (4·79),

East Midlands (3·29), West Midlands (5·10), South West (3·79), East Anglia (1·67), and South East (17·13).

   [5] Parliamentary Question No. 2929, 20 June 1972. The figures relate to mid-1971 population estimates.

   [6] Yorkshire and Humberside, North West, North and Scotland.

   [7] These projections are made by the Registrar General and the Government Actuary. The latest forecast is to 1991.

   [8] For details on all of this see *Population of the United Kingdom*, 1st Report from the Select Committee on Science and Technology, House of Commons Session 1970/71, HMSO (1971).

   [9] Crosland seemed to argue at one point that the North West was over-populated but later changed his argument.

   [10] See the chapter on the UK in the manuscript of J. L. Sundqvist's forthcoming volume 'Population Distribution Policies in Western Europe' (possible title), Brookings (1974).

   [11] The best discussion of the use of IDC controls is in *The Intermediate Areas*, Committee of Enquiry under the Chairmanship of Sir J. Hunt, Cmnd 3995, HMSO (1969).

   [12] The effects of the preference given to development area suppliers are obscure, though it is clear that there are two forms of preference:

(a)   In the *general scheme*, firms in development areas are given every opportunity to tender for public contracts (from the government itself, public bodies and the nationalised industries). When price, quality, delivery and other considerations are equal, the DA firm is given preference.

(b)   In the *special scheme*, government purchasing departments review the initial competitive tenders and if at least 25 per cent is not awarded to DA producers then an offer is made to the first unsuccessful bidder in the DA and, provided the overall cost of the purchase is not increased, an amount of up to 25 per cent of the overall purchase can be awarded to this bidder. If he refuses to accept the offer, the next lowest tenderer is offered a contract and so on.

   [13] That is approximately 60,000 jobs for those currently unemployed and a similar number to cover the registration of those currently unemployed but not registered officially as such.

   [14] A job multiplier of between 1·15 to 1·20 is assumed.

   [15] DTI statistics show that approximately only 12,000 jobs were generated by overseas companies setting up plants in the development areas between 1965 and 1971.

   [16] John Firn, of the Department of Social and Economic Research,

University of Glasgow, is presently undertaking research into the formation of new companies in the Clydeside and West Midlands conurbations
with a grant from the SSRC.

[17] In the first year of the Industry Act, the government claimed that
22,000 additional jobs were likely to be generated in the assisted areas from
selective assistance under Section 7. There was no indication of the period
to which this job creation referred, *Guardian* (28 June 1973).

[18] The measures include rent rebates, transfer allowances for staff and
offsets to relocation costs of offices.

References

Brown A. J., 'Regional problems and regional policy' *Economic Review,*
NIESR (1968).

Brown A. J., *The Framework of Regional Economics in the United Kingdom*, Cambridge (1972).

Cameron G. C. and Clark B. D., *Industrial Movement and the Regional
Problem*, University of Glasgow, Social and Economic Series, Occasional Paper no. 5, Edinburgh (1966).

Cameron G. C., 'Growth areas, growth centres and regional conversion'
Scottish Journal of Political Economy, 21 (1970), pp. 19—39.

Cmnd 5322, *The Dispersal of Government Work from London*, HMSO
(1973).

Department of Applied Economics, *Economic Review*, NIESR (1972).

Department of the Environment, *Long Term Population Distribution in
Great Britain*, HMSO (1971).

Expenditure Committee (House of Commons), *Sub-Committee on regional incentives, session 1972/1973*, HMSO (1973).

Firn J. (forthcoming), *The components of regional economic growth*,
(mimeo), Department of Social and Economic Research, University of
Glasgow.

Forsyth D. J. C., *U. S. Investment in Scotland* (1972).

Foster D. D., 'Public finance aspects of national settlement patterns'
Cities, Regions and Public Policy, Gordon C. Cameron and Lowdon
Wingo (eds.), Edinburgh (1973).

Hart P. E. and Macbean A. I., 'Regional differences in productivity, profitability and growth' *Scottish Journal of Political Economy*, 8 (1961),
pp. 1—12.

Keeble D., 'Employment mobility in Britain' *Spatial Policy Problems of the British Economy*, Michael Chisholm and Gerald Manners (eds.), Cambridge (1972).

Lee C. H., *Regional Economic Growth in the United Kingdom since the 1880's* (1971).

Luttrell W. F., *Factory Location and Industrial Movement*, NIESR, (1962).

McCrone G., *Regional Policy in Britain*, University of Glasgow, Social and Economic Series (1969).

McCrone G., 'The Location of economic activity in the United Kingdom' *Cities, Regions and Public Policy*, Gordon C. Cameron and Lowdon Wingo (eds.), Edinburgh (1973).

Moore B. and Rhodes J., 'Evaluating the effects of British regional economic policy' *Economic Journal*, 83 (1973), pp. 87–110.

Ridley A., 'Regional policy – theory and practice' *Urban Studies Association Conference, Oxford* (unpublished), (1972).

Rhodes J. and Kan A., *Office Dispersal and Regional Policy*, Cambridge (1971).

Samuelson P. A., in *Backward Areas in Advanced Countries*, E. A. G. Robinson (ed.), (1969).

Sant M. E. C., 'Inter-regional industrial movement: the case of the non-survivors' *Essays in Honour of S. H. Beaver*, B. J. Turton and J. Phillips (eds.), (1974).

Simpson J. (forthcoming), *The Northern Ireland Experience of Job Creation*, University of Glasgow Urban and Regional Discussion Paper, Glasgow.

Thomas R. L. and Storey P. J. M., 'Unemployment dispersal as a determinant of wage inflation in the U.K. 1925–1966' *Manchester School of Social and Economic Studies*, 39 (1971).

West E. G., ' "Pure" versus "operational" economics in regional policy' *Regional Policy for Ever?*, G. Hallett, P. Randall and E. G. West, International Economics Association (1973).

Wilson T., 'British regional policy in the European context' *The Banker* (1973), p. 168.

2 The Effects of Regional Economic Policy in the United Kingdom

Barry Moore and John Rhodes

The nature of the regional problem

For more than forty years there has been a significant imbalance in economic activity between the more depressed, peripheral regions of the UK such as Scotland and Northern Ireland (designated as development areas) and the more prosperous areas such as the South East of England and the Midlands. This imbalance in activity results in unemployment rates in development areas (DAs) substantially and persistently above those in prosperous areas; in activity rates below those in other regions and in a high rate of net outward migration. Thus the central feature of the 'regional problem' is a persistent disequilibrium in the labour market, which arises from the fact that the rate of growth of the supply of labour in DAs has over a long period of time exceeded the rate of growth demand for labour (in contrast to the prosperous regions where the reverse has generally been true).

The underlying causes

This disequilibrium may stem from the supply side or the demand side of the regional labour market. An above-average rate of population growth, as for example in Northern Ireland, is a major demographic factor leading to a more rapid growth in labour supply than in other regions.[1] On the demand side, inter-regional differences in industrial structure are of central importance. Some areas have an industrial structure dominated by agriculture, in which employment is declining in all regions of the UK. But the older industrial areas such as South Wales, Scotland and Tyneside also have an industrial structure detrimental to growth. In these areas the declining industries are coalmining, shipbuilding and the more traditional textile and heavy-engineering industries. It is in this context of decline that the growth pole theory (in reverse) is more relevant in the British case

43

— for example the decline of the shipbuilding industry on Clydeside has had downward multiplier effects on manufacturing firms in West Central Scotland. Also important on the demand side is that the peripheral nature of these regions deters the establishment of new growth industries.[2]

The inadequacy of adjustment mechanisms

In the absence of a regional policy, economists look to two types of adjustment mechanism for a possible solution to the regional problem. Firstly, one might seek a solution to regional unemployment disparities by increasing the pressure of demand in all regions by the use of fiscal and monetary policy. But regional variations in the pressure of demand make the achievement of this kind of solution inconsistent with the overall objectives of the government's demand-management policy — namely the avoidance of excessive demand inflation and a satisfactory balance of payments. The overall pressure of demand that would be required to secure a growth of employment consistent with full employment in DAs would imply serious production bottlenecks and delivery problems in the regions of low unemployment. This would automatically lead to an increase in imports which would therefore cause, *inter alia,* severe problems for the balance of payments. Therefore the upper limit to the permissible growth in total demand can be thought of as that which secures the desired pressure in the low-unemployment regions, in which three-quarters of the UK labour force live and work. Thus there is a conflict between the objective of full employment in *all* regions and the general demand-management objectives of the government.

Secondly, when considering possible market adjustment mechanisms, it is pertinent to ask whether such mechanisms exist which will automatically increase the demand for labour in the high-unemployment regions, without at the same time increasing the pressure of demand in the regions of full employment. It is often contended that if one or more of the following conditions prevailed then such automatic adjustment would in fact take place: if factor prices in the regions of high unemployment were flexible downwards, relative to those in regions of low unemployment; if shortages of labour and increasing private and social costs induced firms to divert investment and the demand for labour to regions of high unemployment; if net outward migration from DAs occurred at a rate sufficient to eliminate the excess supply of labour arising in these regions. These conditions either do not prevail or, to the extent that they do, the persistence of substantial regional unemployment disparities over long periods of time suggests that these mechanisms work very slowly.

Factor prices in the development areas, although still below the national average, have shown a tendency to rise relatively, rather than fall. The main reason for this is the process of central wage bargaining by trade unions and employers at the national level but there is also increasing pressure from the regions for wage parity. Thus there are no relative downward movements in wage rates to bring about labour-market equilibrium in these depressed regions.

Secondly, shortages of labour in regions of low unemployment have generated some diversion of firms to development areas but the evidence suggests that such effects have been small and cyclical in character (Cameron and Clark, 1966, Moore and Rhodes, 1973). In spite of labour shortages from time to time, firms have preferred to expand in fully employed areas, partly because they do not internalise the social costs of doing so and also because they are willing to pay higher wages to attract labour from other firms.

Thirdly, the rate of net outward migration from development areas has been running at a high level for many decades. Scotland alone lost 360,000 people between 1960 and 1971. Even this degree of mobility of labour has not brought about the required adjustment, mainly because a high rate of net outward migration reduces both the supply *and* the demand for labour in the development areas. It has been estimated that 100 occupied persons might carry between eighteen and thirty jobs with them (Brown, 1972). Net outward migration over a long period is also highly selective in that it takes out of the development areas young and qualified people on whom the economic future of these regions depends.

The role of regional economic policy

The existence of these market imperfections and the failure of outward migration to correct the imbalance between the demand and the supply of labour suggest that specific measures to stimulate demand in the DAs are necessary. It is the role of regional policy to bring about a net diversion of demand for labour away from fully employed areas to the development areas.

It is important therefore, in considering how regional policy operates, to examine the effects of regional policy on the pressure of demand in *all* regions. More specifically, as we have argued elsewhere (Moore and Rhodes, 1973), it is important to distinguish between 'income effects' and 'diversion effects' of regional policy measures on the pressure of demand

45

in the regions of low unemployment. The diversionary effects of regional policy *reduce* the pressure of demand in the fully employed regions by diverting the demand for labour to the DAs. Income effects *increase* the demand for labour in *all* regions.[3] Regional policy must therefore be considered not only in relation to its effects on individual firms and the development areas but also in relation to the effect on the overall growth and management of the economy.

This framework also focuses attention on the interaction between inter-regional changes in the demand for labour and the consequences for the inter-regional pattern of labour supply. For example the effects of regional policy in raising demand in development areas may reduce the rate of outward migration and raise activity rates in these regions, thus changing both the inter-regional growth of the demand and the supply of labour. This is a crucial factor in analysing what would be required of regional policy if unemployment rates were to be reduced to levels comparable with those in the more prosperous regions of the country. It is the failure to take due account of these interactions which has led people to conclude that, because unemployment disparities have remained large, regional policy must have been ineffective.

Implicit in this analytical framework are the following three objectives of regional policy: (a) in the short term, the alleviation of unemployment in DAs; (b) in the medium term, the increase in national employment, output and income and (c) in the long term, the promotion of a more even distribution of population amongst regions.

What would have been required from regional policy to have achieved equilibrium in regional labour markets in the period 1960–70?

A solution to the regional problem must necessarily be arbitrarily defined. We have chosen a definition in terms of achieving the following objectives: equalisation of unemployment rates between regions; the elimination of net outward migration from development areas; equalisation of activity rates between regions.

If these objectives were to have been met then the solution to the regional problem would have required that 800,000–1,000,000 additional jobs be provided in development areas over the decade 1960–70. In practice it may be possible or even desirable to stop short of such a 'perfect' solution, although as we shall show later an active regional policy in Britain in the 1960s has succeeded only to the extent that it has prevented regional disparities from getting worse.

Measuring the employment contribution of regional policy in the development areas

In Figure 2.1 we give the results of earlier research into the numbers of jobs created in development areas as a direct result of regional policy. In order to identify the effects of policy we compare changes in actual employment with an 'expected' series in active and passive regional-policy periods. The expected series tells us what would have happened to manufacturing employment if each industry in the DAs had experienced the same growth rate as its national counterpart. From 1950 to 1963, a period in which regional policy was relatively dormant, the actual and expected series moved closely together. In the strong policy period of the 1960s actual employment diverged sharply from expected employment and by 1971 was about 12 per cent above what might otherwise have been expected. There are strong grounds for believing that this divergence of 150,000 jobs represents the effects of a strengthening of regional policy. [4]

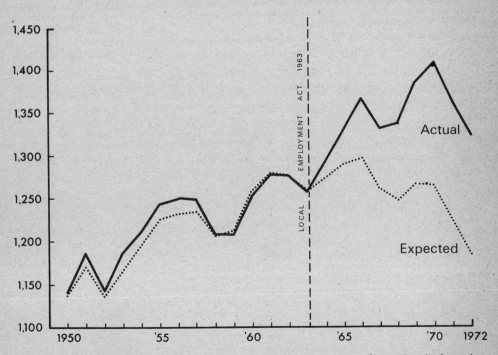

Fig. 2.1 Actual and expected employment in manufacturing industries (excluding shipbuilding and metals) in the development areas*, 1950–72.

* Defined as Scotland, Wales, Northern England and Northern Ireland

47

In terms of the total number of jobs provided in all development areas we estimate that between 1960 and 1972 regional policy created about 250,000—300,000 jobs (this includes the effect on shipbuilding and metal-manufacturing industries, together with an estimate of the multiplier effects on the non-manufacturing sector).

This estimate is consistent with our recent work on the inter-regional movement of manufacturing establishments, based on data collected between 1945 and 1971 by the Department of Trade and Industry. The number of manufacturing 'moves' to Scotland is shown in Figure 2.2; a similar pattern emerges for the other DAs. This series follows very closely the pattern of intensity with which regional policy has been applied, indicating that a large proportion of jobs created in development areas by regional policy has been diverted from the fully employed areas. A very different pattern, not related to regional policy, emerges from an analysis of movement to fully employed areas. The indications are that about three-quarters of jobs generated in development areas by regional policy are diverted in this way, the remaining quarter being generated within indigenous industries in the development areas.

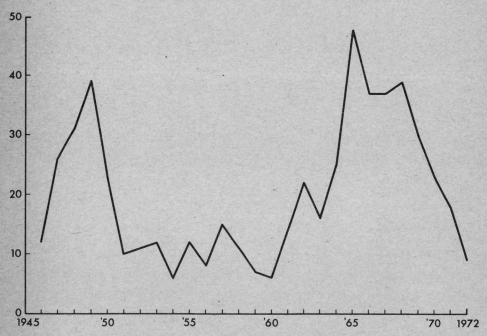

Fig. 2.2   Number of moves of manufacturing establishments to Scotland, per annum, 1945—72

At first sight then, the regional policy effect appears to be encouragingly large, but it has clearly fallen far short of what would have been required to fully correct regional unemployment disparities. Although regional policy has made a contribution to the elimination of these disparities in unemployment (in so far as these disparities would have been worse without regional policy), they have remained at unacceptable levels.

Why has regional policy not been more successful?

Underestimation of the size of the problem

Throughout the 1950s no one foresaw (or could perhaps have been expected to foresee) the extent to which the declining industries of DAs were going to shed labour. But even when the large job losses began to occur in the early 1960s there was a reluctance to assess realistically just how big the problem was and how long it was likely to go on. At no stage have successive governments stated the objectives of their regional policies in terms of the number of new jobs needed to be created in the development areas. It is this failure on the part of everyone concerned to appreciate the size and persistence of the problem that has contributed to a tendency to do too little too late, in terms of policy formulation and implementation. Further, it has also encouraged rather short-term panic reaction when the situation in the DAs deteriorated in a national recession. This brought about frequent policy changes. There has been a general lack of appreciation that the time-scale required to bring about a substantial improvement in the regions is one of decades rather than years.

Optimism on the effectiveness of regional policies

Frequent policy changes have also been encouraged by the frustration of seeing different policy instruments failing to solve the problem and the introduction of new measures by successive governments in an attempt to be more successful within the space of a five-year Parliament. New measures have been accompanied by, in the event, rather optimistic statements about their likely effectiveness. The strength of policy required to overcome inertia and divert a given amount of economic activity to development areas has not until recently been measured, even in broad orders of magnitude, and has implicitly been underestimated.

The slow rate of growth of the UK economy

Regional policies work most effectively in a rapidly growing economy. It is under these conditions that firms build new capacity which regional policies can divert to development areas. At a given strength of regional policies, industrial moves to DAs at times of more rapid growth have substantially exceeded those in periods of recession. It is all the more unfortunate, therefore, that the period of most active regional policy in Britain, between 1966 and 1971, coincided with a period in which the rate of growth of the national economy was relatively low.

The poor image of development areas

Areas of industrial decline with rather poor access inevitably have an image which expanding firms find initially unattractive. The possibility of excess transport costs (relative to other locations) and the lack of services and amenities of all kinds increase the uncertainties attached to a development area location. There is always additional concern about the availability of skilled labour. In this connection some of the DAs have a particularly poor reputation for industrial relations and this is partly borne out by statistics on industrial disputes. After allowing for differences in industrial structure, the DAs have been particularly prone to strikes.

Concentration on diverting manufacturing industry to development areas

Regional incentives and controls in the UK have been directed mainly at the manufacturing industries on the assumption that a large part of all potentially mobile economic activity is to be found in this sector. But the potential mobility of the manufacturing sector is dependent on how quickly it is growing. The UK manufacturing sector has been growing slowly in recent years — indeed in terms of employment it has actually declined since 1966. This has led some people to the view that regional policy ought to be directed more towards the rapidly growing service sector — or at least to that part of the service sector which serves a national market (Rhodes and Kan, 1971). In 1973 the government moved a little in this direction with the introduction of grants for private offices moving to development areas and the announcements of more dispersal of central-government office jobs into assisted regions. This is a move in the right direction, although it would be wrong to suggest that a full solution to the problem lies in directing service activities alone to these regions.

Over-emphasis on subsidies to capital rather than labour

Until 1967 much the greater part of financial assistance to firms in DAs was given in the form of capital subsidies. This is likely to encourage capital-intensive firms into development areas and stimulate existing firms to substitute capital for labour. A. J. Brown (1968) has shown that capital subsidies have attracted capital-intensive firms into DAs and that much of this investment would have taken place had the subsidy not been given. Few new jobs are created when this happens. Since regional policy attempts to provide new jobs in development areas there is a strong case for subsidising the use of labour rather than capital, thus giving more help to labour-intensive activities. The introduction of the regional employment premium (REP) went a considerable way in this direction, although this policy instrument is currently scheduled to be phased out in 1974.

Too little emphasis on training?

Whilst training grants have been available to firms training new labour in development areas, expenditure on training is only about 1 per cent of total expenditure on regional policies. Perhaps more help should be given towards training so that the basically unskilled, hard-core unemployed in development areas can acquire the necessary skills to man the new growth industries which policy aims to move into these areas.

REP may not be used as was hoped or intended

The Green Paper on the REP indicated an official expectation that REP would be used by firms to reduce their prices (below what they would otherwise be), thus raising their sales and increasing employment. It was intended that REP should be a partial devaluation for the manufacturing sector of development areas (without the disadvantage of higher import prices). But even so it was an extremely small devaluation, amounting to no more than 3 per cent in 1968 — had all the subvention been used to reduce prices. Inflation since 1968 has reduced the real value of REP so that any possible price reduction in 1973 would be nearer to 1·5 per cent. There is also a growing body of evidence to suggest that some firms have not used REP in this way at all but have used it as a windfall addition to profits, or to pay higher wages. In so far as firms have not used REP to reduce prices, the expected effect in terms of new employment is significantly reduced.

Industrial development controls may thwart rather than divert expansion

Some employers feel that the main effect of industrial development controls in the fully employed areas is to thwart expansion plans altogether, rather than to divert new projects into DAs. There are clearly cases where this has happened but the evidence suggests that it does not happen on a large scale.

Regional policy has been wrongly considered to be expensive

The rapid rise in government expenditure on financial inducements for firms in development areas has led to the belief that regional policy is very expensive. This has been reinforced by firms which claim that they have been adversely affected by moving into DAs. This increasing concern about 'costs' is one of the main reasons that a more active regional policy has not been pursued. We believe that much of this concern over 'costs' is mistaken and that attention should be focused, not so much on the increasing Exchequer costs but on the real resource costs. We argue in the final section below that the real costs of regional policy are very low — or perhaps even negative.

Other criticisms made of regional policy

Some observers have claimed that insufficient effort has been directed to the establishment and encouragement of 'growth points' where interrelated industries might gain external economies of scale and thus develop more rapidly. By the same token they argue that too much effort has been put into trying to preserve industries and localities which really should have been encouraged to decline.

Others point to the need for the devolution of more economic and political power and decision-making away from central government in London and into the development areas themselves. They deplore the fragmented administration of regional policy in Whitehall, where several government departments are responsible for various aspects of regional development. They note that Northern Ireland, which has had a substantial degree of autonomy in regional development matters, has had a greater degree of success in attracting new industry than have some of the other British development areas without such autonomy. The 1972 legislation did move a little way in the direction of more devolution of decision-making into the regions and more can perhaps be expected after the Report of the Kilbrandon Committee on the Constitution.

Finally, it is sometimes suggested that British regional policy has concentrated too much on moving branch plants into DAs and too little on encouraging indigenous enterprise and entrepreneurship from within these areas. As with many of the other criticisms of government regional policy it is one thing to point to things which may be wrong but quite another to say precisely where lies the solution.

The real costs of regional economic policy

In this section we argue that the Exchequer cost associated with regional policy (about £300 million per annum in recent years) has diverted attention from the real possibility that the resource costs associated with regional policies are close to zero, or even negative. This is because the extra demand injected into the economy by regional policy expenditures is offset by what is in effect an increase in labour supply.

It is clear that in order to identify the full effects of regional policy it is necessary to take into account the indirect effects of regional policy on the fully employed regions, as well as the effects on the development areas. In addition we submit that the government pursues its overall macro-economic demand-management policy as it would have done in the absence of regional policy (namely a policy of achieving the highest level of employment consistent with the absence of inflationary pressures generated by excess demand and an acceptable balance of payments). Thus, if we ignore for the moment the complications introduced by changes in inter-regional migration, the balance of payments and inter-regional variations in productivity, it can be said unambiguously that whenever regional policy increases employment and output in the development areas there must be a net increase in employment and output in the country as a whole. This is because, *ex hypothesi*, employment and output is what it would have been in the fully employed areas had a regional policy not been carried out.

The appropriate demand-management policy required to maintain output and development unchanged in the fully employed regions depends on the relative size of the 'income' and 'diversionary' effects of regional policy on the pressure of demand in these regions. As noted above, diversionary effects of regional policy *reduce* the pressure of demand in the fully employed regions and increase it in the DAs, whereas income effects *increase* the demand for labour in all regions. Thus, if the diversionary effect exceeds the income effect falling on the fully employed areas, there is a net reduction in the pressure of demand in these regions and the appropriate counterpart demand-management action is a *reduction* in tax

53

rates (or an increase in public expenditure and/or monetary relaxation). In these circumstances, because regional policy expenditure has led to a reduced demand for labour resources in the fully employed regions, the resource cost is *negative* and real disposable income in *all* regions is higher than it would otherwise have been. If the diversionary effect is less than the income effect, then tax rates are higher and a *positive* resource cost arises from regional policy expenditures.

A detailed discussion of the effects of relaxing the assumptions on inter-regional migration, the balance of payments and regional productivity differences is to be found elsewhere and in what follows we indicate only the main outcome of the analysis and the more important empirical results. First it is possible that the productivity of additional policy-induced employment in development areas may be less than the productivity of labour in the same industries in the fully employed areas. The important point is, however, that *any* output produced by this additional employment is a net addition to output for the economy as a whole and thus the overall output gain could only be eliminated for this reason if the productivity of this new employment were near to *zero*.

The impact of an effective regional policy is to reduce the rate of net outward migration from development areas and, to the extent that a proportion of these migrants would have been in employment in the fully employed regions, the increase in output and employment as a result of regional policy is lower. On the other hand, in so far as there are savings in infrastructure expenditure, housing and other public services, there are important indirect economic *benefits* resulting from the reduction in migration caused by regional policy.

Finally there are the effects of regional policy on the balance of payments. Because regional policy, combined with counterpart demand-management measures, raises the level of national output, imports will increase. However, the effect of regional financial incentives is also to encourage import substitution and make exports more competitive. If the former exceeds the latter then any resource gains from regional policy will be reduced and *vice versa*.

After taking account of these three qualifications, we estimated that regional policy in the United Kingdom had generated a net increase in employment of between 250,000 and 300,000 jobs over the period 1960 to 1970. The addition to annual output (GDP) is estimated at between £400 and £500 million by 1970 and we estimate a small reduction in general taxation, suggesting that the resource cost of regional policy was *negative or close to zero*. If this is so, then people in the prosperous regions are in no sense 'paying' for regional policy.

Preliminary estimates of the economic and Exchequer implications of regional policy 1963–70

In this section we give the results of a first attempt to estimate the size of the benefits arising from regional policy. In presenting these figures we aim only to indicate broad orders of magnitude.

Two sets of results are presented in Table 2.1. The difference between the two sets of estimates, *A* and *B*, is the degree to which it can be assumed that a successful regional policy reduces the rate of net outward migration from development areas. In version *A* it is assumed, following the work of A. J. Brown (1972), that the creation of 260,000 jobs in development areas reduced outward migration of the labour force by 35,000 (perhaps 100,000 people). In version *B* the same regional policy effect is assumed to reduce net outward migration of *workers* by the much larger number of 100,000 (say 300,000 people). In each case, the remainder of the 260,000 additional jobs must therefore be filled from the ranks of the registered and unregistered unemployed. A detailed explanation of how the figures in Table 2.1 have been arrived at is given in the Appendices.

Looking at the effects in the country as a whole (i.e. fully employed and development areas together) the differing migration assumptions do not affect the picture very much.[5] In version *A* total employment increases by 291,000 and in version *B* by 254,000. The additional annual output in the UK would therefore be £400–£500 million per annum higher by 1970 if the productivity of the additional employment was similar to the national average. The additional output therefore amounts to approximately 1 per cent of GDP as at 1970.[6] This is a benefit which continues each year and if an active regional policy continues to be pursued in the future this benefit is likely to show a gradual increase. Moreover, if regional policy were now abandoned, a large part of the gain in output and employment would continue into the future, since many of the jobs diverted to development areas by the policy of the 1960s will remain in being, some of them for many years.

It is possible that our analysis summarised in Table 2.1 has made insufficient provision for any increase in the demand for investment goods required to produce the additional output made possible by regional policy. The extent to which additional investment demand occurs is governed by two main factors. Firstly, the existence of spare capacity, particularly in development areas, may reduce the requirement for additional investment. Secondly, some activities diverted to DAs may be less capital intensive than they would have been had they occurred in a region of labour scarcity.

Table 2.1 The effects of regional policy on employment inside and outside development areas before and after restoring the pressure of demand in the fully employed areas. Orders of magnitude for the period 1963–70

	A Employment change in*		B Employment change in	
	Fully employed areas	Development areas '000s	Fully employed areas	Development areas '000s
(a) *Before restoring pressure of demand*				
Income effects of initial Exchequer outlays (including multiplier effects)				
Average for the period Appendix A	+ 25	+ 9	+ 25	+ 9
Income effects deriving from the increase in employment and profits				
Average for the period Appendix A	+ 25	+ 9	+ 18	+ 6
Employment creation in and diversion to DAs (including multiplier effects) Appendix B	– 195	+ 260	– 195	+ 260
Sub-Total	– 145	+ 278	– 152	+ 275

Table 2.1 'continued'

(b) *After restoring pressure of demand*				
Employment generated by government expenditure associated with migration Appendix C	− 20†	+ 14	− 67	+ 47
Total increase in employment required to restore pressure of demand Appendix D	+ 131	+ 33	+ 121	+ 30
Total employment change	− 34‡	+ 325	− 98	+ 352
Change in labour supply arising from reduced net outward migration from DAs Appendix C	− 35	+ 35	− 100	+ 100

* A minus sign indicates a decline in the demand for labour, a positive sign indicates an increase in the demand for labour.

† The net effect on employment in the fully employed areas is zero because the decline in the demand for labour is exactly matched by the increase in the demand for labour required to restore the pressure of demand.

‡ The total employment change is negative because the given pressure of demand in the fully employed areas is in relation to a marginally reduced supply of labour arising from migration.

Some allowance for additional investment demand has been catered for in Table 2.1. Firstly, the increase in output will both require and stimulate the production of investment goods and therefore part of the demand for capital equipment will have been satisfied. Secondly, in estimating the income effects of Exchequer outlays, some expansion of investment demand was also allowed for. Thirdly, some of the investment demand will be met from increased imports rather than from domestic output but the potential resource costs of these imports may well be offset by additional exports stimulated by regional policy. We have estimated that if no allowance is made for increased utilisation of spare capacity or labour capital substitution and if, in addition, we assume that the incremental capital output ratio is as high as the capital stock output ratio then the maximum possible investment demand generated will still leave the gains in output and employment intact and leave room for a small reduction in general tax rates.

In Table 2.2 we show the overall consequences of regional policy for

Table 2.2

Summary of Exchequer flows — orders of magnitude 1963—70

| | Annual average 1963—70 (£m) | |
	A	B
Exchequer outlays on regional incentives gross of directly recoverable items	− 155	− 155
Directly recoverable items	+ 30	+ 30
Reduction in tax rates required. Yield of tax system to maintain pressure of demand in fully employed areas at a given income	− 133	− 122
Change in tax and social security receipts after restoring pressure of demand in fully employed areas at given rates of tax	+ 156	+ 133
Net reduction in infrastructure expenditure and public services	+ 6	+ 20
Net change in increase in budgetary deficit (−) increase (+) decrease	− 96	− 94

the Exchequer. The main conclusion is that if regional policy is effective the budgetary deficit must always be higher (or the surplus lower) if the pressure of demand in the fully employed areas is to be maintained unchanged. In terms of the regional policy package of the 1960s we estimate that the budget deficit has been increased by the order of £100 million. This increase in the budget deficit will be largely financed by additional net savings (i.e. by an increase in demand for additional financial assets, resulting from increased output and income) and therefore has minimal monetary implications.

An increase in the public sector deficit emerges for two reasons. Firstly, tax and social security net receipts (after restoring the pressure of demand in the fully employed areas) approximately offset the initial non-recoverable Exchequer outlays on regional incentives, although the offsetting benefits will only accrue to the Exchequer after some years delay. Secondly, assuming full employment in the non-development areas, the general level of taxation would be lower by over £100 million than the level necessary in the absence of regional policy.

Conclusion

We believe that the analysis summarised in this paper has important policy implications, particularly for the United Kingdom.

Normally changes in government expenditure are viewed in relation to the expected claim they make on scarce labour resources. We maintain that government expenditures on regional policy should not be seen as making such a claim on resources. This is because – unlike most other forms of public expenditure – they bring about an increase in the overall utilisation of labour resources (i.e. an increase in productive potential) which is beneficial to the whole economy in terms of increased employment and output. Further we believe that the real costs associated with UK regional policy expenditures in the last decade have probably been negative. Expenditures on regional policy should not therefore be regarded as competing with other public or private expenditure and increases in such expenditures do not necessarily require sacrifices – either in terms of other public expenditure or in terms of higher taxation. On the contrary *all* regions may enjoy an increase in real disposable income because general taxation is lower (or public expenditure higher) than would have been possible in the absence of regional policy.

Finally, the view is frequently expressed that a solution to the regional problem lies in an unprecedented and sustained increase in the rate of growth of the national economy. Under such conditions it is argued that regional policy expenditures would be superfluous and wasteful. We would argue that such a sustained expansion is constrained by the pressure of demand in the fully employed areas (and by the balance of payments) and that it is in precisely such periods of expansion that an active and effective regional policy is needed to divert the pressure of demand to DAs so that additional resources are brought into use to make the general ·expansion more easily sustainable.

APPENDIX

Income effects

Income effects of Exchequer outlays on regional incentives (see Table A1)

The income effects of Exchequer outlays are an average for the period as a whole, though in practice it should be recognised that income effects were higher in more recent years.

For REP we assumed that 40 per cent of the annual payment was used to reduce prices, 40 per cent to increase profits and 20 per cent to increase wages. This was consistent with the findings of our industrial enquiry.

For investment incentives and grants under the Local Employment Acts we assumed the whole amount was received initially into profits. After corporation tax and the conventional 40 per cent distribution to dividends, we assumed that retained profits were used partly to increase investment and partly to reduce prices.

Finally, for largely recoverable items under the Local Employment Acts such as loans and government-built factories, we assumed that one-third of these was a net Exchequer outlay, the balance being the repayment of loans and factory rents automatically received back into the Exchequer.

The direct[7] and indirect[8] income effects on employment are estimated at 34,000 jobs.

Income effects deriving from increased employment and profits in development areas

This derives from the difference between unemployment and supplementary benefits received (for those registered as unemployed) and the

60

Table A1

Exchequer cost of regional policy –
Total cost of special regional assistance to manufacturing industry over and above that available nationally

Great Britain (£m)

Years	Recoverable or mainly recoverable items			Local Employment Acts				Non-recoverable items[5]				
	Government factory building[1]	Loans	Total	Grants under Section Four[1]	Building grants[1]	Plant and machinery grants[1]	Special operational grants[1]	Investment grants[2]	Free depreciation[3]	Regional employment premium[4]	SET premium[4]	Total premium[4]
46/7	5·7	0·2	5·9									
47/8	12·5	0·3	12·8									
48/9	11·0	0·5	11·5									
49/50	6·5	0·6	7·1									
50/1	5·0	0·8	5·8									
51/2	5·0	0·8	5·8									
52/3	3·7	0·3	4·0									
53/4	3·1	1·1	4·2									
54/5	4·5	1·7	6·2									
55/6	5·9	0·4	6·3									
56/7	4·9	0·3	5·2									
57/8	2·7	0·1	2·8									
58/9	1·5	2·1	3·6									
59/60	5·6	3·1	8·6									

Table A1   continued

60/1	21·0	23·5	44·5	2·7	3·3							6·0
61/2	5·5	16·4	21·9	1·2	1·1							2·3
62/3	5·4	4·6	10·0	1·8	4·4							6·2
63/4	5·6	19·0	24·6	0·7	3·0	2·0						5·7
64/5	12·7	10·4	23·1	0·6	10·0	6·8			3·0			20·4
65/6	12·4	9·6	22·0	0·5	13·8	6·1			45·0			65·4
66/7	14·4	13·2	27·6	0·4	21·1	6·3			25·0			52·8
67/8	11·5	13·7	25·2	1·3	18·5	1·3		72·0	4·0	34·1		131·2
68/9	13·9	17·7	31·6	1·3	21·6	0·5		85·0	–	101·0	25·0	234·4
69/70	18·0	28·1	46·1	1·3	26·3	0·1	10·2	90·0	–	105·0	25·0	257·9
70/1	7·9	28·0	35·9	1·2	30·1	0·2	2·8	90·0	–	110·0	–	234·3

Sources:
1. Annual Reports of the Local Employment Acts.
2. Investment Grants: White Paper, *DTI Journal* vol. 10, no. 4, 25 January 1973.
3. Department of Economic Affairs and HM Treasury Progress Report No. 55, August 1969.
4. Financial Statistics: CSO.
5. A small figure of about £3m per annum should be added to cover development area training grants.

average wage. For the unregistered (mainly women) unemployed the additional income is equal to their wages. There is no income effect for those who would otherwise have migrated to work elsewhere. There is also a small income effect deriving from increased profits.

The direct and indirect income effects on employment are again equal to 34,000 jobs on assumption A (low migration effect) and 24,000 jobs on assumption B (high migration effect).

All the jobs arising from income effects will be spread fairly evenly throughout the country. We therefore allocated one-quarter to development areas and three-quarters to non-development areas.

Employment creation in and diversion to development areas by regional policy measures 1963–70

Employment creation in development areas is estimated at 260,000 jobs. This figure is based on earlier work on the number of manufacturing jobs created in development areas by regional policy (Moore and Rhodes, 1973) incorporating more recent research into the effects of policy in the Merseyside development area but excluding the effect in Northern Ireland. A multiplier of 1·4 was again used.

It was argued in the text that a substantial amount of employment generated by regional policy in development areas represented a *diversion* of economic activity from fully employed areas. Some of the 185,000 *manufacturing* jobs generated in development areas between 1963 and 1970 may not have involved a reduction in demand in fully employed areas prior to restoring the pressure of demand in these areas — for example: the 'creation' of new jobs arising from foreign companies which would otherwise have expanded outside the UK; new firms starting in DAs, which would otherwise not have existed at all; and employment in firms winning export orders from foreign competition because of REP.

The precise contribution of 'diversion' and 'creation' is not known but the evidence suggests that 'diversion' is much the larger. We have assumed that one-quarter (65,000) of the jobs arising from regional policy were 'created', i.e. would not have been in the UK at all in the absence of regional policy, and that three-quarters (195,000) have been diverted from the non-development areas.

In the case of employment newly created in development areas there are no negative service multiplier effects in fully employed areas.

The effects of regional policy on inter-regional migration and the consequential changes on the demand and supply of labour in the regions

The effects of regional policy on net outward migration from development areas

The increase in DA employment arising from regional policy can be expected to narrow regional differentials in unemployment rates compared with the non-policy alternative position. The effect of this will be to reduce the level of net outward migration from development areas to fully employed areas.

The causes of migration are extremely complex and not limited to economic factors. There is therefore considerable uncertainty as to how far an effective regional policy reduces the rate of net outward migration from DAs. For this reason we thought it wise to undertake two sets of calculations. The first estimates (version A) are based on recent empirical work on regional migration published by A. J. Brown (1972). These results indicate that 'a rise of one percentage point in the regional unemployment rate relative to the rest of the country goes with an increase of about 3 per thousand in the net outflow of men of working age in the region'. On this basis we estimate that regional policy reduced the level of net outward migration from DAs to other parts of the country by about 35,000 employed persons between 1963 and 1970.

In the calculations labelled B we assumed that the creation of the 260,000 jobs in development areas would reduce net outward migration by 100,000 employed persons.[9] We regard this as an upper limit, based on the rather special case of a sparsely populated area in central Wales.

The consequential changes in the supply and demand for labour

Under assumption A the effect of regional policy on migration is to increase labour supply in development areas by 35,000 and to reduce labour supply by the same amount in the fully employed areas. Assumption B increases the regional change in the labour supply to 100,000.

On the demand side, two effects are distinguished. Firstly, there are those effects which result from the switching of personal consumers' expenditure when people migrate from one region to another. A. J. Brown (1972) has calculated that 'a hundred occupied persons moving in conditions of slack demand might carry between 18 and 30 jobs with them' (p. 276). Secondly, whenever people move from one part of the country to another, this can affect both the geographical distribution and/or the overall amount of public sector social capital expenditure (e.g. housing, schools and hospitals) and associated current public service expenditure. Thus, if net outward migration from development areas is reduced, some employment associated with public expenditure is diverted to development areas (depending on the utilisation and quality of existing public service provision). But other employment associated with public expenditure that would have been required in fully employed areas at the higher rate of net outward migration may now not be necessary. We have assumed that half the expenditure is diverted to development areas and the remainder is not required at all.

Estimates of the social-capital requirements of migrants, and employment generated in providing these public services, were made using information on average requirements derived from the *National Income and Expenditure Blue Book*. We adopted a marginal rate of public service provision equal to half the average requirements.

Estimating by how much taxes are lower if the pressure of demand is maintained in the fully employed areas

We have estimated that, as a result of government regional policy in the 1960s, aggregate demand must be expanded by the equivalent of 164,000 jobs (on assumption *A*) and by the equivalent of 151,000 jobs (on assumption *B*) to leave the percentage unemployment in the non-development areas unchanged. This potential reflation enabled by regional policy can be considered as deriving from a reduction in taxation, an increase in public expenditure, or expansionary monetary policy. We consider only the first of these possibilities.

On the assumption that a 1 per cent addition to employment will add 1 per cent to GDP, if the pressure of demand is held constant, we calculate the GDP equivalent of the additional employment assuming that short-run multiplier effects have had time to work through. We assume that the reduction in yield of taxes is brought about half from changing the standard rate of income tax and half from an across-the-board reduction in purchase tax. We estimate that, taking income tax and purchase tax together, a reduction in these taxes of £100 generates an increase in expenditure at factor cost of £75. The required tax change was thus calculated for each year as the regional policy effect increased and an annual average figure was obtained for the period as a whole.

Increase in tax receipts (reduction in social security payments) after restoring pressure of demand in fully employed areas

In Table A2 we summarise the estimated additional revenue which would have accrued to the Exchequer between 1963 and 1970 as a result of the increased employment and output brought about by regional policy. The various tax revenues are calculated using ratios for each year based on the *National Income Blue Book*.

The estimates are based on a cumulative series of the additional output

Table A2

Exchequer claw-backs from regional policy 1963–70
(£m)   (current prices)

	Migration A	Assumption B
Employers' and employees' national insurance contributions	185	161
Corporation tax*	221	201
Tax on distributed profits	44	38
Income tax	268	235
Indirect taxes	322	281
Sub-Total	1,040	916
Reduction in unemployment benefits[†]	207	145
Grand Total	1,247	1,061
Annual average 1963–70	156	133

*   Including corporation tax of 40 per cent on that part of REP received into profits.
†   Including national assistance and supplementary benefit paid to unemployed persons. Under assumption *A* it is assumed that the registered unemployed are reduced by 150,000. Under assumption *B* the reduction in registered unemployed is 105,000.

and employment generated by regional policy in each year and an annual average was then taken.

In a conventional appraisal of the flow of costs and benefits arising from an item of public expenditure a discounting procedure would normally be adopted. This should be done in due course but in any event the overall conclusion that regional policy leads to negative resource costs is not likely to be affected, although the measure of the benefits will be. On the one hand, the benefit will be reduced in so far as the Exchequer outlays and income effects precede the clawbacks and diversion effects of regional policy. On the other hand, the benefits as we have measured them (increased output in the years 1963–70) are underestimated in that, even if regional policy were to be abandoned, much of the benefit in terms of increased output would continue for many years into the future.

The effects of regional policy on the balance of payments

If it was the case that the effect of regional policy was to increase imports more than exports, this external imbalance would have to be corrected by a change in the terms of trade and some resource cost would result. In reality, however, we think that the balance of payments effects are small and broadly neutral.

The increased output arising from the operation of the investment incentives and the IDC policy will lead to increased imports and thus worsen the balance of payments. In so far as investment incentives make development area firms more competitive than they would otherwise have been, and attract foreign firms which would otherwise not have come to the UK at all, there will be offsetting benefits to the balance of payments. The overall effect on the balance of payments is probably unfavourable.

REP, on the other hand, because it makes DA firms more competitive than previously — particularly if it enables prices to be held below what they would have been — will stimulate exports and encourage import substitution. The net effect on the balance of payments of this measure is probably favourable and little or no resource cost emerges if the terms of trade are adjusted by use of an REP type of policy instrument, because a large part of the additional exports are produced in development areas where unused resources are available.

We estimate the additional imports generated by regional policy to be about £40–£50 million per annum for the period 1963–70. This is not likely to be fully offset by exports generated by REP from 1967 onwards which we estimate at about £40 million per annum for 1967–70. However, the balance of payments position is improved when regional policy attracts foreign firms which would otherwise have gone elsewhere. The inflow of foreign investment improves the capital account and the excess of additional exports over imports generated specifically by these firms improves the current account.[10]

Notes

[1] A. J. Brown (1972) has estimated that in the case of Northern Ireland 'between one-third and one-quarter of its excess unemployment seems to have been attributable to its excess of natural population increase.'

[2] Excess transport costs and remoteness from very large conurbations in which agglomeration economies may accrue are but two of the disadvantages deterring new industries from moving to the more peripheral areas.

[3] These income effects arise in three different ways. First there are those which derive directly from the Exchequer outlays associated with regional policy financial incentives. These find their way into profits, wages, or prices which then generate increases in income, output and employment. The second income effect arises from the increase in income of those employees who would otherwise have been unemployed but for regional policy. The third income effect arises from any increased investment required to produce the additional output arising from regional policy.

[4] For a more detailed discussion of this analysis see B. C. Moore and J. Rhodes. For confirmation of this result see A. J. Brown (1972).

[5] A number of different assumptions on migration and other variables were tried, two of which are presented above. It appears that the overall outcome of the analysis is not very sensitive to a wide range of alternative assumptions about income effects, migration and multipliers.

[6] This does not imply that the growth rate is 1 per cent higher, merely that GDP is 1 per cent higher after seven years of regional policy than it would otherwise have been.

[7] In calculating direct output and employment effects of a subsidy or income change we adopt the following conventions: $S = 0.15$ (higher than average to take account of progressive taxes); direct taxes $= 0.3$; indirect tax content of consumption 0.15; marginal propensity to import $= 0.2$; corporation tax at 0.4, dividends $= 0.4$ of after-tax profits; 0.3 of retained

profits used for further investment; output/employment relationship of 1:1.

[8] A multiplier of 1·4 was used.

[9] This higher migration figure is based on research published by the Development Commission for mid-Wales, which indicated that, *at least in sparsely populated rural areas*, for every ten new jobs created, the net outward migration of employed persons declined by four or five.

[10] A study of American firms moving into Scotland in the post-war period suggests that regional policy was a powerful force in attracting some of these firms to the UK and that their favourable contribution to the balance of payments was substantial. See D. J. C. Forsyth (1972).

References

Brown A. J., *The intermediate areas: note of dissent* Cmnd 3998, HMSO (1968), pp. 155–65.

Brown A. J., *The Framework of Regional Economics in the United Kingdom*, Cambridge (1972).

Cameron G. C. and Clark B. D., *Industrial Movement and the Regional Problem,* University of Glasgow, Social and Economic Series, Occasional Paper 5, Edinburgh (1966).

Forsyth D. J., *U. S. Investment in Scotland* (1972).

Moore B. C. and Rhodes J., 'Evaluating the effects of British regional economic policy' *Economic Journal*, 83 (1973A), pp. 87–110.

Moore B. C. and Rhodes J., *The economic and exchequer implications of regional policy*, Evidence to the House of Commons Expenditure Committee, HC 42 XVI, HMSO (1973B).

Rhodes J. and Kan A., *Office Dispersal and Regional Policy,* University of Cambridge, Department of Applied Economics, Occasional Paper 30, Cambridge (1971).

3   Regional Policy in the EEC

Wolfgang Stabenow

Introduction

The 1957 treaty establishing the European Community laid down essential aims for the Community, which included raising living standards of the population and reducing the differences existing between the various regions and the backwardness of the less favoured regions.

How does all this appear in reality in 1973?

Income per head in the more well-to-do regions is five times greater than it is in the poorest.

Congestion, both of space and labour, frustrates policies aimed at facilitating labour mobility within the Community and also constitutes a serious impediment to the absorption of workers from outside the Community. Those factors add yet another difficulty to the well-known social and economic problems involved — for migrating workers and host countries alike — in the pursuit of labour mobility.

In other Community regions, notably in the large peripheral areas, there is underemployment and unemployment. Jobs are lacking in industry and in the services sector. Infrastructure is substantially lacking — roads, telephone communications, water supply, hospitals, training schools, and cultural and recreational facilities. The conditions for an orderly economic development of these regions are therefore less than adequate.

Freedom of movement for workers is a basic right within the EEC. This right only attains its full meaning if the individual can make use of it of his own free will. Where freedom is largely dictated by necessity it is freedom without substance. It is essential also in this context that work should be available where people want to live.

Finally, economic and monetary union, which we want to establish by 1980, might be jeopardised by continuing regional stresses: Great Britain, Eire and Italy are still unable to conform to common rules in respect of currency and are the countries of the European Community experiencing the hardest regional structural problems.

A rational — and also a rationally possible — political decision took place when it was decided to merge the economies of the nine member states and to opt for European union. Rational consequences must therefore follow. This implies above all that economic and monetary union

71

should be furthered in three ways. There must be:

1   A Community monetary policy (in particular a reduction in exchange rate differences and a uniform approach to other currencies throughout the world).
2   A common medium-term economic policy and a common budgetary policy (more especially with regard to measures to fight inflation).
3   A common regional policy (in particular with regard to co-ordinating measures by member states and to the employment of Community mechanisms for regional development).

The Paris Conference, 1972

The final communiqué of the 1972 Paris Summit Conference is clear, up to the following point, on regional policy. It states 'the Heads of State or of Government agreed that a high priority should be given to the aim of correcting, in the Community, the structural and regional imbalances which might affect the realisation of Economic and Monetary Union.'
    Turning to detail, the conference laid down the following guidelines:

1   The Commission was asked to prepare a report analysing the regional problems which arise in the enlarged Community and to put forward appropriate proposals for the removal of imbalances.
2   Member states were committed to co-ordinating their regional policies.
3   The institutions of the Community were asked to create a Regional Development Fund before 31 December 1973 and therefore from the beginning of the second phase of economic and monetary union – that is to say, basically from 1 January 1974; this will be financed from the Community's own resources.

    The Commission has, to a large extent, carried out this mandate.

1   Its report (the Thomson Report) on regional problems in the enlarged Community was presented on 3 May 1973. This considers the present economic situation of regions within the Community and furnishes details of the policy guidelines to be followed, which will, in particular, be reflected in its proposals. These deal with: regional development in member states; degree and character of the principal regional imbalances; aims and instruments of regional policy in member states.

The report was discussed in the Council of the Communities in May and was the subject of a major debate in the European Parliament at the beginning of July 1973.

2   The Commission laid before the Council on 26 July 1973 the draft for a decision establishing a Committee for Regional Development. This committee is to facilitate the co-ordination of regional policy by member states.

3   At the same time, 26 July 1973, the Commission presented to the Council a proposal for a regulation establishing a European Regional Development Fund.

The Council, the European Parliament and the Economic and Social Committee had to deal with these proposals in depth and also at great speed, in order to meet the timetable laid down at the Paris Conference.

We shall shortly consider the Commission's proposals in greater detail. Community regional policy is no invention of the Paris Summit Conference; but the latter has probably given this policy its first major political thrust.

Previous policies and proposals

I shall not devote time here to details of regional economic policy as reflected in the treaties for European integration, nor to the thorny path which led from the Community conference on regional policy of 1961 to the Paris Summit Conference of 1972. We cannot, however, ignore certain of its aspects.

1   The Community has been endowed with an instrument of regional policy with the creation of the European Investment Bank. From 1958 to 1972 the bank issued loans of 2·6 billions of units of account (approximately £1,100 million). Seventy-five per cent of this has been entirely devoted to regional policy purposes. The treaty establishing the European Coal and Steel Community provides for financial contributions by the Community for economic reconversion in the coal industry and for the retraining of workers. In this particular field the Community has contributed towards the establishment of 110,000 new jobs and to retraining some 500,000 workers.

Additionally, contributions from the European Social Fund for re-establishing and retraining workers are concerned substantially with measures designed to promote regional development. The revised fund of 1971 offers greater possibilities than its predecessor for co-ordinating social and regional policy at Community level.

2   Both the European Parliament and the Commission sought throughout

the 1960s to bring the debate on regional policy within the Community to concrete results. All these endeavours were unsuccessful.

When the idea of economic and monetary union began to take hold in 1969, the Commission laid a proposal before the Council for a decision on the means to be employed for furthering regional policy (CEC, 1969). It followed this up with further proposals in following years, which were designed to complete and amplify the basic decision on regional policy. The proposals were as follows:

— A Regional Development Committee should be established in order to provide the expertise for co-ordinating regional policy.

— Community procedure should be used to ascertain the economic situation of development areas and programmes of member states with regard to the areas in question.

— There should be improved co-ordination between available Community financial mechanisms for purposes of regional policy: (European Investment Bank, European Agricultural Guidance and Guarantee Fund, budgetary allocations of the European Coal and Steel Community, European Social Fund.)

Following a Commission proposal in 1971, finance of proposals from the Agricultural Fund outside agriculture and the food industry was made possible for the first time. Contributions were authorised on behalf of farmers and agricultural workers in agricultural programme areas — namely those leaving agriculture and following agrarian conversion with a view to enabling both them and their children to find new employment in industry, handicrafts, and the services sector. 250 million units of account were made available to this end.

— A European Regional Development Fund was to be established and principally designed to provide interest rebates more particularly by way of contributions to servicing interest on loans issued by the European Investment Bank. It was also proposed to introduce a system of guarantees for regional development.

— A Community information network should be created for investors in the private and public sectors who might contribute to the realisation of regional development programmes.

The Commission also raised the question in 1972 as to whether a Regional Development Corporation might be created in which the Commission might participate, together with other public and private companies. This corporation should not, however, limit itself to informing and recruiting investors. It should also provide technical aid notably with regard to the establishment of industrial sites. The Commission also emphasised that the

74

corporation should contribute to undertakings in the development programme areas.

The Council, the European Parliament and the Economic and Social
Committee debated the comprehensive proposals of the Commission in
full. The Council in particular linked the Commission's proposals to its
negotiations over economic and monetary union, the third programme for
medium-term economic policy and structural reform for agriculture. It
never went beyond declarations of principle. However, it agreed that part
of the means available to the Agricultural Fund should, from 1972 onwards, be used for regional development purposes. The regulation required
to put this decision into force has to date never been discharged. A preliminary decision for the Regional Development Fund was taken in the spring
of 1972, which was timed to produce concrete results before the end of
the year.

These negotiations occurred during the final phase of the Community
of Six. Developments at that time were overtaken by the Paris Summit
and the accession of new member states. It is to be hoped that they came
in useful in both contexts.

The Thomson report: main proposals

The (1973) proposals for a Regional Policy Committee and a Regional
Development Fund replace the 1969 and 1971 proposals to a large extent.
The proposal to use means available to the Agricultural Fund for regional
policy purposes is still with the Council. It is to be assumed that it will be
implemented together with the new proposals. The Commission is also
prepared to renew its proposals for a guarantee system and for a Regional
Development Corporation.

The Regional Policy Committee

Co-ordination of regional policy is an integral part of co-ordinating the
overall economic policy of member states. It must therefore follow the
same institutional rules as overall co-ordination of economic policy and
especially integration. These are that the Commission has the right to
propose — indeed it has a virtual monopoly in this respect — while the
Council has the task of decision. The European Parliament can only take
note of the Council's decision until such time as it possesses the greater
powers more in keeping with those of a real Parliament.

Although the Commission has now proposed that a Regional Policy

Committee be set up equally responsible to the Council and the Commission, this will imply no change in the institutional system nor in the present balance of functions between the institutions of the Community. The committee's task will be solely consultative and designed to further co-ordination. It is to provide a platform upon which responsible representatives of member states and the Commission may realistically debate conceived regional policies. The outcome of the committee's work, taking the form of reports, will be binding neither on the Council nor on the Commission in the context of their legal acts.

The Commission intends that the Regional Policy Committee shall be modelled on the Monetary Committee and the Committee for Medium-Term Economic Policy. It has withdrawn its 1969 proposal whereby the committee would only be responsible to the Commission.

The solution is not one of ideology but solely of practical application. However, any notion that the committee is solely responsible to the Council must be rejected. This could only prejudice the Commission's right of initiative and introduce distortion into the institutional balance.

The member states and the Commission will each nominate two representatives to the committee. The European Investment Bank will be represented by an observer.

An important departure from the 1969 proposal is the widening of the field of opinion in the committee to include not only the institutions of the Community but the regions themselves and both sides of industry. In this respect the Commission is mindful of the need to make a prudent start in the light of the fact that the European Community is conceived as a community of member states. The Community must be enabled to seek the various views represented in the regions. Since the question of regional representation in the nine member states is not only very varied but in part almost entirely undecided, much will depend on success in developing a dynamic practical approach. Community regional policy on the one hand and regionalism on the other are still two different concepts. That they will always remain so is an open question.

The final communiqué of the Paris Summit Conference sets store on an increased participation of both sides of industry in the European unification process. The Commission has given further form to this thought in its proposal for a programme of work in the social field. The draft decision for the creation of a Regional Policy Committee also foreshadowed the proposal that representatives of trade unions and employers might participate in the committee.

Another open question still is that of a dialogue between the committee and central organisations of local authorities. The Commission, for its part, has maintained over the years a regular liaison with the Council of European Municipalities and with the International Union of Local Authorities. But, as in the case of participation of regional corporations, there is a long way to go before there is proper participation of local authorities.

What questions of expertise will the committee have to handle in detail?

The Commission has described the substance of the co-ordination of the regional policy of member states as follows: 'On the one hand there must be targets progressively co-ordinated and on the other hand clearly defined measures and a uniform method of approach to regional development in the Community.' This leads on to a whole list of individual subjects which enter the field of co-ordination and with which the committee will have to deal. Some examples are:

1 The committee should study and compare aims and means, methods and experience in regional policy.
2 The committee should construct an up-to-date picture of the manner in which the economic and social situation develops within the various regions of the Community.
3 Regional development programmes constitute one of the essential instruments of regional policy. The committee's task will be to examine programmes presented by member states, together with specific development targets, more especially for the Community programme areas. Whoever lays down regional development programmes does not act in any way from academic or bureaucratic motives. Rather does he approach the matter from the angle of spending public monies that are all too often limited. We must achieve a clear-cut relationship between national and Community expenditure — however much this may in the first instance fall as a burden upon the administration of one or other member state.
4 In recent years it has been possible to achieve a first step in co-ordinating rules for aid in member states. An upper limit of investment has been fixed in the so-called central areas and a number of additional rules have been made for granting regional aid. This co-ordination must be furthered, both from the angle of regional policy and that of considerations regarding competition. It will be a task of the committee to seek to bring uniformity into aid systems of member states. This task will not prejudice the powers of decisions which the Commission possesses in controlling state aids within the Common Market.
5 Parallel with the 'incentives for programme areas' there will need to be preventive measures in areas of concentration. These may take the form of

administrative control of investment, prohibitive measures of taxation or contributions for the resettlement of undertakings. Legislation in France, Great Britain, Italy and Eire provides for such measures in one form or another and with varying intensity. At the present moment the Netherlands Parliament is considering a government proposal for measures dealing with the selective control of investment.

Harmonisation of these measures is needed under the different angles: decongestion, environment, competition.

The Regional Development Fund

The European Fund for Regional Development is the essential instrument for Community regional policy but the financial operations of the fund should not be ends in themselves. The fund must also play its part in achieving co-ordinated policies of member states.

We must not, at this point, lose ourselves in the details of the Commission's proposals for a regulation nor in the special budgetary details relating thereto. It is much better that we should stay with the main problems which are as follows:

1   Perhaps not the most important but certainly the most spectacular question concerns the size of the fund: how much should it be? A clue to the answer is already contained in the Paris final communiqué: 'Intervention by the Fund in co-ordination with national aids should permit ... the correction of the main regional imbalances in the Community.' This should be an indication of the means required, even though it is not yet possible to estimate this requirement exactly in financial terms.

The Commission has therefore decided not to lay down a precise size for the fund in its proposal for a regulation but considered that the means required should figure on a yearly basis in the budgetary estimates of the Community. In this way quantities would alter in the light of requirements calculated over the short term and of experience acquired with time. This should also comply with the fact that the basis for the fund does not derive from natural contributions but is based on the Community's own resources.

The Commission proposed that 500 millions of units of account (about £200 million) should be credited to the Regional Fund for 1974. It is thinking in terms of 750 millions of units of account for 1975, rising to one milliard of units of account for 1976.

To this we should add the 50 millions of units of account deriving annually from the Agricultural Fund to create jobs outside agriculture for those previously employed therein. This gives the impressive total of 2·4 milliards of units of account for the years 1974–76, which the Community will add to the national means available for regional development.

In making these proposals the Commission is not only requesting effective aid for the less prosperous regions of the European Community. Whoever proposes expenditure on this scale for discussion and decision is at the same time raising basic questions as to the meaning of European union. The Commission shows clearly in its relevant reasoning in the matter that it is well aware of this.

2   Our second question concerns those regions which are to receive aid from the Regional Fund.

The proposal of July 1973 already indicates the basic criteria to be employed for selecting these areas. They must be areas where the gross domestic product per head of population is below the Community average. The development areas must also be either of a nature where agriculture predominates, or where industrial change is taking place, or where structural under-development occurs. The Commission is able, with the aid of statistics, to pin-point the characteristics whereby the development areas may be identified.

A further condition for demarcating the regions for intervention by the fund arises from the nature of Community aids: Community development areas will be only those where national rules for regional aid apply. On 10 October 1973, the Commission submitted to the Council its proposal for a Council regulation on the list of regions and areas qualifying for Community regional aid. The map resulting from this proposal covers about 52 per cent of the surface area and about 32 per cent of the population of the Community.

This proposal has been criticised, in some quarters, for the size of the specified areas. However, the Commission felt then that this would best implement the political mandate of the Paris Summit Conference: to use the fund only in co-ordination with national regional aids. However, this concept would also permit use of the fund's resources in those regions most in need.

3   The next question concerns the kinds of projects to be assisted by contributions from the fund.

The Commission proposes that both production investment and infrastructure should be subjects for Community development. Contributions from the fund will be made in respect of industrial projects and those connected with services, in so far as the member states concerned also contribute thereto. Investment costs will have to be more than 50,000 units of account in each case; smaller projects will be reserved to exclusively national actions for regional development. Projects to which the

European Regional Fund contributes must lead either to the creation of new employment or to the guarantee of existing employment.

Contributions from the fund may be made to projects for infrastructure, in so far as these are necessary to industrial or service undertakings. It is worth noting that the Commission considers that social and cultural infrastructure should be left to national authorities. However, it has no wish to be dogmatic about the kind of infrastructure in which the Community might participate.

4 How much should be contributed by the fund in each particular case? With regard to investments in industry or in services, it is considered that contributions from the fund might be up to 15 per cent of investment costs. The Community contribution should, however, be no more than half the total of national aid.

In the case of projects for infrastructure, there should be a maximum contribution of 30 per cent from the fund to public works. This may also take the form of interest rebates on loans issued by the European Investment Bank.

5 We must also question under what conditions the fund may participate in projects for regional development.

The Commission has not insisted on tight business criteria for individual projects. This does not seem necessary in view of the link between national and Community development.

From an economic viewpoint, a project in receipt of a contribution from the fund must, above all, be able to make a contribution to increasing employment. Additionally there should be evidence that the project will contribute to the economic development of the region in question. Consideration must also be given to the impact on the environment of projects for development.

Special care should be taken in the case of a project for which the investor comes from another member state. Such investments across frontiers will have an essential part to play if they intensify capital where labour is available. Further encouragement in this connection may be anticipated in the future, particularly with regard to taxation.

Finally, there will be particular interest in investment projects situated on the frontiers of two or more member states and designed to develop regions forming a natural economic connection.

The essential condition for interventions from the Regional Fund is, however, that projects may only qualify if they are included in a regional development programme. It should certainly suffice up to the end of 1975 if the region in question has specific development targets which are not yet part of an integrated programme — the Commission's proposal includes, moreover, a number of guidelines for the content of regional development programmes.

It is intended that the Regional Policy Committee shall examine programmes and targets. It will then be the task of the Commission to decide whether they comply with Community aims.

This is the decisive link between Community co-ordination and financing of regional policy.

6   Lastly, we may ask: according to what procedure will contributions from the European Fund to regional development be sanctioned?

In principle the decision rests with the Commission. As is the case with the management of the Social Fund and the Agricultural Fund it will be assisted by a special committee for this particular fund. The Commission will preside over this committee, on which member states will be represented. In the case of a difference of opinion between the Commission and the committee, acting by qualified majority vote, the Council shall decide — also by qualified majority vote.

The foregoing decisions on each individual project for industry or service activities will apply to cases involving expenditure of 10 millions of units of account or more and to projects for infrastructure involving at least 20 millions of units of account. In the case of smaller projects there will be global decisions on the basis of quarterly estimates for each development area. All applications must be submitted by member states.

Conclusion

The Commission proposals for a Community regional policy give a definite answer to certain specific demands which were made at the Paris Summit Conference. But political realities mean that we shall certainly have to learn to live with compromises which may ultimately result in a whole package of decisions marking the transition to the second stage of economic and monetary union starting in 1974.

As the instruments of the common regional policy become operational, the Community will be faced with new trials. The allocation of financial resources will constitute an acid test. Assistance from the European Regional Development Fund may be granted, in the context of the other basic conditions, only according to the relative severity of regional imbalances. The contribution made by a national economy to the Community budget can be no more decisive here than the influence of one member state as compared to another in the Community decision-making process.

Once again, it is not a question of creating an equalisation fund but of developing a comprehensive economic policy.

A comprehensive regional policy of the European Community is only conceivable, however, if we destroy behind us all the bridges which keep the path open to non-binding economic co-operation. A policy which is meant to act on the very foundations of our social and economic existence can allow for no ways of escape.

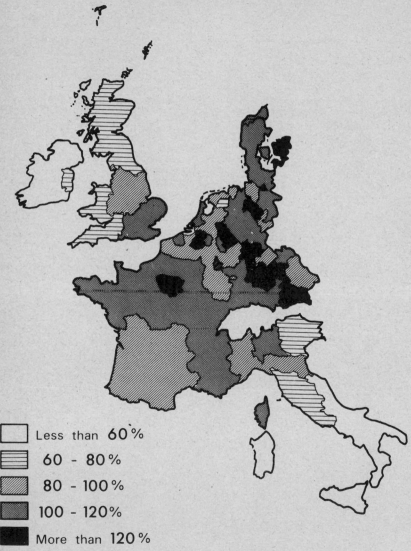

    Less than **60**%

    60 - 80%

    80 - 100%

    100 - 120%

    More than **120**%

Fig. 3.1   GDP per head of population in the EEC, 1970, by region (Index: average of Community of Nine = 100)

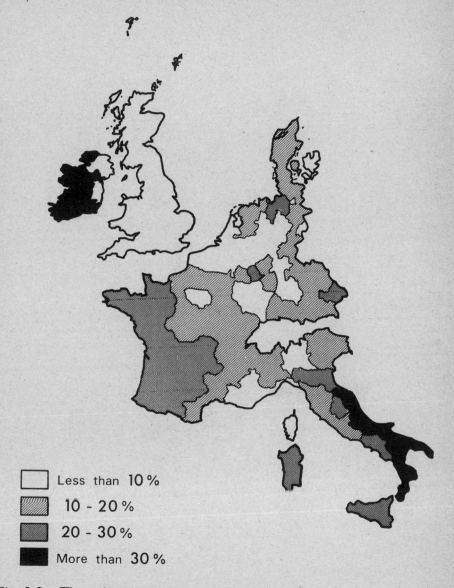

Less than **10** %

10 - 20 %

20 - 30 %

More than **30** %

Fig. 3.2   The primary sector as a proportion of total employment in the EEC, 1970, by region

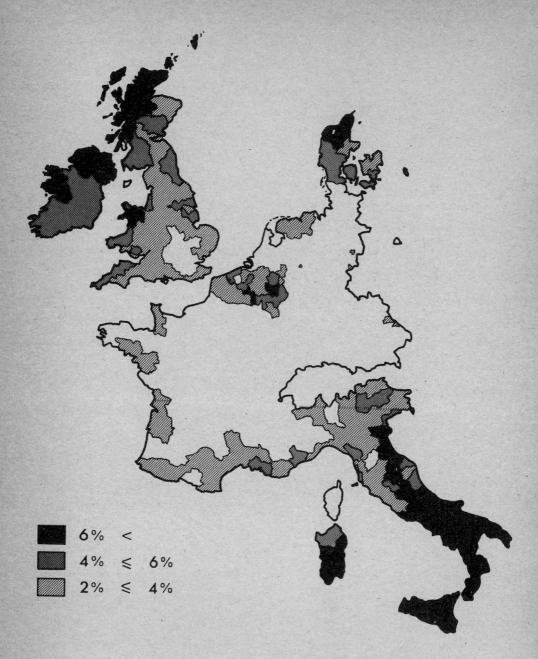

Fig. 3.3 Average unemployment rates in the EEC, by region
(rates derived from 4-year period 1968–71)

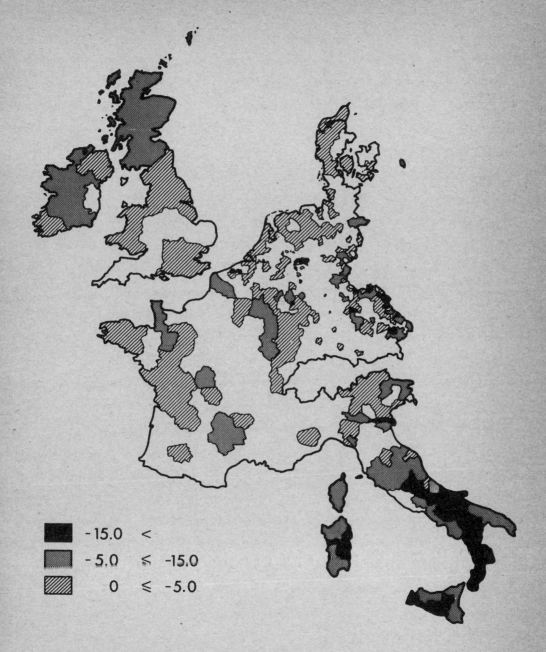

Fig. 3.4   Out-migration in the EEC, by region (average per annum; rates per thousand resident population in the 1960s)

References

Commission of the European Communities, *A Regional Policy for the Community*, Office for Official Publications of the European Communities, Luxemburg (1969).

Commission of the European Communities, *Report on the Regional Problems in the Enlarged Community*, Brussels (1973).

4 European Regional Policies[1]

Kevin Allen

This paper is in two parts. The first examines the differences and similarities of the regional policies pursued by individual EEC member countries. The second is concerned with regional policy at Community level.

The policies of member countries

A key characteristic of European regional policy is diversity, with the intensity, nature and reasons for policy varying considerably among countries.[2] In some, the attempt to simulate conditions in the more prosperous areas through growth areas and infrastructure is a vital component of policy. Italy and France are the prime examples, where even the industrial mobility incentives discriminate in favour of the growth areas while in others, and particularly the UK, growth-area policy is not a major part of development strategy and, indeed, certain aspects of policy (the special development areas, for example) are in direct contradiction of growth area policy. The use of state industries in regional policy is extremely important in Italy (and to lesser degrees in France and Germany) but relatively unimportant in any direct sense in Britain. Industrial mobility financial incentives are found in all countries. Yet while in the UK, Italy and Belgium they play a major role in regional-development policy, they are seen as being substantially less important in France. The financial incentives available in the various countries show an enormous variety of tax concessions, grants, loans at subsidised interest, equity finance, relocation compensation and labour subsidies.

That there should exist this degree of diversity is not surprising. First, the nature and intensity of the regional problems differ between countries, thereby requiring differing forms of policy.[3] A growth-area policy is, for example, generally considered as more relevant for backward agricultural areas than depressed industrial areas. Secondly, regional policy inevitably reflects political factors — which determine both the extent of policy as well as the form. An Istituto per la Ricostruzione Industriale, for example, playing a regional role is probably not politically feasible in the UK at the present time. Thirdly, regional policy is often an adjunct or modification to national systems and policies or a reflection of peculiarly national conditions. The heavy use of subsidised loan capital for regional development in continental Europe reflects to a large extent the importance of fixed-interest loans for company finance relative to the UK. The Italian social-security concession for southern Italian firms exploits the system of social-security finance operated in Italy, by which the great majority of contributions is paid by employers. The Italian use of the State holding sector for regional (and other) roles has been made possible by the historical accident which created at least part of that sector.

The great diversity of regional problems and policies in Europe makes international comparisons difficult and is likely to be a major problem during the evolution of a more co-ordinated regional policy in the Community — a point to which I return later. At the same time, the differences of political, economic and social conditions among the nations make it especially difficult to reach firm views on whether particular parts of regional policy in specific countries have relevance for the UK or other countries. Without taking account of the broader economic context, within which regional problems and policies have evolved or operated in the individual countries, the conclusions can in fact be misleading. Too few international regional problems and policy comparisons have taken adequate account of these broader aspects of context.

But alongside the differences in European regional policy are a number of interesting and instructive similarities. Some of the major ones are listed below:

1   All the European countries have substantially increased their expenditure on regional policy over the post-war period and particularly during the 1960s and early 1970s — years of radical structural change, often to the detriment of employment in the problem regions. The cost per job 'created' has also risen markedly. Perhaps surprisingly, this increased expenditure and intensification of policy was not associated with any detailed evaluation of the economic worthwhileness of regional policy. This is not to say that the possible contributions of regional development to national growth of regional policies were ignored but the claims were generally qualitative and vague. Only in very recent years have active attempts been made to quantify, even if only partially, some of the costs and benefits of regional policy. In Italy, quite detailed analyses of the infrastructure savings arising from a more active southern policy have been made (Cafiero and Busca, 1970) and, at a less quantitative level, the consequences of inadequate southern policy for national cycles have been analysed (Ventriglia, 1972). Outside Italy, earlier work by Needleman and Scott (1964) — which primarily concerned transfer costs — was com-

plemented by a cost/benefit 'model' (or framework) designed by an EFTA regional policy working party (EFTA, 1971). Moore and Rhodes have attempted a quantification of the costs and benefits of UK regional policy and reported on their work. Few would argue that further effort along these lines would be superfluous, particularly work which relaxes the 'full employment in the pressured regions' assumption, even though this will then set up a number of difficult hares — and particularly those concerned with discounting.

2 Not only has expenditure on regional policy increased substantially over the post-war period but policies have also been changed frequently. The UK is not exceptional in her post-war shifts from large development areas to small development districts and back to development areas again; from a position where growth area policy was the solution to one of SDAs; from grants to depreciation allowances and back to grants again; from tight to slack IDC; from a hailing of REP as the new solution to its threatened abandonment. Other countries have had similar experiences. These frequent changes have disadvantageous effects on investment decisions but, more than this, they reflect the paucity of economic analysis and data in regional policy. The operation of macro-economic policy is difficult on a number of counts — ignorance of the current state of the economy, the direction in which it is moving, the speed at which it is moving and what happens if policy measures are initiated. Regional economics is certainly in no better condition.

3 A particularly intriguing similarity among the European countries, with the exception of France, is the lack of policy for service mobility. Where such policy does exist it is generally weak, relative to that for industry, and usually more in the form of decentralisation policy than regional policy in the normal sense of the term. It is not easy to say whether this neglect reflects the fact that much of the base of regional economics is international trade, excessive faith in export base theory or a view that services are 'unproductive'. Certainly there is no bonanza of jobs from service mobility. Many of the characteristics of the service sector make for difficulties in encouraging inter-regional movement — dependence on local markets, small scale of activity, importance of females in key jobs, the incremental pattern of growth as opposed to the lumpy nature of manufacturing growth (Rhodes and Kan, 1971). But some parts of the sector are good potential candidates for movement. Success in respect of service mobility has so far been slight in most countries and has mainly concerned government departments.[4] But without more positive incentive schemes, one would not expect great success in the private service sector. There is little reason to believe that the dislocation costs of a

service unit are substantially inferior to those for manufacturing plant. Consideration of service mobility has, perhaps, in terms of sophistication been taken further in Europe than in the United Kingdom. In Switzerland and France, for example, interest has been shown in a concept with an important service component called *spatial functional disintegration.* The basic idea is that a firm is a set of functions which have different location requirements and that with modern transport and communication systems there is no reason why these functions should not be spatially spread according to their location needs.[5] The Swiss have been working in terms of five functions: processing, administration, distribution, training and head office. There is some evidence that the process is at work in Switzerland even in the absence of relevant policy. It could be a trend which it might be worthwhile examining in more detail, and, if possible, stimulating.

4   All economic policies must pander to political forces and regional policy is no exception. In Europe this has shown itself in the inability to introduce radical spatially discriminatory policies. In both France and Italy growth-area policy has been diluted (through the designation of a large number of growth areas) into a policy of dispersed concentration rather than concentration *per se*. It is not by accident that Italy has at least one growth area (or nucleus) for each southern province. In the United Kingdom, political factors played some part in seeing the gradual erosion of growth-area policy (though the economic case always seemed weak) to the current situation in which, if a growth-area policy exists (and there is doubt in this), then it is covert rather than overt. Similar political factors have also doubtless played a part in the almost complete European lack of policies for area decline. Plans for growth abound but except for the 'D' areas in the north-east of England, plans for decline do not appear to have been formulated. And yet a large number of areas in Europe are declining and in many such areas realistic assessment would indicate little hope for a reversal of this trend. The need for decline policies is particularly acute when growth-area policies are being pursued (unless one believes in substantial and medium-run spread efforts). Few would argue against the need to plan for growth but there seems a reluctance to accept the need to plan for decline, in spite of the strong economic and social arguments for such policies.

5   Realism is generally lacking in respect of European intraregional spatial policies but it also seems to be deficient in the view of the time scale of regional development. Too often this has been optimistic. When the Cassa was created in 1950, there was an expectation among observers that the Southern Problem could be resolved within the Cassa's envisaged life

(10 years). The Cassa still exists, and with funds now substantially greater than in 1950, while the North/South disparities are as serious as ever. In spite of the fact that regional policies have been operated in the European countries over much of the post-war period (and even before in some countries) and in spite of a continual toughening of this policy, there are no major European problem areas which have been removed from the designated list. Regional development involving, as it does, industrial and often settlement restructuring, is almost inevitably a slow process. Currently the structural problems remain serious, while the potential for industrial mobility is not limitless. Higher incentives can only operate at the margin and most countries are now at the stage at which policy has already creamed off the 'easy' units. It may become even more difficult in the future to secure inter-regional industrial mobility, particularly with the increased need for industrial mobility to achieve urban reorganisation and restructuring objectives in the pressured regions. There has, in recent years, been a growing recognition of the long-term nature of regional development. A number of economists in Italy now see a process lasting for decades rather than years, though the politicians find this difficult to accept — as they do in the United Kingdom where a recent statement by one minister was to the effect that the regional problem was unlikely to be resolved in the life of this government! The optimism with respect to time scales is found not only in individual countries but also in the EEC *per se*, where there still remains the hope that, aided by additional EEC funds, substantial headway can be made in resolving the various regional problems before 1980. We return to this point later. One final comment deserves to be made on the slow process of regional development and this concerns the appropriate policies. There is surely a case for arguing that regional programmes have concentrated too much on *development* policies and given too little attention to more short-run policies (generous unemployment and early-retirement benefits in particular) to alleviate the social problems which inevitably result from the slowness of the development process. The UK is less at fault in this respect than many of the other European countries.

6   A common feature of European regional policy has been the disappointment concerning the secondary impact of firms on the area of designation. The expression 'cathedrals in the desert' has become common. Ancillary development around new plants is often sparse and much of their demand for material and semi-finished imports goes not to local industry but to firms outside the region with a consequential low multiplier effect. In the UK, Lever's (1974) analysis of a panel of firms in Scotland revealed that 80 per cent of their material and semi-finished inputs

came from outside Scotland. This would appear to be a common phenomenon in Europe and a particularly acute problem in the industrialisation of southern Italy. The Italians have, however, taken active steps to try to ease this problem and three are of particular interest. First, incentives have been oriented towards firms who are likely to have links with other southern units — either as suppliers or buyers. In addition, higher equipment grants are paid when their equipment is purchased from southern producers. These policies represent a move towards using multipliers as one of the bases for incentive awards, suggested a number of years ago by this author (Allen, 1969) and not very far from Wilson's regional super-multipliers (Wilson, 1968). Secondly, the Italians have tried to make use of the State holding sector to increase the impact by planning the large State holding units on a scale which should encourage the spontaneous development of ancillary industries (Alfa-Sud being an example of this) and by using the sector to develop ancillary industries around major plants. The results have, however, not been impressive.[6] The secondary development arising from Alfa-Sud was poor until Fiat located some of its plants in the South, while the sector's role in ancillary development was limited by the fact that it has never been successful in the running of small and medium-sized firms. Thirdly, the Italians have led Europe in the development of the inter-related-industrial-complex idea. Tosco's Bari/Taranto complex is well known. It was an attempt to plan a complex (in engineering) based on primary and secondary units, with a view to building the primary units to such a size that their demands would give sufficient economies of scale to promote the development of secondary or ancillary units in sufficient numbers to supply the main needs of the primary units. The complex should have got round the usual problem of regional development because of which industry A doesn't come to an area because industry B (a supplier) is not present and industry B doesn't come because its main market, industry A, is not there. It would also have given rise to large multiplier and super-multiplier effects. The plan did not succeed but without doubt further attempts will be made to develop other complexes in Europe along similar lines.

Other similarities in European regional policy could be mentioned beyond those listed above — the orientation of incentives towards capital rather than labour (or some neutral feature like value added); the excessive concentration of regional policy on new firms rather than indigenous ones (reflecting political factors and the shortcomings in our understanding of entrepreneurship); the growing tendency towards selectivity in incentives but often at a pragmatic level, rather than through a careful analysis of objectives and priorities.

Both the similarities and differences of European regional policies have implications for a Community regional policy — the topic of the next section.

Regional policy and the EEC

So far, the EEC has had relatively little effect on regional policy in the member countries with the exception of Belgium and, to a very limited extent, Italy, where a proposal for a transport subsidy in the mid-1960s was objected to by the EEC. Whether the failure of the Italians finally to introduce this subsidy was a result of the EEC's stand or the lack of funds available to the Cassa is, however, a moot point.

Not only has EEC control of member-country policy been slight but, until very recently, Community regional policy has been weak. No body specifically concerned with regional development existed and funds for regional-development purposes were small. The Investment Bank, it is true, allocated three-quarters of its monies to the backward regions but there was no element of subsidy in these funds. Part of the Agricultural Guidance and Guarantee funds went to structural changes in the backward regions but the guidance section (responsible for structural change) has always been the Cinderella of the fund and the greater part of the fund's expenditure has been through the Guarantee section and to French farmers. There is a case for saying that in some countries the guarantee policies offset any of the regional benefits of the guidance section.[7] The Social Fund, with its resettlement and training grants, has had little money and only an indirect (and not necessarily beneficial) effect on the regional problems. The European Coal and Steel Community financing system has probably had more of an impact on the regional problem than all these other bodies put together, though it has not touched the major agricultural-problem areas of the Community.

This lack, or weakness, of Community regional policy has been in spite of the preamble to the Treaty of Rome in which the signatories expressed themselves 'anxious to strengthen the unity of their economies and to ensure their harmonious development by reducing the differences existing between the various regions and by mitigating the backwardness of the less favoured'. It is also in spite of widening — or at best stagnating — regional differentials. 'It must, however, be realised that these differences that already obtained when the EEC was established, have not become any smaller; on the contrary, they show a tendency to grow.'[8] The lack of policy is in spite of a Community in which 'the physical poverty of the underprivileged regions is matched only by the mounting environmental poverty of the areas of concentration.' (Commission, 1973, p. 5)

Only in the last few years have active steps been taken to implement and operate a Community regional policy with proposals first, that part of the guidance section funds should be used for the creation of industrial jobs in rural areas; and secondly, that a regional development corporation be set up having both advisory and technical assistance tasks as well as acquiring 'temporary and minority holdings in the regions qualifying for aid';[9] and thirdly that a regional development fund be created to give grants and interest subsidies for industrial, service and infrastructure projects in the problem regions. All three proposals still have to be agreed by the Council. It will be particularly interesting to see the Council's reaction to the Commission's proposal that 2,400 million units of account (for a three-year period) be allocated to the Regional Fund. This sum, which includes 150 million units of account from the agricultural fund for the creation of alternative jobs in rural areas, is higher than most observers expected. The Regional Development Fund is to be the 'principal vehicle for mobilising community resources as a complement to actions primarily carried out in the Member States.' (Commission, 1973, p. 13)

The Commission's general view of its involvement in regional policy is that 'Community regional policy cannot be a substitute for the national regional policies which Member States have been conducting for many years', but that 'the role of community regional policy will progressively increase as the Community increases and improves its instruments of intervention, together with the co-ordination of national regional policies which will be undertaken in the light of the varying extent of regional problems' (Commission 1973, p. 12). In the light of this statement there are three major requirements for a meaningful Community regional policy and each of them gives rise to difficulties.

The first is the isolation of problem regions and the ranking of these in terms of priority and need. As the Community increases its own regional instruments and as it seeks to co-ordinate (read control) the policies of member states this will increasingly become a key issue. Even ignoring the political factors the isolation and grading of the peripheral regions will not be easy. First, statistical methods for measuring the various features of a regional problem (unemployment, activity rates, migration and income per head, etc.) still differ considerably among the individual countries. The Italians, for example, measure their unemployment in such a way that the results are not directly comparable with the UK rates.[10] Secondly, even without these methodological problems (and there has been some standardisation of EEC statistics, particularly labour, in recent years), there remains the problem of interpretation. Southern Italian unemployment rates may be low relative to, say, Scotland but this may be explained in part by other features of the South's economy — low activity rates, high proportion of self-employed and agricultural workers, low unemployment benefit, etc. Social, political and economic factors play a major role in determining the statistical intensity of a regional problem and without firm and deep understanding of the individual economies it is difficult to reach anything like a standardised view. Thirdly, there is the problem of what represents need. Are social factors to predominate here? Is it to be need relative to the non-problem regions in the particular member states or the EEC as a whole? How are we to compare a region having, say, low unemployment with one having high migration?

The second requirement is the harmonisation of policies in the member states such that priority peripheral regions get favoured treatment. One would hope that this was not attempted through the existing blunt and limiting criteria of transparency currently operated in the central areas (virtually restricting assistance to capital grants). But if more wide-ranging policies are to be allowed there are two ancillary requirements before comparison (subsequent control) of incentives is possible. First, a system is required to allow a meaningful summation of the various national incentives such as to measure their overall value. (Should these be set against total or value added? What is the right discount rate? Should account be taken of national industrial structure, industrial structure of new firms attracted in the past or those expected in the future? How do we set about measuring the locational disadvantages of the various areas to get a net measure of the incentive value?) Secondly, a comparison of incentives requires an enormous amount of background context material such as tax rates, capital markets and accounting systems. Thirdly, apart from industrial incentives *per se,* how can other regional development policies be compared and co-ordinated — infrastructure and state industries in particular? Our economic knowledge and analysis is still insufficient to allow realistic inter-country policy comparisons to be made.

A third requirement for a meaningful Community regional policy is the development of new tools for its own policies beyond simply picking up the chits for member country policy. Stabenow says something of Community thinking in this respect in his paper. One suspects, however, that active consideration is being given to two main forms of policy. The first is control of development in the pressured areas. Unless some system for seriously limiting the inflow of immigrants from non-EEC countries can be found, the need for this is very great. The form of this control could be along the lines of the British IDC but one wonders whether the Italian-,

95

Dutch- and French-type penalty systems for their pressured regions would have advantages: first, in that they would avoid excessive demands on the European bureaucracy and, secondly, monies collected could be used to swell the Community's regional development funds. The problem of isolating regions for such control mechanisms will be serious.

A second strand of Community policy to which thought is obviously being given is that of a regional-development corporation. In late 1972 the view seemed to be that this should be rather low key. It would be interesting to know whether a more dynamic role (along, say, the lines of IRI) is now being considered — perhaps involving the take-over of a number of key European firms. Certainly an IRI-type system could not work along the lines recently suggested by the Commission (involving itself in small and medium firms in the problem regions), for if IRI is the model then the point needs to be stressed that IRI has never been successful in the field of small and medium-sized firms. There may be a case for a European corporation based on key European firms — particularly if Townroe's (1971) thesis of the satisficing firm is right — but the caution must be that this can be an expensive (in the real resource sense) form of policy and, unless the corporation was gigantic, and probably then unwieldy, could only make a limited contribution to EEC regional development.

To a large extent the great interest currently being shown in Community regional policy is a result of the Community's seeming objective of economic and monetary union by 1980.

> For it is clear that rapid progress towards Economic and Monetary Union would be arrested if national economies had not undergone the transformations needed to avoid excessive divergencies between the economies of member states. The reduction, by appropriate means, of regional imbalances is therefore a factor for accelerating those economic changes upon which the strength of economic and monetary union will depend when it comes to abandoning recourse to parity changes as a way of restoring a fundamental balance. (Commission, 1973, pp. 6–7)

Implicit in this statement appears, however, to be the view that the new Community involvement in regional policy will secure at least a substantial reduction of regional imbalances. Without doubt, regional funds deployed by the Community, on top of national funds, will help the peripheral regions but surely the time scale is too optimistic. We have already made the point that the correction of regional imbalances is a long-term process. National governments have been slow in recognising this fact; the Commission seems to have ignored it. If economic and monetary union depends on the substantial reduction of regional problems, one suspects that it will be well beyond 1980 before it is achieved. But not only is there an unjustified optimism in expecting that the Community's efforts will succeed, when years of expensive national policies have failed; there is also an implicit assumption that regional problems, when solved, are solved for good. Yet these problems often have a dynamism of their own.[11] Like the poor, one suspects that they will always be with us.

One final point in respect of the Community's regional policy needs to be made and stressed, even if only briefly. Comments by a number of observers seem to argue that the Community's regional policy (expanded, of course) could, when economic and monetary union is secured and when countries become regions, be the substitute for devaluation. This is totally mistaken. The current incentives in most countries are equal to less than 5 per cent of total production costs and are in consequence the equivalent of only a very low devaluation. To use regional policy types of measures for a meaningful 'national' devaluation would involve almost inconceivable levels of labour or capital subsidy and enormous inter-country exchequer transfers.

Notes

[1] I am grateful to Professor T. Wilson and Mr D. Yuill, both of Glasgow University, for comments on an earlier draft.

[2] For a good description of the differences in regional policy between EEC member countries (and other OECD countries) see the various papers produced by the seemingly eternal OECD working party no. 6 and particularly *The Regional Factor in Economic Development*, OECD (1970). Differences between EFTA countries have recently been described and discussed in EFTA (1971). The most up-to-date — even though cryptic — description of EEC member country policies can be found in the 'Thomson Report', Commission (1973).

[3] Detailed and up-to-date statistics on the various European regional problems can be found in the Thomson Report, op. cit.

[4] Even with government departments, the advocacy for regional decentralisation is often cautious. One wonders, cynically, whether the Danish case has become well known. The Danish regional development department had for a number of years advocated the decentralisation of a number of departments to the regions. One of the first results was the shifting of that department itself into the problem areas!

⁵ The idea is by no means new. Analysis on basically similar lines can be found in R. M. Haig (1926).

⁶ In other respects the role of the state holding sector in southern development has been substantial — accounting for some 50 per cent of southern industrial investment during the 1960s.

⁷ This is certainly the case in Italy where the EEC pricing system has impeded agricultural product switching. See report of Ministero del Bilancio e della Programmazione Economica (1972).

⁸ Part of a speech by F. Crijns, Regional Policy Directorate, to the European Movement conference on Scotland and the EEC (October 1972).

⁹ W. Stabenow, 'Regional Policy in the Enlarged European Community', cyclostyled paper given to the Regional Studies Association (October 1972), p. 9.

¹⁰ For a very good discussion of the problems of making international comparisons of unemployment figures, together with attempts at standardisation, see Robert J. Myers and John H. Chandler (1962A, 1962B).

¹¹ See A. Bergan 'Aspects of Regional Problems and Policies in Scandinavia', Conference on Large Scale Development in Remote and Rural Areas, University of Aberdeen (March 1973).

References

Allen K. J., 'The regional multiplier: some problems in estimation' *Regional and Urban Studies: A Social Science Approach,* S. C. Orr and J. B. Cullingworth (eds), (1969).

Cafiero S. and Busca S., *Lo Sviluppo Metropolitana in Italia,* Rome (1970).

Commission of the European Communities, *Report on the Regional Problems in the Enlarged Community,* Brussels (1973).

EFTA, *Industrial Mobility,* Geneva (1971).

Haig R. M., 'Towards an understanding of the metropolis' *Quarterly Journal of Economics,* 40 (1926), pp. 179–208 and 402–34.

Lever W. F., 'Manufacturing linkages and the search for suppliers and markets' *The Industrial Firm and Location Decisions,* F. E. I. Hamilton (ed.), (1974).

Ministero del Bilancio e della Programmazione Economica, *Programma Economico Nazionale 1971–5*; Allegato Secundo: *Programma 1966-70: Obiettivi e Risultati,* Rome (1972).

Myers R. J. and Chandler J. H., 'International comparisons of unemployment' *Monthly Labor Review* (1972A).

Myers R. J. and Chandler J. H., 'Towards exploring international unemployment rates' *Monthly Labor Review* (1972A).

Needleman L. and Scott B., 'Regional problems and location of industry policy in Britain' *Urban Studies,* 1 (1964), pp. 153–73.

OECD, *The Regional Factor in Economic Development,* Paris (1970).

Rhodes J. and Kan A., *Office Dispersal and Regional Policy,* Cambridge University, Department of Applied Economics, Occasional Paper 30, Cambridge (1971).

Townroe P. M., *Industrial Location Decisions,* University of Birmingham, Centre for Urban and Regional Studies, Occasional Paper 15, Birmingham (1971).

Ventriglia F., 'Meggi e modalita della ripresa dopo due crisi congiunturali' *Rassegna Economica* (1972), pp. 927–55.

Wilson T., 'The regional multiplier – a critique' *Oxford Economic Papers,* 20 (1968), pp. 375–93.

5 The National System of Cities as a Framework for Urban and Regional Policy

J. B. Goddard

The convergence of urban and regional policies

Recent reviews of urbanisation strategies in a number of different countries have suggested that the concepts, objectives and practices associated with the traditionally separate fields of urban and regional policy are beginning to converge (Bourne, 1973; EFTA, 1973). Here urban policy means policy concerned with single cities or, in some cases, groups of interrelated cities within a single region, and regional policy refers to attempts to achieve a balanced development between major regions of a country. For example, it is now recognised that the short-term and limited economic measures traditionally associated with regional policy need to be supplemented by longer term objectives and policies that take account not only of economic but also of social and environmental factors. Long-term objectives clearly demand selective and concentrated efforts rather than dispersed effects spread over large areas of the country concerned. Concentration implies an urban focus and consequently a co-ordination of both urban and regional policy measures. The principal argument of this paper is that such co-ordination can probably best be achieved through a national settlement strategy which acts as a framework for all aspects of public policy that have a bearing on spatial distribution at the national, regional and local levels.

Table 5.1 is an attempt to illustrate this convergence on the national system of cities as the most appropriate strategic framework. The table selectively draws upon experience in a number of different countries, principally the EFTA countries, including the United Kingdom (EFTA, 1973), together with Canada and Australia (Bourne, 1973). The table does not apply to any single country; in fact, there is probably no single country which has a national settlement strategy in which all of the dimensions of Table 5.1 are represented. As in any attempt at tabular summary, there are many arbitrary and possibly erroneous classifications, while many themes have obviously been ignored. Nevertheless, the table illustrates an

Table 5.1   Examples of the convergence of urban and regional policies towards national settlement strategies (modified from Bourne, 1973)

	Urban policy		National settlement strategies	Regional policy		
	Previous or current perspective	Evolving perspective →		← Evolving perspective	Previous or current perspective	
Concepts & definitions	Physically defined city or built-up area	City region or daily urban systems (e.g. labour-market area)	Interdependence within and between a hierarchically ordered system of cities	Functionally integrated region (e.g. based on economic interdependencies)	Uniform structural region (e.g. based on industrial structure)	Concepts & definitions
Goals	Spatial & physical form	Management of processes of economic and social change	The regulation of the total environment; a contextual and open-systems perspective	Equality of economic, social and physical development	Economic balance	Goals
Problems	Incompatible land uses / Spatial concentration of industrial and office employment	Social polarisation / Mis-matching of employment opportunities and occupational structure	Monitoring of indirect distributive effects and externalities	Specialised occupational structure / Problems of access to specialist information	Specialised industrial structure / Inaccessibility for transport of goods	Problems
Institutions	Independent sectoral authorities (education, health, transport etc.)	Unitary authorities	Hierarchy of spatial planning: national, regional and local	Super-ministries with regional offices	Independent national ministries (transport, housing, planning etc.)	Institutions
Policies (a) Physical	Local over-spill schemes	Major expanded cities as counter-magnets	The national system of cities as a framework for the spatial, intersectoral and hierarchical co-ordination of public policy	Control of several major cities	Control of physical growth of single metropolis	Policies (a) Physical
(b) Economic	Industrial dispersal	Dispersal of offices as well as industry		Selective spatial and sectoral controls and incentives for offices and industry (decentralisation)	Blanket industrial location controls and incentives (dispersal)	(b) Economic
(c) Social	Aspatial policies in education, health etc.	Selective urban priority areas		Occupational re-training and spatially selective subsidies (e.g. passenger transport)	Aspatial social policies (e.g. unemployment benefits)	(c) Social

evolving perspective to public policy that would not otherwise be apparent.

The remaining paragraphs of this opening section of the paper are used to comment upon Table 5.1. The rest of the paper then examines in greater detail what some policy-makers see as the likely goals and forms of a national-settlement strategy. Before proceeding any further it should be made clear immediately that a 'national-settlement strategy', as the term is used here, does not refer to an idealised spatial and size distribution of urban settlements within a given country.

Convergence of concepts and definitions

At the urban scale the need to consider the implications of the relationship between a city and its surrounding regions is now generally accepted. Such intraregional relations are most powerfully expressed in journey-to-work flows to employment cores from their commuting hinterland. These types of flow define what has come to be called the 'daily urban system' in terms of sometimes overlapping labour-market areas (Hall, 1971). Conceptually, if not in terms of administrative areas, functional definitions of urban regions have therefore displaced physical delimitations. At the interregional scale it is similarly appreciated that such daily urban systems lock into regional and national systems of cities through complex networks of social and economic relations. Social inter-dependencies are most clearly expressed in terms of migration flows between cities at different levels in the urban hierarchy (Figure 5.1). On the economic side, the growth of multi-unit corporations means that linkages within and between organisations, expressed in terms of flows of money, goods and information, directly and indirectly connect distant urban regions into a unified spatial system (Figures 5.2 and 5.3). It is now widely appreciated by academics that the links in such systems of cities from the principal channel through which development process and policy effects are spread (Boudeville, 1966; Berry, 1972; Pred, 1973). Nevertheless, in most countries, regional-policy measures are still directed through uniform structural regions, regions which emphasise internal homogeneity rather than the heterogeneity and complementarity that characterise functional regions.

Convergence of problems and goals

An emphasis on inter-urban dependencies inevitably leads to the adoption of an open-systems perspective on regional-development problems (Emery and Trist, 1972). Open-system thinking highlights the overlaps that exist both between spatial sub-systems and between different policy areas. Thus

103

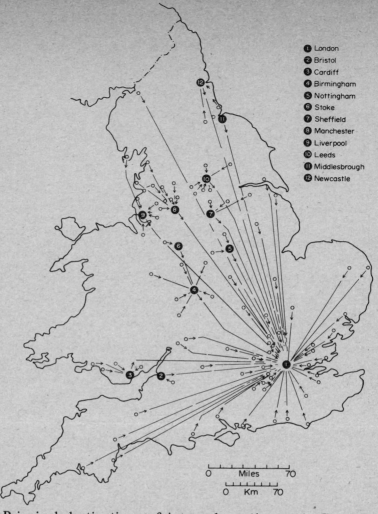

Fig. 5.1   Principal destinations of inter-urban migrants in Great Britain, 1965–66 (standard metropolitan labour-market areas)

problems of an individual city have to be seen in the context of its relations with the surrounding region *and* with other cities in the national system of cities. For example, some of the problems of the inner metropolitan area, such as social polarisation, must be seen in the context of problems of persistent structural unemployment in cities in the DAs, as well as unbalanced local dispersal of jobs and people.

The increasing overlap of policy areas has in turn created a need to specify clearly the goals of public policy in general and to consider how

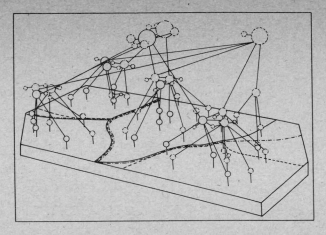

A graphical model of three organisations, made up of units which are linked together but at the same time divided in hierarchical levels and spread out over geographical space. Size of sphere indicates level. Organisation A unbroken lines, B dashed lines and C dashed-dotted lines.

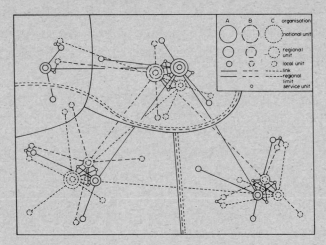

Units, links and regional boundaries of organisations projected on a map.

Fig. 5.2 Spatial structure of three hypothetical organisations (after Wärneryd)

spatial factors might influence the achievement of these goals. So both urban and regional policy have witnessed a change from spatially defined goals, such as 'concentrated urban form' or 'regional balance' to a consideration of how the spatial dimension affects the attainment of equity and

105

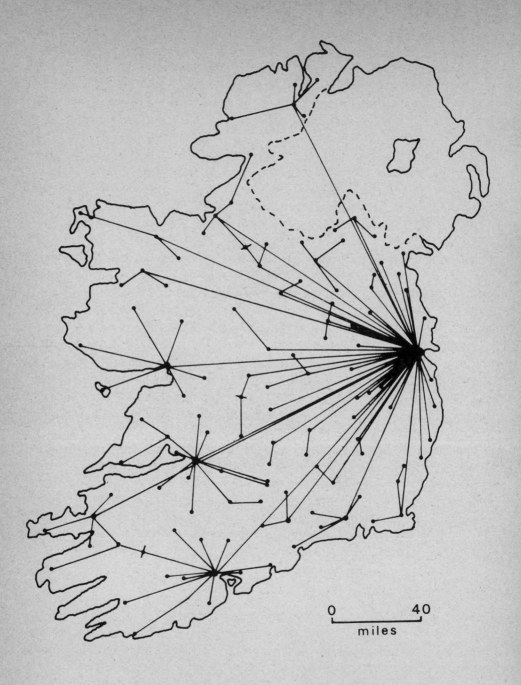

Fig. 5.3 Principal destinations of telephone calls in the Irish Republic (after O'Sullivan, 1968)

growth goals. In this respect, an emphasis on the social consequences of urbanisation has come to characterise thinking at all levels. The indirect distributive effects and externalities created through spatial planning within cities are increasingly well documented (Harvey, 1971). Although less widely discussed, the inter-urban differences in environmental conditions are probably greater than the intra-urban differences from which they derive.

Adjustments in a dynamic and open urban system will always produce new socially undesirable side effects, so the need continually to monitor processes of change is increasingly accepted. But an emphasis on social monitoring at the total expense of economic and physical considerations would be as undesirable as a previous emphasis on these latter factors at the urban and regional levels respectively. This is because it is now more widely appreciated that social, economic and physical factors interact with one another in a complex way. For example, the persistent problem of slow rates of industrial growth and change in the development areas could be as much the result of poor access to specialist information and knowledge as to problems of physical inaccessibility for the transport of goods (Thorngren, 1970; Tornqvist, 1970). Since there is a close correlation between the availability of specialist information and the distribution of job functions within organisations, the economic problems of development areas may be closely related to social problems of occupational structure — i.e. a preponderance of manual and clerical jobs. So, from an economic and social point of view, occupational structure becomes as important a dimension to regional development as problems of industrial structure, such as an excessive dependence on declining heavy industries (Goddard, 1973A). Similarly, at the urban scale, social problems are created not simply by the dispersal of employment in aggregate but from an unbalanced dispersal of different types of job opportunities and population in different occupational groups. A short-run mis-match between the population and employment may therefore arise.

Convergence of institutional forms

Consideration of labour market problems, although relating both to economic and social conditions, represents only part of the total environment. At both urban and regional levels the effect of differential physical access to all sorts of amenities, such as recreation, education and welfare services, is now widely accepted as a factor influencing the achievement of equity goals. This implies spatial co-ordination of the location decisions of different public sectors, from national down to local levels. The

107

emergence of unitary authorities at the urban scale and super-ministries at the national scale represents an attempt to achieve such inter-sectoral co-ordination. Regional offices of national ministries may also encourage co-ordination among hierarchical levels.

Convergence of policies and practices

The process of urban-system change has always created new problems which have generated specific policy responses. In physical planning at the intraregional level, local over-spill schemes have been replaced by major expanded towns which have a long-term objective of acting as counter-magnets to the large metropolis. At the inter-regional level, control of the physical growth of a single metropolis has been replaced by controls over several major cities. In the economic sphere, the importance of office employment in urban and regional development has led to policies that cover both manufacturing and tertiary sectors. Since office employment is so clearly an urban function, the need for selective, spatial and sectoral control rather than blanket incentives covering extensive parts of a country and broad sectors of the economy has been repeatedly stressed. Selectivity in educational priority areas has become the keynote of both urban policy and regional — for example, through the identification of growth centres and mobile sectors of the economy.

But growth centre and related industrial-mobility policies raise a number of fundamental questions, basically concerning matters of location. For example, from where and to where in a country should mobile industry move? What types of environments are appropriate for different economic activities? What types of centres should be designated as growth centres and where are these to be located? How are the benefits of growth centres to be confined to the development areas rather than spreading back to the congested regions?

When it comes down to the specifics of implementing such policies, the need for a hierarchy of objectives with different time horizons soon becomes apparent. Comprehensive long-term strategies are needed as a framework for spatial and non-spatial policies that are designed to deal with more immediate problems. Although a growth centre policy may be regarded as a relatively broad economic-development strategy, many authorities do not consider such a strategy sufficiently comprehensive for the achievement of long-term goals. For example, 'growth centre policy has to be considered within the context of an inter-related system of centres and requires the manipulation of the entire system of cities taking into account the direct effects of policy measures and the indirect effects generated by existing relations.' (EFTA, 1968) Here, growth centres are seen not merely as limited tools for encouraging development within a peripheral region, but also as part of an overall strategy for the entire settlement pattern of a country.

Opinion converges on the same conclusion from the urban level. Here the need for corporate planning of the urban environment is now widely accepted. It is fully appreciated that numerous public and private decisions, such as those relating to the location of homes, work-places and transportation facilities, interact with one another in a very complex fashion. The chief function of corporate planning is to manage the daily urban system in such a way as to balance the needs of all sections of the community, both firms and households. The point of convergence with regional policy is that the system of all settlements within a nation operates in a similar way as a single city; each unit is but one sub-system within an interdependent system of cities. An urban policy decision such as a town-expansion scheme has a direct effect on the local community but also can have many indirect consequences for a large number of other settlements. The control of these indirect efforts is extremely difficult but their very existence demands consideration of the settlement system as a whole. It is therefore important to consider the impact of urban policy not only in relation to spatial distribution and resource allocation within a city or region but also in the wider context of the national settlement system.

The co-ordination of urban and regional policy through a national-settlement strategy

The preceding paragraphs have touched upon selected policy themes from a number of different countries. To summarise, the convergence of concepts and definitions emphasises the importance of interdependencies within and among a hierarchically ordered system of cities as the principal mechanism through which development processes spread. The goal of spatial and aspatial policies is to manage changes in this system in order to achieve equity and growth objectives and minimise undesired side effects. This goal is most likely to be achieved by using the national system of cities as a strategic framework for the inter-sectoral and hierarchical co-ordination of public policies.

The goals of a national settlement strategy

A national settlement strategy should not be seen as an end in itself but a means towards the achievement of specified national goals. The essential first step in formulating such a policy therefore requires the translating of national goals into specific objectives for the development of the national system of cities. Because such a policy affects the population as a whole — not just the distribution of economic activity — this translation process must take account of all possible objectives that are seen to be the concern of central government — covering both social as well as economic welfare. As in national planning at the aggregate level, it will be necessary to be aware of possible conflicts between different sets of goals and the need for value judgements in balancing priorities.

Because of the importance of goal formulation and the difficulty of translating from national to urban system levels, and the problem of goal conflicts, it would perhaps be helpful to consider the development of the urban system in a temporal perspective. Thus one economist has recently been 'tempted to think of economic growth in terms of urban growth and to treat the national system of cities as a spatial form of organisation adopted by the industrial economy to achieve its growth goals.' (Richardson, 1972) How far the existing urban system represents an optimal arrangement for achieving national goals of economic growth is far from clear; indeed, from a practical point of view, such an optimal pattern is probably not feasible, since economic conditions are continually changing. But it is probably reasonable to assume that over a long period of time the spatial structure of the urban system has evolved principally in response to economic forces. In very general terms, the present urban structure has therefore been shaped by the sum of past economic conditions and demands. But economic processes do not stand still. Contemporary forces are at work within the framework of the existing settlement structure that in the long run will contribute towards shaping new patterns of settlement. However, from the point of view of population distribution, this process of change may be particularly painful, because there are often time-lags between evolving patterns of industrial and service location and commensurate adjustments in the population and settlement structure.

In the short term, discrepancies often appear between the supply of job opportunities by type and the pattern of population demand. Unfortunately such discrepancies often seem to work to the detriment of households. For example, many existing small settlements are located at the sites of now exhausted natural resources or were once associated with single companies that have long since closed down or moved to new locations. At certain times such settlements offer economies to commercial enterprises, perhaps in the form of monopoly positions in local labour markets. Similarly, large urban agglomerations were necessary from an economic point of view as long as technological conditions imposed severe limitations on the movement of goods and people. Such agglomerations still dominate the urban scene, even though the technological conditions that brought them about have since changed considerably. Large cities still produce economic benefits for particular types of activities, especially those for which personal contact is important. However, space-demanding productivity processes, coupled with reduced transfer costs of goods and standardised information mean that the costs of the largest urban centres may eventually outweigh the benefits for many types of economic activity. As a result, certain activities are seeking out new locations, leaving behind in the metropolitan areas considerable social costs, partly created by their earlier environmental requirements — including a population with insufficient skills or resources to follow.

In terms of economic goals, one of the objectives of an urban policy could be to foster the variety of economic environments that seem to be necessary for the evolution and subsequent expansion of new forms of economic activity. Most research on the operation of the existing settlement system would suggest that this goal could be achieved with little modification of existing trends, other than through the encouragement of industrial mobility, since variety is an essential characteristic of an hierarchical structure of urban units. A hierarchy offers advantages, since at one point in time various enterprises will be at different stages of development and each will have different environmental requirements. For example, the largest urban areas can offer considerable advantages to newly established firms, particularly in the form of each access to technical knowledge; but, at a later stage, as processes become more standardised, a less varied environment might be more profitable. The same factors could equally well apply to various parts of the same enterprises — ranging, for example, from the highest level decision-making functions through to more routine productive processes (Figure 5.4).

However, it does not follow that the most appropriate settlement structure on economic grounds is *necessarily* the most appropriate if full account is taken of social considerations. The preceding discussion has suggested that, in an unplanned situation, the economic benefit of the settlement structure depends in part on the transfer of social cost to the community. Partly because of technological change, the equilibrium on which the social justice of a settlement system depends is a long-term goal that may never be achieved, particularly in spatial terms. Thus one settlement's benefit may be gained through another's cost.

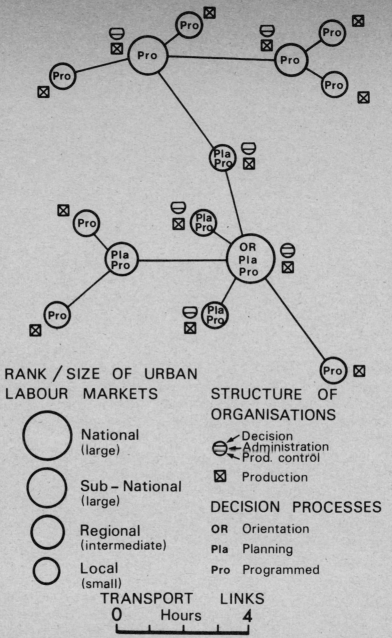

RANK / SIZE OF URBAN
LABOUR MARKETS

○ National (large)

○ Sub – National (large)

○ Regional (intermediate)

○ Local (small)

STRUCTURE OF ORGANISATIONS

⊖ ← Decision
← Administration
← Prod. control

⊠ Production

DECISION PROCESSES

OR Orientation

Pla Planning

Pro Programmed

TRANSPORT LINKS

0 ⊢⊣⊢⊣ Hours ⊢⊣⊢⊣ 4

Fig. 5.4 A theoretical classification of urban contact environments for a hypothetical system of cities
(Each unit is characterised by the parts of a multi-unit organisation and the type of decision processes that are most suited to the contact environment of the local area and its pattern of accessibility to all other units in the city system.)

112

Unfortunately, these costs are not equally shared among different sections of the community. Most governments are aware of the inevitable inequalities in the distribution of the costs and benefit of the economic system at the national level and attempt to achieve some reallocation of resources through taxation and welfare policy. But what is seldom realised for individuals (although it is common knowledge in the case of firms) is that access to resources of all types — employment opportunities, public and private service and recreation — that together determine an individual's 'real income', is determined not only by that individual's position in the social system but also by his location within space (Harvey, 1971). Here, 'real income' covers not only the monetary rewards of employment and property ownership but also all the costs and benefits that in combination determine the welfare of the individual. Thus, just as economic activities gain all manner of benefits by locating in appropriate urban environments (and frequently these benefits are not always directly measurable in terms of short-run profits), so the same set of urban environments contributes towards the total welfare of individuals to varying degrees.

The key to understanding the spatial determinants of real income or welfare can probably be found in the three words 'demand',[2] 'supply' and 'access', which all have particular spatial and temporal connotations, in addition to their usual economic and social interpretations. The supply of resources in the form of job opportunities of different types and of public and private service facilities varies considerably among settlements. In addition to problems associated with shifts in employment location that have already been outlined, many established public and private service facilities (like hospitals) have been concentrated in space in the process of seeking narrowly defined economies of scale. Generally these developments favour the metropolis, especially when seen in connection with the introduction of new types of services, which first appear in the larger centres and slowly filter down the urban hierarchy. Looking at the pattern of very broad terms, the working party felt that individuals in different settlements would have similar basic job and service requirements, related particularly to their stage in the life cycle. Regardless of preferences, all individuals need access to employment, retail and welfare services and recreational amenities. Needs are more extensive than narrowly defined economic 'demand', although there are some geographical variations, associated with such factors as the age distribution of the population and trade-offs connected with environmental factors, in the main the pattern of individual needs should follow the distribution of the total population in a spatially unbiased way. But, as a result of the fact that

113

patterns of supply and demand do not coincide in space *and* time, inequalities of access to resources arise.

The time dimension is important in a number of respects; for example, in order to have access to — i.e. to use — facilities, the individual is necessarily involved in travel. There are numerous constraints on the individual with respect to access, but perhaps the most important, after account has been taken of income differentials, is the distance he can travel in a reasonable time (Hägerstrand, 1970). As a result of differences in the level of personal mobility and variations between urban units in the number of opportunities available within a given time distance, discrepancies emerge among people in the degrees of freedom they have in the allocation of their time. Although, within a daily perspective, all individuals are endowed with the same fixed time resource, differences emerge in the degrees of flexibility a person has in allocating his time to different activities — a fact partly determined by the type of environment in which the individual lives. Thus, time taken up in long journeys to work is not available to be spent with the family or in recreation. Because of all manner of time constraints, certain basic resources may simply not be available to the individual living in particular urban units. Despite the expectations voiced in some circles in the past decade, the completely mobile society is unlikely to come about within the foreseeable future, if ever (Webber, 1963 and 1964; Pahl, 1969).

Similar problems of demand, supply and access emerge when these factors are viewed in terms of the life span of the individual. In this context, questions of accessibility to educational, employment and, most obviously, medical service, can be seen as important determinants of life chances. Job opportunities that cannot be reached by daily travel involve migration but here again individuals are constrained to varying degrees in their ability to move to new urban areas in order to take up the type of job determined by their personal qualification. Some people may prefer not to move because of local ties but are forced to do so because of economic circumstances; either ties are broken or long extra journeys are required to visit relatives or friends. For others, the local environment may impose restriction on their daily activities but lack of employment or housing opportunities elsewhere prevents them changing this environment for one more suitable to their needs. For instance, the variety offered by very large cities can be advantageous for the young, single and well-to-do but for the old and those with less disposable income, this variety may be unavailable. Such people pay many of the costs of urban agglomeration but seem to gain few of the benefits — and yet they may still be locationally tied by employment to the city. So just as there are variations between individuals in their degree of personal mobility on a daily scale, so on a life scale the same pattern-variation emerges in a person's ability to turn residential preferences into actual locational choices. In the long run, therefore, all sorts of problems arise in matching patterns of demand for jobs and living conditions to the supply of these items within and among urban areas, problems that have a fundamental bearing on the distribution of resources in relation to desired social objectives (Figure 5.5).

At present governments have more control over this sort of problem than is fully realised, principally through their influence on the location of public services and continually increasing public-sector employment. But unfortunately in few countries are the activities of different public sectors conceived — let alone co-ordinated — in a spatial context, especially at a national scale. So, although equality of availability is a basic tenet for the provision of welfare facilities, one social administrator has pointed out that there are such considerable differences between urban areas in social provision that the equality objective needs to be connected to one of 'territorial justice' (Davies, 1968). Unfortunately the increasing application of narrowly defined cost-criteria to public-sector activity has tended to result in the concentration of service facilities into larger units and fewer and larger urban areas, a process which could be working against the desired equality goal of the social services.

In the manipulation of the environment through planning processes, governments therefore have a power to influence the achievement of not only economic but also social goals. In spite of a long history of welfare policies, it has only recently been recognised in Britain that planning at the local and regional scale 'affects the distribution of resources in a particular spatial context and thus affects the access of people at different locations to these resources' (Strategic Plan for the South East, 1971). The same argument applies, with possibly even greater force, on the national scale to the issue of planning the urban system and regional development. To continue with the quotation from the same official report:

> ... some sections of population living in particular areas gain by having better job opportunities or better access to facilities and others lose by the very fact that investment is elsewhere or by suffering, for example, from the noise and danger of new harbours, airports and motorways. The achievement of some social goal depends upon the spatial distribution of jobs and homes as well as upon non-spatial social policies. Spatial and non-spatial policies must be seen together in the light of social goals and this is a chief justification for combining social and economic policies with government decisions on investment.

115

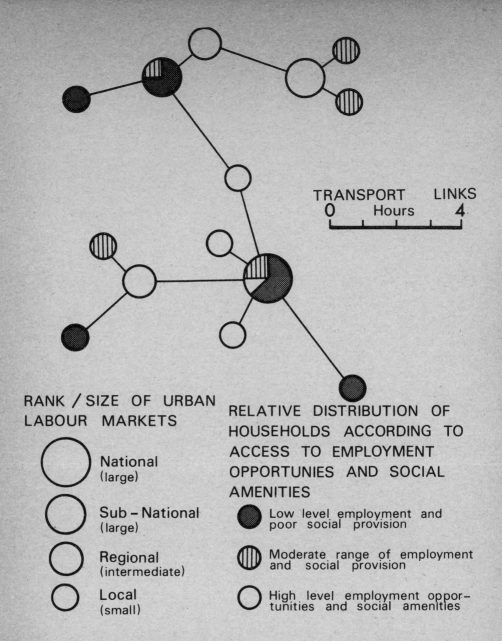

TRANSPORT   LINKS
0   Hours   4

RANK / SIZE OF URBAN LABOUR MARKETS

National (large)

Sub – National (large)

Regional (intermediate)

Local (small)

RELATIVE DISTRIBUTION OF HOUSEHOLDS ACCORDING TO ACCESS TO EMPLOYMENT OPPORTUNIES AND SOCIAL AMENITIES

Low level employment and poor social provision

Moderate range of employment and social provision

High level employment opportunities and social amenities

Fig. 5.5   A theoretical classification of social environments for a hypothetical system of cities

(Each urban unit is characterised by the proportion of households having high, moderate and low levels of access to a range of employment opportunities and social amenities, both locally and elsewhere in the city system. Undivided circles indicate that all households fall into a particular address category.)

116

As a result of such considerations a principal objective for a national-settlement policy would be to develop a pattern of urban units that would help the attainment of social objectives of equality of opportunity, while at the same time not being undesirable or unfeasible from an economic point of view. In this respect particular attention has to be paid to the occupational structure of the labour market of urban units. Occupational structure is an important but previously neglected dimension, because it refers both to the job that an individual does — i.e. his role in an organisation — and to his position in society — i.e. the resources at his command. Occupation therefore links economic and social environments. Although emphasis is placed on social goals, it must be borne in mind that such goals can only be induced through careful direction of present and future economic opportunities, including the steering of employment to new locations. Thus trends in the location of employment should not have been viewed as a necessary determinant of the evolving form of the urban system but as one possible means for achieving social ends.

The forms of a national settlement strategy

A national settlement strategy should obviously provide a very broad outline for the development of the national system of settlement rather than the form of a rigidly defined spatial plan. The strategy would provide a framework for decision-making at the national level by public and private agencies and a basis for more detailed planning of spatial structure at the regional and city levels. As a long-term strategy, the settlement policy would also provide a focus for the operation of shorter-term regional policy measures, such as industrial incentives and employment relocation, and would ensure that such decisions were integrated with all aspects of environmental planning.

The distinctive feature of the strategic approach is that it integrates spatial planning with other aspects of government activity not traditionally associated with it, such as regional and economic policy and social policy. Thus the measures taken in response to a strategy might include long-term planned investment in urban renewal, transportation links and New Towns' construction and also incentives and controls, both short, and long-term, designed for the creation and desired distribution of employment and the proper location of welfare facilities.

Such measures are not new in themselves; the novelty lies in the sectorally and spatially integrated approach to the many aspects of the problems of population distribution. Population is a basic national resource in which people cannot clearly be divided into social and economic entities. The same people are members of households in a social setting, demanding certain supplies of service and job opportunities, and employees in an economic setting providing the necessary facilities. It is thus impossible to plan for the distribution of economic activities without taking account of labour-market conditions; just as the supply of labour forms part of the economic environment of a particular urban unit from the point of view of an industrial enterprise, so the supplies of different job opportunities form part of the total social environment from the point of view of the individual. Job opportunities combine with housing conditions, service, educational and welfare provisions and recreational amenities to determine the total living conditions or 'quality of life' of a particular urban unit. Together, these factors influence migration and ultimately the distribution of population and these, in turn, affect labour-market conditions; the population distribution is clearly the focal point of this complex set of inter-relationships, representing the outcome of numerous interacting forces.

Because a large number of different agencies have a role in determining the many aspects of environmental conditions in different urban units, the task of integration and co-ordination is likely to be extremely difficult. For this reason, there is a case for establishing a hierarchy of planning, with more detailed planning at lower levels of the hierarchy, set within the context of broader strategies at a higher level. The number of levels in the hierarchy will depend on the size of the country and the size of the problem involved. The fact that all forms of decision-making have a spatial manifestation means that geographic space, structured in the form of a strategic plan, can act as a potentially unifying dimension. A national settlement development strategy would thus serve as a framework for central and local government and private investment on a national scale. At the next level of the hierarchy these strategies would provide a basis for more detailed decision-making for urban units. The emphasis in a national strategy is therefore placed on the resource allocation among, rather than within, cities.

Obviously the national strategy would need to be mainly based on the existing settlement structure; opportunities for fundamental changes in this structure are limited, given the inherent inertia of the urban system. Emphasis would therefore have to be placed upon the management of processes of change within the existing framework. This might imply the planned contraction of certain settlements and the controlled growth of others, so ensuring that people do not suffer as a result of too rapid changes. Such planned changes in the context of the settlement strategy

118

imply that provision will often have to be made in new or expanded settlements in advance of need, in order to minimise disruption for both people and firms and to act as a stimulus for planned expansion.

In its concern for the total environment the strategy would have to take account of the needs of both firms and households. In certain respects, these two sets of needs can be jointly met through the management of labour-market conditions within and among different settlements. One clearly definable objective of the settlement strategy could be to create in each unit labour-market conditions that can be adjusted to changing economic circumstances. This would imply a wide range of *occupational* skills, as well as a varied structure free from excessive dependence on single industries. While regional policies have long recognised the need to diversify industrial structure, the importance of access to a range of skills and information, and the needs of people for occupational mobility must be stressed. By providing possibilities for occupational mobility within the local labour market, the settlement strategy should help reduce the incidence of forced long-distance migration between different settlements. If there is not too great a variation among urban units in the basic essentials of life — of which career possibilities are probably the most critical component — people would be free to stay or to migrate on the basis of less fundamental environmental preferences.

Some policy instruments associated with a national settlement strategy

A variety of policy instruments could be used to achieve these objectives. A preliminary step might be to classify *all* major urban units according to their nationally-determined long-term growth and functions. Such a classification must cover the whole settlement system, not just those parts that have problems caused by size, rapid growth or rapid contraction. A national settlement policy is therefore a more comprehensive tool than the identification of growth centres within regions or a strategy of control in the congested areas.

The essence of a classification of urban units is that it can be used as a basis for the selective application of government incentives in some settlements and controls in others. Specific places can be chosen to be the focus of both industrial location measures and investment in infrastructure. In terms of industrial mobility, a major advantage of such a classification of settlements is that possibilities for active promotion are considerably greater than is the case with blanket policies covering extensive and often heterogeneous regions; it is obviously easier to promote the image of a limited number of identifiable units than extensive tracts of country loosely labelled 'development areas'.

The adoption of a goal-orientated classification scheme can create a conflict between the need for long-term commitments, on the one hand, and the need for flexibility in order to meet changing organisational and technological conditions, on the other. While changes in the planned functions of some settlements may be necessary, the classification should also identify, from amongst the full range of classified settlements, those that are likely to contribute most towards reducing economic and social differentials within the settlement system. From the very outset those strategic settlements that appear to have the greatest potential in this respect will need to be the focus of some fixed commitments. In countries where problems of regional imbalance can be attributed to the excessive growth of a few major cities, this might imply identifying those settlements that have a possibility of operating in some respects as national alternatives to the largest urban units. Nevertheless, emphasising such strategic centres should not disguise the fact that a classification scheme should encompass all settlements in the urban system, though with varying levels of commitment.

Focused investment in infrastructure (including housing, cultural, welfare, and educational facilities and intra- and inter-regional transport) within the framework of the settlement strategy would be necessary to enhance the status of major strategic centres relative to the capital, a process that will be essential if differentials within the settlement system are to be reduced. This investment would need to be accompanied by a pattern of 'concentrated decentralisation' of top administrative jobs from the capital, in order to secure the functional independence of the strategic centres. Decentralisation would ensure that many linkage requirements could be met by the strategic centres within the regions, so reducing the leakage of non-industrial multiplier effects from the area of their origin. Concentrated decentralisation is therefore essential if the strategic centres are to function as information sources rather than simply as staging posts for the capital.

Since a single strategic centre could not provide all national — i.e. unique — functions, an objective of equality of availability would require a pattern of investment in passenger-transport facilities that link the strategic centres not only to their immediately surrounding settlements but also to other strategic centres in the system. At present, the hierarchical ordering of passenger transport, with a dominant focus on the capital to the exclusion of cross-country links among other major centres, only serves to reinforce centralisation of control and regional inequalities in development potentials. Decentralisation of decision-making functions would therefore need to be linked with the reinstatement of links across the settlement hierarchy. In view of the likely costs, selective investment in advanced telecommunications could be of critical importance in fostering such linkages.

In addition to the direct economic benefits to the development areas, a pattern of concentrated decentralisation can create more long-term social benefits than is possible with a greater dispersal of investment. Concentration plus decentralisation of administrative employment can ensure that labour markets offer possibilities for occupational mobility without enforcing geographical mobility; the urban units can therefore intercept migration flows and so reduce the pressures on the congested regions. Medium-sized labour markets can also offer an acceptable range of employment opportunities and ensure that journeys to work are not over long. Finally, moderate concentrations of population can provide sufficient support for a high level of provision of social amenities.

Above all else, it is the political problems associated with classification which militate against the adoption of a selective approach to urban policy at the national level. The selection of some places as centres for major investment inevitably implies that some other settlements are not selected. One possible solution to this sort of problem is to recognise openly the different time horizons to which the various policies apply. Regional inducements to industry have traditionally been problem-orientated rather than goal-orientated. Such an approach could conflict with a necessarily longer-term national settlement strategy, since the creation of new employment in small centres needs additional commitment in urban infrastructure. It may therefore be argued that short-term policies will probably be most effective if they are 'person-orientated' rather than 'place-orientated'. That is, people who chose to live in places that were not viable in the long term could be given personal financial assistance, e.g. to run private transport as an alternative to fixed investment in public-transport facilities, but they could not be guaranteed a large choice of employment opportunities or social amenities. At the other extreme of the urban hierarchy, problems created by the sheer size or too rapid contraction of the big cities are probably most effectively tackled in the short run by person-orientated policies which need to be reinforced by long-run balanced dispersal of population and employment.

Because national settlement policy has to be place-orientated it must emphasise long-term objectives; in so doing, the policy must ensure that short-term measures do not conflict with these objectives. For example, a policy that can be readily implemented, that of dispersing civil service

121

employment from the capital, would need to be related to the long-term objective for fostering major centres in the development areas; if civil service employment were widely dispersed, and this dispersal were not associated with a decentralisation of some decision-making functions, it would contribute little to the development areas and only serve to reinforce the position of the capital. At the same time co-ordinated (public) and unco-ordinated (private) dispersal of employment from congested cities must not be allowed to counteract long-term social goals. For example, the dispersal of manufacturing and clerical employment from London that is in part the result of location controls could be contributing to a potentially serious degree of social polarisation.

The successful operation of a national settlement strategy will almost certainly require new adminstrative arrangements. A corporate approach to spatial planning at the national level would create many problems for existing institutions, in addition to those of scale. Perhaps the greatest obstacle is the sectoral nature of national budgets and the practical effects of national standards of provision, e.g. for schools, hospitals and housing, which are too often narrowly drawn. Usually resources for such items are distributed between settlements on a per capita basis in order to meet nationally agreed standards. But in spatial terms this amounts to no more than trend planning or, as some would call it, 'bottleneck' planning. In other words the existing distribution of population is accepted and resources are allocated accordingly. However, the very essence of a national settlement strategy is its selective approach to resource allocation, with facilities in certain instances provided with future needs in view — as in the case of British new and expanded towns. Clearly selective allocation of resources across a broad front requires some completely new form of spatial budgeting. While this objective might be achieved through separate block allocations of funds to different regional authorities, some form of central control is still essential to ensure that a national perspective is maintained.

The correct balancing of national and regional objectives is at the heart of the successful implementation of a national settlement policy. On the one hand, a need for a national view suggests a high degree of central administrative control. On the other hand, the objective of regional balance calls for physical dispersal of administrative employment from the centre, coupled with the decentralisation of authority — especially in budgeting matters.

An example of an institution that would probably be essential to the successful operation of a settlement strategy is some central form of *location executive*. Its duties would be to operate location incentives and controls within the framework provided by the settlement strategy. In view of the importance of office activities in shaping the development of the urban system and determining the occupational structure of individual urban units, the executive would have to have particular responsibility for the location and relocation of office employment. Arguably, the advisory role of the agency could be more important than its formal powers — by providing information to enable firms to match their own locational requirements to the opportunities created through the national settlement strategy. This could be a very important function of the executive since many location decisions are made on the basis of inadequate information concerning the range of possible alternatives (Webber, 1972; Cyert and March, 1966). The uncertainty which has generally discouraged firms from moving long distances could be reduced by the provision of information about, for example, contact opportunities in the new location. In addition the increasing importance of non-economic factors in decision-making — for instance the perceived desirability of particular residential urban units — suggests that the executive should be involved in the presentation of the public images of selected units.

Another key function of a location executive would be to plan relocation both from the point of view of the economic performance of the organisation and living conditions of its employees — the latter because relocation of decision-making functions implies that people are likely to move with their job. While this will not directly contribute to providing jobs for those currently living in the development area in the short run, such moves will obviously bring indirect and long-term benefits. A relocation of employment to a number of major urban units would therefore provide a compromise between moving jobs to people where they now live, on the one hand, and moving people to the present location of jobs.

The continual need to monitor the process of location adjustment and change from all points of view must be strongly emphasised. In particular this should include consideration of the regional effects of non-spatial policies. For example, the consequences of changes in the structure of large corporations, changes in the organisation of health and educational services or changes in national external economic relations. These are clearly tasks for a programme of policy orientated research. A number of additional research topics suggest themselves. First, there is a need for a reliable data base on locational change to provide a basis for detailed research studies. In particular, an early-warning mechanism reporting on pending office relocation and expansion needs to be established. But since locational change represents only a minor part of the process of the adjustment of organisations to changing conditions, more research is urgently required on the way units interact with different spatial environments. For example, studies of the communications patterns of units in different locational situations could give guidance as to the type of function that will be needed to create viable employment centres in the development areas and minimise the leakage of multiplier effects.

The consequences of relocation and structural changes in organisation need to be studied in terms of cost and benefit for both giving and receiving communities. For example, it is vital that the dispersal of civil servants planned in many countries is carefully monitored in terms of costs to the capital resulting from the dispersal, as well as the benefits accruing to the new community. Indeed, there might be a case for slowing down the rate of unplanned dispersal because of the adverse effects this could have on the occupational structure of the capital. In addition to the directly spatial effects, careful study is required of the consequences of dispersal on career paths. It is vital that this sort of information is fed back into the decision-making process in order to provide a basis for a continuing revaluation of dispersal policies.

Conclusions for regional policy in the UK

Many of the emerging themes that have been discussed in this paper are embodied in British urban and regional policy, yet the UK still lacks a national-settlement strategy. The need for corporate planning of the total urban environment is widely accepted along with the need to set such planning within an intraregional strategic framework. Each of the regional strategies that are now in preparation may provide a basis for the co-ordination of a wide range of decisions in both the public and private sector; but there is no published national framework linking each of the regional strategies. In regional policy, issues of social and physical development are increasingly considered, although the weight of regional policy is still concerned with economic matters. Some degree of selectivity is implied in the hierarchy of assisted areas from special to intermediate areas but this selectivity does not have an urban focus.

Thus, in spite of recent developments, regional and urban policy in the UK still remain separate at the national level. As a result, major investment decisions, particularly in the transportation sector, but also in urban infrastructure, are being made without a co-ordinating spatial framework within which national effects could be considered. Such decisions as the Third London Airport, the rapid-transit system for Manchester or the dispersal of civil service decision-making functions from London are likely to have direct and indirect effects that spread throughout the urban system and therefore have an important bearing on questions of regional development and regional balance.

In the highly integrated economy of a country the size of Britain, standard regions can no longer be treated as closed or isolated systems. One of the reasons for the fact that some policy measures have effects throughout the country is the growth of large corporations with units located in many cities. Links between the administrative parts of large corporations frequently control the spread of indirect effects. These administrative units are principally urban office functions. The control of such indirect effects clearly demands office policies that are related to the urban system. Along with other factors, this urban focus implies a selectivity in urban and regional policy that focuses on the settlement system rather than broadly defined and heterogeneous development areas. And, as regional policy evolves within the EEC, such selectivity and concentration in the application of financial incentives and control is likely to become a dominant theme. Altogether, these considerations clearly point the need for a national settlement strategy as the most appropriate framework for co-ordinating regional and urban policy in the UK.

Notes

[1] This paper draws upon a report prepared by the author for a working party of the Economic Development Committee of the European Free Trade Association on new patterns of settlement, EFTA (1973).

[2] Potential 'demand', i.e. needs, and not demand in a strict economic sense.

References

Baker L.L.H. and Goddard J.B., 'Inter-sectoral contact flows and office location' *London Studies in Regional Science*, vol. 3, A.G. Wilson, ed. (1972).

Berry B.J.L., 'Hierarchical diffusion: the basis of developmental filtering and spread in a system of growth centres' *Growth Centres in Regional Economic Development*, N.M. Hansen, (ed.), New York (1972).

Boudeville J.R., *Problems of Regional Economic Planning*, Edinburgh (1966).

Bourne L.S., *Regulation of Urban Systems: A Comparative Review of Nation-*

al *Urbanization Strategies (Australia, Canada, Britain and Sweden)*, Ministry of State for Urban Affairs (mimeo). Ottawa (1973).

Cyert R.N. and March J.G., *A Behavioural Theory of the Firm*, Englewood Cliffs, New Jersey (1963).

Davies B., *Social Needs and Resources in Local Service: a Study of Variations in Standards of Provision of Social Service Between Local Authority Areas* (1968).

EFTA, *Examination of the Growth Centre Idea*, European Free Trade Association, Geneva (1968).

EFTA, *National Settlement Strategies: a Framework for Regional Development*, European Free Trade Association, Geneva (1973).

Emery F.E. and Trist E.L., *Towards a Social Ecology: Contextual Appreciations of the Future in the Present* (1972).

Goddard J.B., *Office Linkages and Location: A Study of Communications and Spatial Patterns in Central London*, Oxford (1973A).

Goddard J.B., 'Information flows and the development of the urban system: theoretical considerations and policy implications' *Proceedings of Urban Economics Conference*, Centre for Environmental Studies (1973B).

Goodwin W., 'The management centre in the United States' *Geographical Review*, 55 (1965), pp. 1–16.

Hägerstrand T., 'What about people in regional science?' *Papers, Regional Science Association*, 24 (1970), pp. 7–21.

Hall P., 'The Spatial Structure of Metropolitan England and Wales' *Spatial Policy Problems of the British Economy*, M. Chisholm and G. Manners (eds), Cambridge (1971).

Hall P. *et al.*, *The Containment of Urban Britain:* Vol. 1: *Urban and Metropolitan Growth Processes* (1973).

Harvey D., 'Social processes, spatial form and the distribution of real income in an urban system' *Regional Forecasting*, M. Chisholm and A. Frey (eds) (London) (1971).

Pahl R.E., 'Is the mobile society a myth?' *Whose City?* R.E. Pahl (ed.) (1970).

Pahl R.E., 'Property and the urban system' *Spatial Policy Problems of the British Economy*, M. Chisholm and G. Manners (eds), Cambridge (1971).

Pred A.R., *The Growth and Development of Systems of Cities in Advanced Economies*, Lund Studies in Geography, Series B, no. 38 (1973).

Richardson H.W., 'Optimality in city size, systems of cities and urban policy: a sceptic's view' *Urban Studies*, 9 (1972), pp. 29–48.

Thorngren B., 'Regional economic interaction and flows of information'

Proceedings of the Second Poland/Norden Regional Science Seminar, Studies vol. 33, Polish Scientific Publications, Warsaw (1967).

Thorngren B., 'How do contact systems affect regional development?' *Environment and Planning*, 2 (1970), pp. 409–27.

Törnqvist G., *Contact Systems and Regional Development*, Lund Studies in Geography, Series B, no. 35, Lund (1970).

Törnqvist G., *Contact Requirements and Travel Facilities: Contact Models of Sweden and Regional Development Alternatives*, Lund Studies in Geography, Series B, no. 38 (1973).

Webber M., 'Order in diversity: community without propinquity' *Cities and Space: the Future Use of Urban Land*, L. Wingo (ed.), Baltimore (1963).

Webber M.N., 'The urban place and non-place urban realm' *Explorations into Urban Structure*, D.L. Foley *et al.* (eds.), Philadelphia (1964).

6 European Integration, Urban Regions and Medium-Sized Towns

Jacques R. Boudeville

Introduction

The European Community as a social and political system remains rather unshaped and in constant structural evolution. The relations within itself and with the environment do not yet show the self-regulating mechanisms which will secure stability in the evolutionary path of the system and its ultimate survival. However, as with all systems in process of formation, Europe can be defined by the progressive coherence of its objectives, by its socio-economic structures and by its instruments of action.

The basic trends in contemporary Europe seem to be, firstly, a spontaneous and spectacular modification of the type of urbanisation, and secondly, a voluntary, but difficult, tentative form of integration.

In the European analysis, integration appears as the main objective. As those of most social systems, this objective is complex and multi-dimensional. One must take care not to bias objectives in simplifying them as unique factors. European integration means, firstly, a reduction of disparities between levels of living and types of behaviour. For example the Mezzogiorno, whose economic distance from the rest of Europe is increasing, is badly integrated in its regional and urban economy. However, the links between market, industrial and urban sub-systems are one of the clues of European homogeneity.

A second side of European integration is the increasing interdependence of the nations composing it. It is well known that the intensity of trade within the community is increasing more rapidly than the trade of Europe with the rest of the world. Intra-European trade amounted to 39 per cent of the total in 1962 and 49 per cent in 1971, forming a regional bloc more integrated than the United States and Canada (33 per cent). But the exchange of goods is only one side of integration. One must add the exchanges of labour, of capital and of information, which pertain to the study of the urban complexes. The inter dependence thus illuminated can be either hierarchical and dominating (the Ruhr in Germany, London in the UK), or generalised between equal and organised partners. This is one of the aims of the European Community.

The third aspect of integration is the existence of an international consensus and a coherence in national decisions. This is not simply the study of the creation of a new political organism. It is also the determination of the level of collective decision-making, of the strength of decisions and of their impact in the different fields of action. One of the fundamental domains and one of the privileged fields of impact is, as this paper shows, the town.

The town is the expression, the fundamental structure and the essential channel of the organisation of European territory. The large urbanisation of European activity and population is reflected in the new strength of current developments. In the Federal Republic of Germany in 1970 76 per cent of the population was urban, in Denmark 80 per cent, the UK 78 per cent, the Netherlands 82 per cent, Belgium 72 per cent, and France 70 per cent. All the demographic growth will materialise in the towns; in France it will be augmented by a rural exodus. The rate of growth of the French urban population will result in an 80 per cent urbanisation at the end of this century. The urban population will thus double in thirty years.

The French space is unique in the European context. The population densities of Belgium and the Netherlands are 320 and 356 inhabitants per square kilometre, for Germany and the United Kingdom the figures are 240 and 228 and, in Switzerland and Italy, 150 and 100 inhabitants per square kilometre, whilst France has only 93 per square kilometre. It is important to know if this difference will lead to the development of divergent types of towns within countries with the same rate of urbanisation or industrialisation.

Urban systems seem indeed to have had a rapid evolution in Europe and two distinctive types of system coexist. Firstly, there is the classical urban structure of *polarized regions* as described in France by Hautreux and Rochfort (1964), in Great Britain by Smailes (1944), in the Rhine basin by Christaller (1933) and Juillard (1961) and in the United States by Harris (1943). This type is different from the recent *urban region* of central Western Europe, including Randstad, the north of France and Belgium, the Ruhr and the Swiss plateau.

This urban-regional texture is beginning to develop at present along the lower Seine valley, along the Rhône valley and the Mediterranean seaboard. The urban region becomes a great homogeneous space with a high demographic, industrial and tertiary density, with a diversified urbanisation and with a discontinuous frame with agricultural interruptions. This new urban texture substitutes for the hierarchy based on the metropolis and medium-sized towns and forms a new kind of solidarity and complementarity. The urban region poses new transportation problems and new organisational difficulties. The density of concentration of numerous towns gives birth to different kinds of social behaviour and necessitates a new administrative and political organisation. As this new urban structure develops without taking into account political borders (the more so with the disappearance of custom boundaries), it is probably time to take advantage of a generalised phenomenon which creates new problems for all governments and to find new European economic solutions.

This is the aim of this report. It is a comparative study in an evolving system. Its analysis tries to clarify a process of information and to choose between alternative strategic policies.

Urbanisation processes in Europe

To what extent are different urban forms and policies linked with the evolution of European networks of towns?

Urban life is a social system widely opened. It is linked by predominant external relations with the rural world and with other cities. The town is not only a type of settlement, it is a network of relations with the environment and among different economic and social groups within itself. The town, a privileged node of the national system, is a microcosm of the entire society, with its culture, its economic activities and its social connections. In short, it is a sub-system whose generalisation tends to make a perfect image of the entire society. But it is a sub-space which is diversified and subject to evolution. It is not sufficient to stress that medium-sized towns (between 30,000 and 200,000 inhabitants) tend to grow more rapidly than the towns with more than 200,000 inhabitants. It is also necessary to discover if these medium-sized towns pertain to one of two urban systems in competition: the system of hierarchical interdependency and traditional tertiary functions of the polarised region; or the system of the high urban density and diffuse interdependency of the urban regions.

We will first study economic structures corresponding to the traditional hierarchical urban systems in Europe, with reference to the French policy of *métropôles d'équilibres* and medium-sized towns. With respect to the latter, it is important to note the wide variety among medium-sized towns. Lajugie distinguishes six different types of medium-sized towns: those included in a conurbation; immediate satellites; isolated towns; distant satellites; specialized towns; and constellations.

We will observe, secondly, the structure and policy of the urban regions in the Netherlands, Germany and the UK, as well as in the north of France and the Paris region.

We will finally try to sketch, for the medium and long term, the coexistence, the relations and the simultaneous evolution of the two urban systems.

Classical urban structure

Whatever might be the social structure and the density of the industrialised countries, the town is never an isolated unit in its own region. A town must be defined in relation to the urban system to which it belongs. Originally, in Germany and in the UK, as in France, this network was, to different degrees, hierarchical. The differences of hierarchical strength of the urban network define the polarised region, not the similarities of the towns included.

The theoretical scheme of the European polarised region can thus be described as a hierarchical set of a metropolis, its satellites and the rural world within their command. It is a heterogeneous space, parts of which are complementary and maintain among themselves, and more specially with the dominant metropolis, more trade than with any neighbouring region. It is, in fact, a locus of interchanges of goods, services and information, whose internal intensity is larger in each point than the external intensity. The polarised region is integrated. It is not self-sufficient (Boudeville, 1970).

The beautiful symmetry of this construction was unhappily based on a trade economy sufficienty described by its tertiary circuits and functions (Prost, 1965). The Christaller rule, as generalised by Beckmann and applied to the Rhine region, enables the population of a town to be deduced from its rank in the hierarchy and is the ultimate theoretical effort accomplished in this direction (Boudeville, 1973). From another point of view, the town typology built in France on the principal components of the urban functions and the stimulating studies from Hautreux and Rochefort (1964) are of the same nature.

In fact French research went much further than a typology and tried to integrate it within an economic development policy. The sectoral polarisation policy of François Perroux (1964) thus met the geographical urban hierarchy and the 'equilibrium metropolis' policy. But it showed that the classical symmetry of the tertiary world was destroyed by the asymmetries of industrial networks. The diffusion of innovations no longer followed the tree of Hägerstrand (1967). It was necessary to find a new type of hierarchy, distinguishing (a) central places; (b) the growth poles; (c) the development poles; and (d) the integration poles.

(a) The *central place* is a classical tertiary city, often historical and animating the rural environment. It is also the destination of agricultural migration. Its frequency is at its maximum in Italy.

(b) The *growth pole* is a town which is industrial and diversified, but passive, one in which the rhythms of growth of the population and of income depend on the propulsive effects coming from the development pole. They form a large proportion of the independent medium-sized towns with between 20,000 and 200,000 inhabitants and are growing rapidly in Germany and in France (the rest of the medium-sized towns being integrated in the urban regions).

(c) The *development pole* is an intradependent agglomeration endowed with innovative firms and is thus propulsive; at each moment investment has important effects on the growth poles. The failure of Italian policy within Bari and Taranto is a result of the fact that both towns remained growth poles far away from the propulsive north.

(d) An *integration pole* is a multi-focal development pole, connecting two urban systems which remained separate from each other, thus creating propulsive circuits and feedbacks in each of them. It gives birth to new propulsive nodes and to new evolutionary possibilities.

Observation of the French economy shows a great number of such integration poles in formation.

1 The triangle Caen—Rouen—Le Havre (850,000 inhabitants) constitutes a set of complementary urban centres capable of integrating the disintegrated high and low Normandy (Boudeville, 1973, p. 188) but with major political difficulties.

2 The triangle Pau—Lourdes—Tarbes on the border of Aquitaine and Midi—Pyrénées constitutes a similar phenomenon between Toulouse and Bordeaux.

3 The well-known triangle Mulhouse—Belfort—Montbéliard, whose interdependence (led by major industrial companies, e.g. Peugeot, Althom, Bull) is also a trans-regional integration pole facing the polarisation of Basel in Switzerland.

4 On the border of Germany and France stands the problem region of Nancy—Metz—Saarbrücken, with their evolving connections. Once realised, the unity of the enlarged Lorraine agglomeration and the Metz—Saarbrücken region could constitute a new axis described by Juillard as a miniature Essen—Düsseldorf.

It appears that the notion of the integration pole leads directly to that of the urban region, from which it differs, but to which it gives greater precision.

The structure and policy of urban regions

A new form of organisation illuminated for the first time by Jean Gottmann (1961) in the United States, under the term 'Megalopolis', is now developing in Europe. It does not constitute, in either case, a fantastically large town, but a space with high urban and demographic density with commuting to industrial and tertiary employment; in short, a dense and diversified mass of towns and agglomerations, separated by agricultural spaces. This is a new notion on the qualitative and quantitative level. It creates a new style of life and transcends the borders of regions, provinces and states. It needs new technical solutions in order to solve the problems of a new type of human establishment. It is through the urban region that European integration will necessarily be built.

(i) Definitions of urban regions in the EEC

The European urban space presents itself in a manner still open to controversy. The statistical solution of its delineation could be found if the statistical office of the European Community could generalise the French notion of 'zones de peuplement industriel ou urbain' (zones of urban or industrial settlement).[1]

Another approach would start from the metropolitan area concept, which is of American origin, but utilised in France for the study of the prospective urban organisations of OREAM and OREAV (Organisation Régionale d'Etude des Aires Métropolitaines and Organisation Régionale d'Etudes d'Aménagement des Vallées). The Parisain region and North region are conceived as metropolitan areas and their kernel of high urban density is assimilated into the total planning region. The two notions are distinct from the equilibrium policy followed in the other parts of the country. The generalisation of OREAM made in Alsace and Midi—Pyrénées comes from the necessity of a regional perspective and not from the pure idea of a metropolitan area. The OREAV of the Oise and Loire Moyenne were themselves closer to the notion of urban areas in formation.

The metropolitan area differs from the polarised region in its homogeneity: density of population and urbanisation. It is no longer a city with its distinct functions and set of towns linked to it. It is rather an urban space, dense but discontinuous, made up of towns for which proximity ensures a community of life, of trade and of infrastructures (Figure 6.1). A great number of these areas are the result of growth of the capital from which the agglomeration expands towards its closer satellites and induces the growth of medium-sized towns which are more distant. But this simple scheme is not the only one. There exist mononuclear metropolitan areas, such as the Paris region (9 million inhabitants), which the new towns try to re-structure. There exist also bi- or multi-nuclear areas, such as Tokyo–Yokohama, Metz–Nancy, Cologne–Düsseldorf, some of which have a leading core, as do *Lyon*–St. Etienne–Grenoble, *Lille*–Roubaix–Tourcoing, *Manchester*–south east Lancashire–north east Cheshire, *Birmingham*–West Midlands and Frankfurt in the Rhine–Main region (3 million inhabitants). One must add Brussels–Antwerp–Ghent (3 million inhabitants). Some of them are multi-national: Aachen–Maastricht–Liège and Basel–Freiburg–Mulhouse–Belfort–Montbeliard (Figure 6.2). All are politically sensitive.

For simplification, one can propose the following as examples:

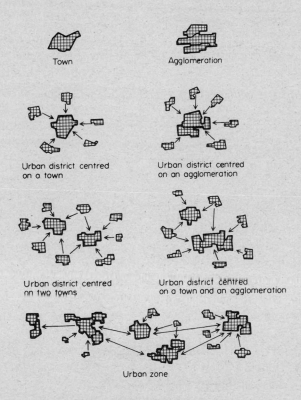

Fig. 6.1   A schematic illustration of urban systems

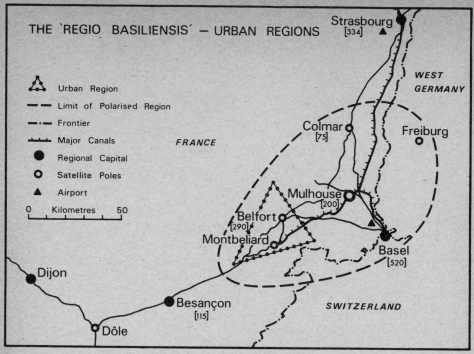

Fig. 6.2   The 'Regio Basiliensis' (populations in thousands)

— Paris region: mononuclear (9 million inhabitants);
— Rhine—Main—region: polynuclear with a predominant centre: Frankfurt (3 million inhabitants);
— Rhine—Ruhr—region: polynuclear with a dominant bi-pole: Cologne —Düsseldorf (10 million inhabitants);
— The Randstad Holland: metropolitan area without a predominant centre (4 million inhabitants).

But these metropolitan regions can be grouped into a large homogeneous set called 'urban regions', which can themselves be included in a megalopolis.

This last notion is the most inclusive. It circumscribes, in its homogeneous urbanisation polygon, other polygons of a more restrictive definition from the point of view of density and green spaces. In its most inclusive form, it has four extreme points in Europe: Liverpool, Hamburg, the Swiss Plateau, Le Havre—Southampton, and thus includes the Paris region. This set of 133 million inhabitants is rather heterogeneous and equals about two-thirds of the population. It is larger than the American megalopolis and is too diversified and discontinuous to give birth to homogeneous solutions (Figure 6.3).

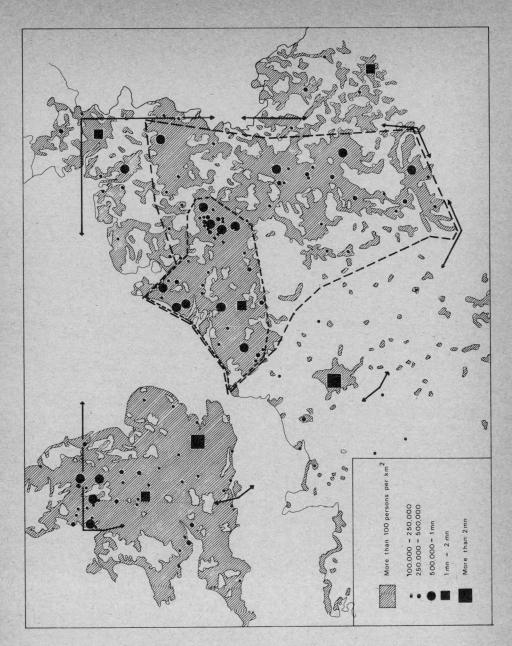

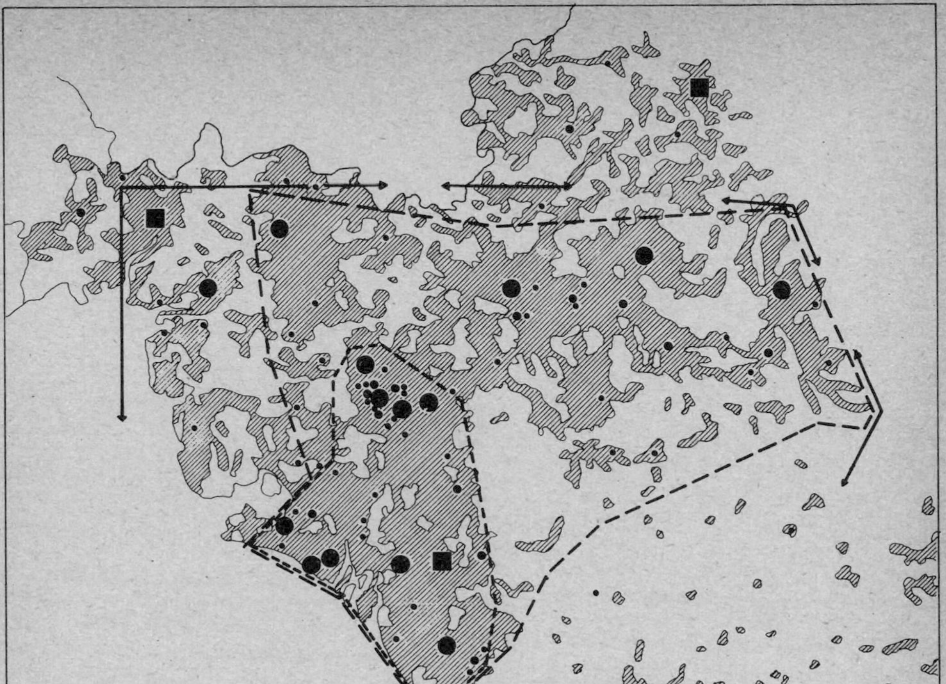
More than 100 persons per km²
100,000 - 250,000
250,000 - 500,000
500,000 - 1mn
1mn - 2mn
More than 2mn

Fig. 6.3 The European megalopolis

On the other hand, a dense set made up of the Benelux — excluding the north of the Netherlands — the French north and Europe from the Rhine up to the Swiss Plateau, forms an urban region of high interdependence (Figure 6.3). The accession of the UK to the European Community and the construction of the tunnel under the Channel would extend this set to the urban region of London, Liverpool and Manchester. The whole set forms a mass of 72 million inhabitants on 265,000 square kilometres — a density of 270 inhabitants per square kilometre. By comparison, Hondo in Japan has 79 million inhabitants on 230,000 square kilometres — 34 inhabitants per square kilometre.

In the centre of this European region — a continental delta between France, Belgium, the Netherlands and Germany — an urban region is constituted by the Randstad Holland, the Rhine—Ruhr region and the French—Belgian metropolitan region. The danger would be that the two continuous urban axes, starting from Rotterdam towards Lille and from Amsterdam towards the Ruhr, would develop without any discontinuity.

But another scheme of a more prospective character has been drawn by OTAM. In the preceding picture, the 'centre—west' axis was the line London—Rotterdam—Essen, bending further with the Rhine towards the Swiss Plateau. For OTAM the picture is different and built on the gross national product per capita (Figure 6.4). Industrial Europe climbs towards the German industrial complex. The scenario is now more orientated north—south. It begins in Lombardy and climbs through Switzerland towards Hamburg. Another branch starts from Barcelona and climbs through Fos—Marseille and Lyon towards the Rhine.

In our view, the problem is different. The centre—west region of Europe and its axis London—Ruhr—Basel, are undeniable facts but this European core must be structured at the international scale. It must also be brought into equilibrium with the remainder of western Europe. The modest urban region of Paris—Le Havre grows only in the surroundings of Paris. The SDAU (Schema Directeur d'Aménagement et d'Urbanisme) of Le Havre will remain a pious hope if it does not integrate itself with the other bases of the Norman triangle: Rouen and Caen.

The true equilibrium strategy is elsewhere: in the Mediterranean urban region, simultaneously industrial and touristic. It is in Barcelona of Catalonia and the metropolis of Perpignan; it is the outstanding effort of Languedoc—Roussillon; it is Marseille—Aix—Fos, a future urban region of 2·2 million inhabitants; and it is Genoa trying to meet the two other great western Mediterranean harbours. Given this second axis, the problem of the north—south junction is to try to find a traditional solution through

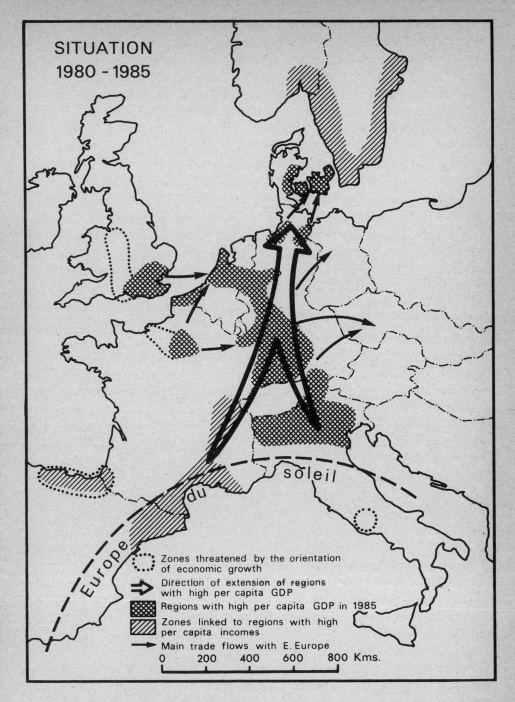

SITUATION 1980 - 1985

Zones threatened by the orientation of economic growth

Direction of extension of regions with high per capita GDP

Regions with high per capita GDP in 1985

Zones linked to regions with high per capita incomes

Main trade flows with E. Europe

0   200   400   600   800 Kms.

Europe du soleil

Fig. 6.4   Axial development in Western Europe: forecasts for the 1980s

Lombardy and Brenner and a modern solution through the Rhône, the Saône and the Rhine.

(ii)   Urban regions and central places

Thus, on one hand, we have the environment of the urban regions, along with their medium-sized towns; and on the other hand we have the network of regional poles and satellites covering the less industrialised and urbanised part of the territory. From this point of view, how do the co-existence and the relations between these two different urban environments present themselves?

To understand one must think in the framework of the diffusion of information and of innovations of techniques and behaviour. It is well known that there are two types of innovation: the innovation of the consumer who modifies his material and cultural behaviour, and the innovation of the producer who transforms his techniques and his organisation. But in underdeveloped countries, as well as in the industrialised ones, the towns appear always as poles, capable of diffusing information through their areas of influence and of diffusing development through social evolution. In Hägerstrand's model, diffusion is accomplished through two different principles: the hierarchical distance and the spatial distance. In a first stage, the innovation is transmitted between towns located at the highest level, in a second stage it goes down the hierarchy.

At each level the distance brake exists: $T_{ij} = \dfrac{K^P{}_i P_j}{d_{ij}^{\alpha}}$
where T is the intensity of transmission between places (P) and d_{ij} is the distance (geographical and hierarchical) between places P_i and P_j. This can be represented schematically as in Fig. 6.5.

The new element is that the hierarchical distance brake disappears in the urban region. It continues to act only in the polarised region.

The α coefficient of d, revealed by correlation analysis, can be broken down to α_1 (geographical distance) and α_2 (hierarchical distance), which is zero in metropolitan areas and urban regions. Thus the hierarchical distance brake disappears in the urban region. It continues to act only in the polarised region.

The scenario 'urban region and rural desert' pertains to the apocalypse of the impossible. The role of medium-sized satellite towns which are not engulfed by the urban tissue becomes clear: it is the role of animating regional and rural life. But to accomplish this mission, they must be exposed to innovations by communication networks (airports, turnpikes, business trains). Their social structure must be open to information leading to diversity of technical cultures. Their size (threshold) must be adapt-

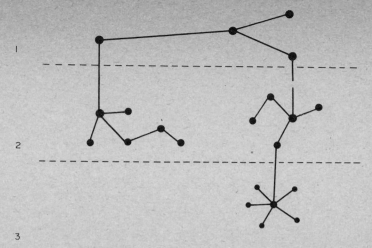

Fig. 6.5 The transmission of innovations in a hypothetical settlement hierarchy

ed to the new techniques. The distinctive qualities of the entrepreneur must be socially accepted.

It is striking, when reading the French regional development plans (PRDE), to see how the concept of town differs from one part of the territory to another. The importance given to the metropolitan area, to the regional capital, to the intermediate towns and to local-activity points varies considerably. All the regions possessing a métropole d'équilibre consider its development as a fundamental objective. Rhône—Alpes and the North speak openly of urban regions. On the other hand, the regions remaining mostly agricultural insist on developing the network of medium-sized towns. In the first category, one insists on promotion of economic development; in the second, on the rational and harmonious organisation of the territory. This is the case of Midi—Pyrénées, of Brittany, of Pays de la Loire, of Franche-Comté, of Champagne—Ardennes.

The systematic study of the medium-sized town whose threshold should be 50,000 inhabitants, is presented by the Basse-Normandie report. Caen transmits growth to Bayeux, Villers Bocage and Falaise; Alençon similarly influences Argentan. Simultaneously Lisieux is integrated in the triangle Caen—Rouen—Le Havre, an urban region of the future with 850,000 inhabitants in 1971, whose model is evidently the Randstad Holland (4 million inhabitants).

The danger is of finding all the concentration of sectors of command, research and high technical levels in the urban regions which are also

141

characterised by a great professional and social mobility – predominantly of the middle classes. This evolution would parallel in the urbanised and polarised regions a deconcentration of plants utilising less-qualified labour and offering as an external economy their labour market. A relative proletarisation could result, reflected in the local level of salaries. This proletarisation, coupled with social mobility, could create a dualism which would only be compensated for by a strong identification with the historic town.

In less developed regions (Mezzogiorno, Groningen, Limousin, Brittany) or in regions close to a national metropolis (Centre, Picardie), there does not exist a strong urban hierarchy and the medium-sized towns are weaker than elsewhere. However, solidarities appear in some cases (in France, Tours–Orléans–Blois or Nîmes–Montpellier–Sète) as urban constellations oriented by some development axes.

Two problems exist: that of the restructuring of the rural world which is at present shrinking and that of the industrialisation of depopulating regions. It is remarkable that the only regions where the rural population does not diminish are 'zones of urban or industrial settlement' (ZPIU). The rural world and the medium-sized towns are different and have not the same future as the regions in which they are situated. Concerning the industrialisation of medium-sized towns, scheduled by the Schiller plan in Germany and the Mezzogiorno policy in Italy, it is necessary to understand the mistakes that have been made and to discover the factors and mechanisms of urban growth, if one wants to promote better strategic choices.

(iii)   Models of urban development

Models of urban development must take into account at the same time the intraurban structure and the system of relations between towns.

One must explain: (a) the domination and expansion of the urban regions; (b) the progress and absence of autonomy of the growth poles; and (c) the processes of decentralisation and integration. It will suffice here to indicate three different models which enable us to draw a rapid scheme of explanation and to generate simulations and scenarios formalised in different ways.

(a)   The urban region
It is defined first by its interconnections; the diversity of its complexes and their integration into a strong whole; second by the fact that it keeps for itself and reinvests the surplus value created by technical progress; finally by its generation of social and technical progress.

Interdependence is defined as a feedback or, more precisely, by the existence of a unique, strong component (Campbell, 1972) such as an integrated industrial complex, propelling the urban region. This urban region would have a diversified activity characterised by the mutual accessibility found in an industrial contiguity graph adjacent to the Boolean matrix of major inputs and outputs. Let A be the contiguity matrix, the accessibility matrix is $B = (I + a)^{p-1}$, where p is the order of the square matrix A. The strong components are shown on the lines of the reciprocal accessibility matrix $B.B'$.[2] The integration thus studied is different in every urban region. It is strongest when reciprocal accessibility appears at shortest distances. Moreover connections appear between different urban regions, including specialised complexes. Their hierarchy is not only a function of the number of feedbacks and of the short closing distances of the strong component but also of the possibility of keeping in the region the surplus values which are created.

A complex A keeps for itself the surplus values of technical progress when its specialised activities create fast productivity profits and couples them with higher wages and higher investments in the region itself. Another complex B, deprived of fast technical progress, can absorb the surplus values created in the complex C if the latter transmits its productivity increase through lower relative prices. The scheme is simple (Bienaymé, 1966).

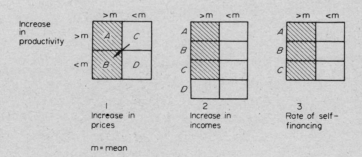

The industry A *retains* the surplus values, the industry B *captures* the surplus values, the industry C *transmits* surplus values. Both industries A and B are regionally favourable; the industry C can be partially favourable if it retains a part of the created surplus through higher wages and self-financing.

All industrial activities participate in technical progress, but with a rhythm higher or lower than the mean. Most of them are also a field of price increases but also with a higher or lower rate: the industries whose

143

price increases are the highest — with or without a productivity progress — are keeping for themselves, or able to capture, surplus values. Some of these industries are characterised by fast salary increases and by higher self-financing rates. The urban regions containing such industries are propulsive. A comparative analysis of European urban regions in this context would be of the highest interest.

The urban region is a privileged environment for the diffusion of the innovations in production and consumption. It substitutes horizontal diffusion for vertical and hierarchical diffusion.

The urban region can be conceived as a polynuclear metropolis whose different nodes are at the same hierarchical level and in rapid contact. The small town, close to the capital, is no more isolated or distant than another very distant metropolis. It is part of the metropolis itself. In the same way, a number of the medium-sized towns which form an urban ZPIU of high density contribute to increase the diversity and the contacts within the set, and increase the probability of innovation. This supposes that urban interconnections have a high intensity of quaternary activities (i.e. high-productivity services and research for industry).

(b)   Polarisation of the growth poles

The hierarchical system of growth poles can be defined by the nature of industrial activities. The growth pole differs from the development pole because it is an isolated medium-sized town in which industries are 'impulsive' and not propulsive ones following the model of Ben Higgins. Of course the impulsive industry can develop itself more rapidly than the propulsive one. This is why polarised satellite towns grow faster than development poles such as London, Paris or Montreal.

This is shown in the following scheme, which makes a distinction between polarisation and multiplication: polarisation is an inducement of investment unexplained by the consequences of input—output relations. It is the consequence of innovation and complementarity of demand.

The polarisation equation can be written as follows:

$$\Delta Ie = a_{em} \, \Delta Im \qquad (1)$$

Ie = induced investments
Im = propulsive investments
a = matricial polarisation co-efficient between m and I

The matricial multiplication can be written as:

$$\Delta Ye = ke \, \Delta Ie \qquad (2)$$

$$\Delta Ym = km \, \Delta Im \qquad (3)$$

144

The three equations show that:

$$\frac{\Delta Ye}{\Delta Ym} = a_{em}\, \frac{ke}{km} \qquad (4)$$

It shows also that an impulsive industry can have a higher rate of growth than a propulsive industry if the condition (5) is satisfied, i.e.:

$$a_{em}\, \frac{ke}{km} > 1 \qquad (5)$$

A growth pole contains only industries of the impulsive type e. A development pole contains simultaneously industry of type e and m. The whole polarised system of towns is necessary to build strong component complexes which differ from urban regions by including hierarchical brakes.

Of course, Higgins and Hägerstrand can be combined by writing:

$$\Delta Ie = a\, \frac{Se\, Sm}{d_{em}^{\alpha}}\, \Delta Im$$

where Se and Sm are the quantified digraph structure of the growth pole e and the development pole m.

A further synthesis can be achieved with the Bienaymé scheme (described above) if we add to the classical Leontief multiplier $|A|$, the matrix $|K|$ of capital coefficients and the diagonal matrix $|\hat{F}|$ of self-financing. We thus have a double feedback with a modification of structure; in other words the problem is a dynamic one.

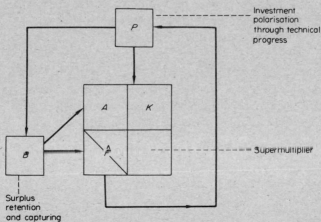

(c)   Decentralisation and integration

The phenomenon of decentralisation consists either in creating accessibilities and completing the strong components as expressed above, or in inducing complementarities and agglomeration economies between industries of the satellite towns.

In other words, the problem is to find what type of industry will create a feedback in the urban system and where to locate it in order to minimise the distance brake and maximise the structural attraction of towns. Industries retaining and capturing productivity surpluses seem to be indispensable in development poles and urban regions.

Urban growth seems finally to state, on the one hand, the problem of quaternary innovation and of the existence of directorial centres in urban regions and, on the other hand, the problem of accompanying manufacturing industries by tertiary growth in medium-sized towns.[3]

The presence of a tertiary activity as a refuge for the rural exodus is in no way a favourable solution, though it is to a large extent the one that can be observed at the present time in a large part of Europe. On the other hand, the presence of a tertiary activity which would not be simply a lagged effect of industrial growth presents itself as an indispensable element of the social equilibrium of the town. Once more, the solution depends on the type of urban system and on the type of region.

Urban strategies

In the face of such multi-dimensional problems, to what extent can different strategies be chosen? Firstly, observation of European planning shows that there exist different responses to the urban problems appearing in similar environments. Secondly, it can be seen that different international systems may help to make more humane, and to integrate, the great transnational urban regions.

European responses

Urban problems are a favourable field for systems analysis. Diversity and community of objectives are mostly linked to the urban structures. In the same manner, the differences between political instruments are linked to the historical heritage. What is important is that everywhere the question is not simply to counteract but also to guide and dominate critical relations in the inter-regional and international fields. It is from this point of view that it is necessary to compare countries with dominant urban regions (the UK, Germany, Benelux) and countries with the urban region in process of formation (France, Italy).

The UK is a country of large urban regions but possessing a dominant metropolis (London). It is also a pioneer in the evolution of urban strategies. It was the first to make a synthesis between the physical planning of the architect and the economic planning of the regionalist. It is the first to evolve from the concept of the new town, relieving congestion in the capital (London), or helping a regional capital in the process of reconversion (Glasgow) towards the construction of a strategy of urban growth built on a constellation of medium-sized towns. The South East Economic Planning Council is in favour of the creation of new urban zones (for example, Milton Keynes and Peterborough) situated at 100 kilometres from London and linked to the metropolis by a few growth axes built along the highways and railways. In addition, Redditch and Telford come to restructure the urban zone of Birmingham. Warrington, Runcorn, Skelmersdale, and Central Lancashire are located between the urban zones of Liverpool and Manchester. Thus, far away from development areas, a linear urban complex (Figure 6.6) is building up with London as metropolitan centre and, on the axis leading to Birmingham and Liverpool, with green intervals and satellites linked by a fast transport corridor (Rodwin, 1970). Until now the problem of urban regional strategy and the problem of helping the classical depressed regions have gone hand in hand only in Scotland. The future European midlands or central region strategy might alter the picture, as we will see. Thus far, the British innovation remains the new town and its administrative instrument: the public development corporations, which serve as a model for Europe. Its transformation during the second generation into an instrument for structuring the urban region is nowadays understood.

Some urban regions are characterised by an absence of a strict hierarchy among the different towns. They are situated mostly in Germany and the Netherlands. These countries are also those where the decentralisation of town and country planning is the strongest. The urban density is, however, different in each of them. In Germany, 50 per cent of the population lives in 24 agglomeration zones and the Rhine—Ruhr region groups 16 per cent of the German inhabitants on 2·4 per cent of the territory, with a density of 1,666 inhabitants per square kilometre. In the Netherlands, the Randstad Holland has about the same geographic size and represents 60 per cent of the population on a surface of 20 per cent of the territory with a density of 870 inhabitants per square kilometre.[4] In each country, urbanism and town planning are the business of municipalities and the co-ordination is realised on the regional level. Very broad directives are established on a national level. In the absence of a primate metropolis (unlike in the UK), a new-town policy does not exist in the Netherlands and Germany. The only exception is the new town of Marl in

147

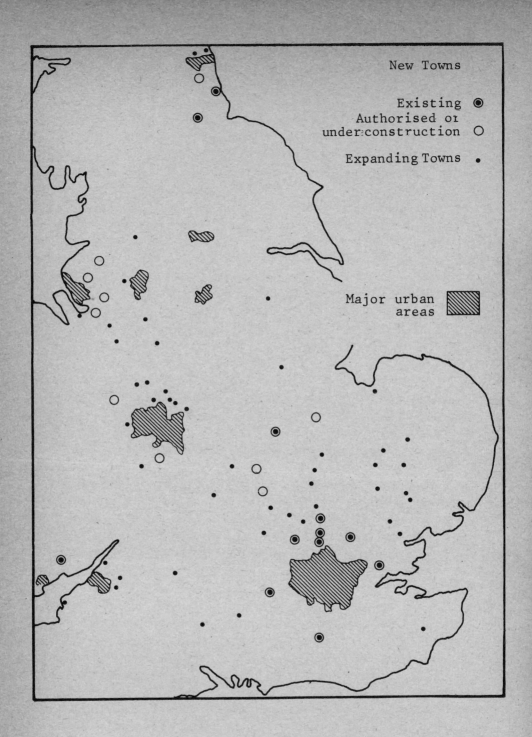

Fig. 6.6   New towns and expanding towns in England and Wales, 1969

the northern part of the Ruhr. Germany is mostly characterised by dormitory towns. On the other hand, the Netherlands may be considered as another model but its strategy is the reverse of the British one. It tries to revitalise town centres (Amsterdam and The Hague are stagnant towns) and tries to put a brake on the invasion of green spaces, namely in the centre of the Randstad Holland. Groningen is the only regional centre to present itself as a classical case of a medium-sized town in an underdeveloped region.

In any case, in the Netherlands, the municipalities are in charge of urban planning and co-ordination is realised by the provinces. The approval of the government is not necessary. The system is decentralised. The most important contribution of the Netherlands in town planning is to have been the first to conceive and to organise urban regions and the urban zones in a system adapted to the well-being of man. Grouped concentration districts are created and separated by green belts and green spaces to constitute urban zones. These urban zones are discontinuous and the city is interspersed with the country. This has been well understood by de Rouvre in his prospective of the French northern urban region.

The problem of the less industrialised countries, in which the urban regions are still in the process of formation, is different. This is true in a densely populated country such as Italy (175 inhabitants per square kilometre) as well as in a sparsely populated country like France (90 inhabitants per square kilometre).

France's low population density, compared with her closest neighbours, and the recent manifestation of her industrial and population growth explains her peculiar reactions towards the urban phenomenon, which is more recent for France than for the United Kingdom or the Benelux. In fact, France is spontaneously concerned by modern urban structures only in the north and in the Paris region. It is the future scenarios of her own life played by its neighbours and the United States which induced France to conceive first the strategy of the OREAM and now the strategy of medium-sized cities. The latter are seen as indispensable in structuring the metropolitan areas in larger urban zones and in animating, well away from the great development axes, some traditional polarised regions which are less industrialised and more rural, if not agricultural. If France does not want to convert herself into regional and national parks, she cannot, as the Netherlands, be interested only in the design of urban regions. If she does not want to put brakes on her cultural development and her industrial integration within Northern Europe, she must build two urban axes: the first would rest on Mediterranean seaports and tourism, the other would be the Rhône axis joining Latin Europe with the Europe of the Rhine. But

France's most important response to urbanisation is to remember that the Paris region will retain a small and antiquated dimension if it does not, in the Dutch or German way, come to terms with the medium-sized towns of the lower Seine.

To realise this double strategy — the creation of modern metropolitan regions and the promotion of medium-sized towns — France possesses forty-seven isolated towns with from 50,000 to 200,000 inhabitants. For their planning, she has an administrative tool which makes use of co-ordination: the SDAU. The prospective SDAU is established for a thirty-year period, supported for ten years by the POS (Plan d'Occupation des Sols). The former OREAM and OREAV have played their role of reference and general orientation. It remains to be seen whether a joint elaboration of the SDAU by the GEP (Departmental Group of Study and Programming) and by the municipalities, districts or communities will be an effective combination. French urban experience is not yet a regional one.[5]

In Italy, the formation of metropolitan regions has also recently materialised. After a first stage of centripetal grouping of population one can observe a second stage of diffusion characterised by the growth of closely spaced traditional settlements, large regional urbanisation and a progressive conurbation of the growing centres. Thus, in the industrial triangle Milan—Turin—Genoa and on the Via Emilia, Italy foresees the formation of a continuous urban region. In the rest of the country, autonomous polarised nodes would remain linked by transportation and separated by large under developed zones. The central problem for Italy is the great lack of operational urban planning and the difficulty of controlling land use. A second characteristic is the centralisation of the polarisation policy created in Mezzogiorno (Figure 6.7). Within this region, the zones and nodes of industrial development represent 9 per cent of the surface and 31 per cent of the population of the territory. The absence of co-ordination between economic planning and physical planning is still obvious in Italy.

Italy has not yet understood that urbanisation is not a growth and agglomeration of towns, but a dispersion of urban elements formely agglomerated. Moreover Italy is dominated by the requirements of an underdeveloped region, and makes a confusion between growth poles remotely controlled from Milan and a polarised and interdependent system on the regional level. However, in 1971, the localisation of the plant of Alfa Sud in the province of Naples broke with the previous mistakes and created at the same time, by the end of 1973, 60,000 direct jobs and 17,000 induced jobs linked to a deconcentration of the metropolitan area.

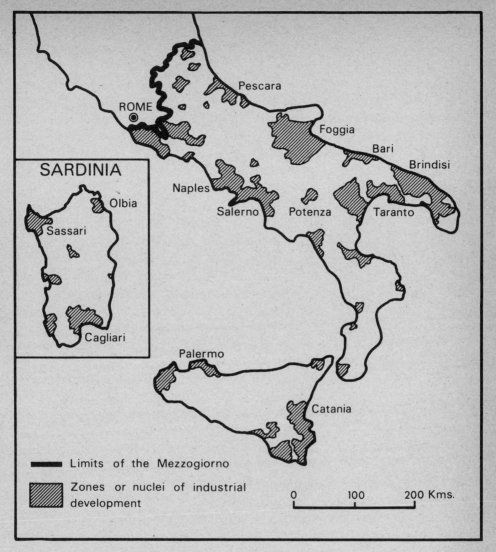

Fig. 6.7   Development areas in the Mezzogiorno

International strategies

Over-riding these different structures and different national responses, which international system will be most suited to help the European integration which will necessarily be built in the long term on the urban system?

To draw a parallel between monetary, regional and urban questions on one side and short-term, medium-term and long-term problems on the

151

other, is too easy not to be superficial. In the same way that regional help is conceived by the UK as a partial substitute for devaluation, the regional approach might be seen as a substitute for urban planning because it is politically more malleable and socially less structured.

Integration resides less in the homogeneity of the styles of life than in the interdependence of the activities and the coherence of decisions. This is why the choice of urban international strategies is based on long-term international options.

(i)   A first option might be sketched in the following way: urban constellations will be developed along major transport corridors (Figure 6.8), crossing borders and thus creating problems of international infrastructure which cannot be dissociated from urbanisation.[6] The role played in this field by the European Investment Bank can only be marginal in the present state of its statutes and of the periods allowed for repayments.

These corridors are mostly formed by river valleys (Rhine–Rhône). The closeness of towns along the borders presents environmental and pollution problems (air, water, soil), which are presently being studied in a complementary way by the European Commission and by OECD. Pollution is essentially an urban phenomenon. It is from the point of view of the polluting towns, as well as from the point of view of polluted river basins, that it can be solved.

A second option concerns the urban restructuring of the rural world: in other words, a policy of animation and reorientation of activities. An expansion of medium-sized towns is not sufficient and the building-up of classical central places will be useless at the end of the agricultural exodus. In any case, the manpower liberated by agriculture will rapidly decrease in Europe. England provides a most useful example in this context.

The solution of the Schiller plan – to create rural industrialisation poles as medium-sized towns of over 20,000 inhabitants – might be compared to the abstract Israeli scheme of creating a Pareto type of urban distribution. In fact, the solution has to be adapted to the possibility of the rural surroundings forming national parks for urban regions.

(ii)   The evolution of the urban environment necessitates an adaptation of objectives and, at the same time, a reform of outdated administrative instruments.

Amongst the urban regions, some are prosperous: the Ruhr, the Netherlands and, to a lesser degree, the north France/Belgium region. There are also depressed urban regions such as the midlands and north in the UK, as poor nowadays as northern industrial Italy. An outstanding exception is Birmingham, whose urban renovation is the sign of dynamism. However, it is not the level of the product per inhabitant which is im-

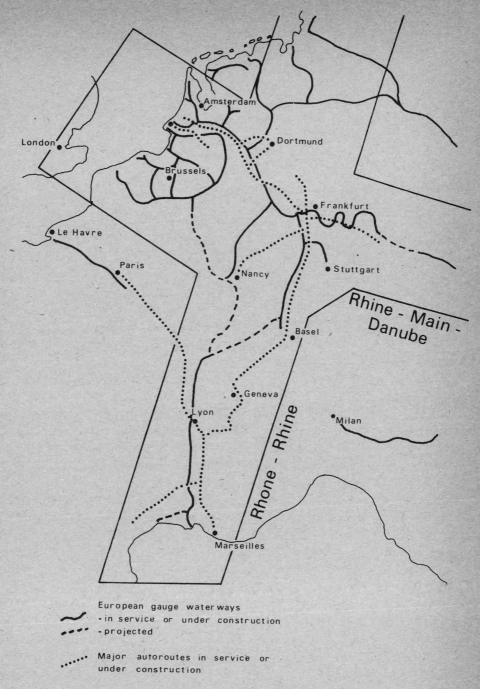

Rhine - Main - Danube

Rhine - Rhine

London
Amsterdam
Dortmund
Brussels
Frankfurt
Le Havre
Paris
Nancy
Stuttgart
Basel
Geneva
Milan
Lyon
Marseilles

European gauge waterways
- in service or under construction
- projected

Major autoroutes in service or
under construction

Fig. 6.8   Transport corridors in the EEC

portant; it is the evolution and perhaps also the total industrial product. But it is also true that urban regions, even the poorest, have to help the rural and tertiary regions in the European Community and their polarised urban hierarchy. Both town and country are a necessity. This is why, as Italy originally tried to, the UK is presently asking for a large regional development fund for its development areas. There is no doubt that through British action the Summit declaration of October 1972 will be honoured.

The efficiency of a production system is not built only on work but also on the environment and on the general organisation. In the same way, prosperity is not only built on industries but also on the town, its management and urbanism and, even more, on its integration in an urban region or in a system of polarised towns. There does not exist any country, even the Netherlands, where the administrative and cultural innovation implicit in a grouping of municipalities has been achieved in a general and satisfactory way. The social and political expression of the new urban community needs a perfect understanding of the underlying system. This should be the inter-disciplinary work of political scientists, geographers, economists and sociologists.

The town is, at the same time, a locus of social life and of production. It is also a built environment, which has only a very slow evolution. The planning of land use has a range of ten years. The horizon of daily life is not sufficient to avoid mistakes as grave as French 'grands ensembles', a birthplace of social instability. One must think on the level of urban organisation and of the participation in the creation of common objectives inside and between towns linked by spatial interdependencies.

Notes

[1] ZPIU is a set of municipalities characterised by its homogeneity of population, namely:
(a)   the small proportion of population living from agriculture;
(b)   significant commuting of employees from home to work;
(c)   the existence of industrial activities created or developed due to the proximity of an agglomeration, the presence of a communication axis or of raw material resources.
[2] $[b_{ij}b_{ji}]$.
[3] In this context three medium-sized towns constitute an important example. The annual rate of growth of Châlons (3·5%), Reims (3·1%) and even Amiens (2%) are explained by an important new industrialisation.

Châlons-sur-Marne, the smallest of the regional capitals (56,000 inhabitants) may be regarded as a political test.

[4]	Area km² ('000)	Population (millions)	Population per km²
Holland	33·6	12·6	375
Randstad	6·8	5·9	870
	20%	49%	
Germany	248	58	232
Rhine—Ruhr	6·2	10·4	1,666
	2·4%	16%	

[5] In particular the connections SDAU—PME (Programme de Modernisation et d'Equipement Publique), which are integrated in the PRDE, are very confused.

[6] For a different point of view see *Survol de l'Europe Travaux de Prospective,* no. 37 (1973).

References

Bienaymé A., *Politique de l'Innovation et Répartition des Revenues,* Cujas, Paris (1966).

Boudeville J. R., Les espaces économiques *Que Sais-je?,* 950, Presses Universitaires de France, Paris (1970).

Boudeville J. R., *Aménagement du Territoire et Polarisation,* M.T. Genin, Editions Techniques, Paris (1973).

Campbell J., 'A structural approach to growth pole theory' *Proceedings of Symposium on Problems of Slow Growth in Developed Countries,* M. A. Micklewright (ed.), St Johns, Newfoundland (1972).

Christaller W., *Die Zentralen Orte in Süddeutschland,* Jena (1933),

Gottman J., *Megalopolis, the Urbanised North Eastern Seaboard of the United States,* New York (1961).

Hägerstrand T., *Innovation Diffusion as a Spatial Process,* Chicago (1967).

Harris C. D., 'A functional classification of cities in the United States' *Geographical Review,* 33 (1943), pp. 86—99.

Hautreux J. and Rochefort M., *La Fonction Régionale dans l'Armature Urbaine française,* Ministère de la Construction, Paris (1964).

Higgins, B., *Pôles de Croissance et Pôles de Développement*, Ministère de l'Expansion Economique Régionale, Ottawa (undated).

Juillard E., 'L'urbanisation des campagnes en Europe occidentale' *Etudes rurales: Ecole pratique des Hautes Etudes*, 1 (1961).

Perroux F., 'La notion de pôle de croissance' *L'économie du vingtième siècle*, Presses Universitaires de France, Paris (1964).

Prost M. A., *La Hiérarchie des Villes en Fonction de leurs Activités du Commerce*, Gauthier—Villars, Paris (1965).

Rodwin L., *Nations and Cities*, Houghton Mifflin, Boston (1970).

Smailes A. E., 'The urban hierarchy in England and Wales' *Geography*, 29 (1944), pp. 41—51.

7 Regional Policy and Sub-Regional Planning in the North West[1]

A. G. Powell

Introduction

The form and content of plans are determined by the problems and circumstances prevailing during preparation. The planning process must therefore be capable of adapting to changing circumstances. The process is more important than the plan.

The first of the modern British regional plans were those for the special areas in the 1930s. These were basically economic in content and social in motivation. Wartime destruction switched the emphasis to physical plans, still with social objectives — yet lacking in social, economic and technological projections and predictions. There were many such plans in the mid-1940s, that of Abercrombie for Greater London being the best known and most imaginative. Plans for the County of London, Greater Manchester, Teesside, central Scotland and the West Midlands conurbation followed. These were 'master plans', intended to be good for all time. They tended to assume a static population, failed to understand evolving patterns of household formation, ignored at least the *scale* of growth of private transport and, perhaps rightly in the then context of the Uthwatt Report (1942) and legislation on compensation and betterment, also ignored economic factors in general and market factors in particular. Compensation and betterment apart, the 1947 Town and Country Planning Act sealed the physical land use approach for two decades. In fairness, it introduced the concept of five-year programmes — though they subsequently fell into abeyance. By granting planning power to counties and county boroughs, the Act also provided the built-in conflicts which produced the bitter over-spill battles, the green belts and — at least outside growth areas such as the South East — the failure to move employment to new towns to which labour was reluctant to move and therefore industry was reluctant either to lead or to follow. The result of these and many other consequences of an imaginative and far-seeing Act was, in fact, to throw the power of decision back to Whitehall and to clog hopelessly the planning machine in the detail of development

157

control to the exclusion of any real planning for the longer term. It has taken twenty-five years for us to appreciate even partially that the environment and changes within it are part of a single and vastly complex process of inter-relationships which even now is only beginning dimly to be understood and whose ramifications and apparent eccentricities will continue to bedevil planning in the future. The inter-relationships of economic, social, technological and physical decisions — especially as they affect people — are what regional plans (or strategies) are all about. The strength of the forces behind economic, social and technological trends must be infinitely better understood than is now the case if the forces themselves are to be used to bend trends and to plan for a better 'quality of life' (whatever this phrase may mean). What makes a great conurbation or city-region tick? Why have the many millions of pounds invested in assisted areas left them little better off (at least in employment terms) than they were two decades ago? Why do workers and employers persistently refuse to accept inducements to move to what, to all appearances, are such superior new towns and modern environments? Why is society polarising between the under-privileged poor of the inner city and the affluent of the suburbs and beyond? What further problems are hidden beneath the apparent affluence of much of the countryside? Why is there so wide a tolerance of low standards, vandalism and litter? And perhaps above all, can the present approach to planning cope? Are we big enough to control our own destiny? Should we accept that a grand design for, say, the Mersey Belt of south Lancashire and north Cheshire is impossible in the absence of a latter-day Michelangelo or Leonardo da Vinci?

The Planning Advisory Group (PAG) Report (1965) of a body of the foremost physical planners, developers and administrators, laid the basis for the new development plan provisions in the Town and Country Planning Acts of 1968 and 1972. Now, for the first time, the economic and social causes and consequences of physical land-use policy were required by statute to be built into the development plans of counties and county boroughs and the foundations of an approach to some form of corporate planning were laid. In theory at least, the Local Government Act of 1972 provides the machinery with which, and the stage upon which, the hierarchy of structure and local plans can be developed. In practice, doubts are already being expressed[2] on the viability of the system within a few months of formal submission of the first structure plans to DOE.

The origin of regional policies and strategies

The National Plan of 1965 has been ridiculed and virtually forgotten —

which is unfortunate, since there has been a continuous search for a means of replacing it. National planning as such in Britain is no new development. Physical planning at the national level has produced the motorway network; railway, port and airport development; accelerated and decelerated housing policies; controlled energy resources and their development; established national parks and recreational areas and policies and, above all, attempted to level out variations in employment growth, largely by means of fiscal controls operating through a variety of agencies and geared into an annual review (i.e. a 'plan') of national expenditure and investment covering both central and local government. But, whatever the intentions, the overall plan behind the policies has been only implicit, never explicit as far as the public or even Parliament are concerned.

The beginnings of regional planning as an explicit means of co-ordinating national and local politics in social, economic and physical fields were almost accidental. Economic Planning Councils (EPC) were established between 1964 and 1966 in each of the administrative regions — which were themselves the periodically adjusted areas set up in wartime for civil-defence purposes and which, in general, have served their purpose as reasonably homogeneous units, each with its own identity and problems. The Planning Councils are non-elective and advisory to central government and their established place in the national machinery is an indication of their accepted value. Their establishment followed closely on the Hailsham study and plan for rehabilitation of the North East in 1963. Their functions were never closely defined and they were left substantially to create their own special role. The clear intention was that they should develop and promote economic planning. In practice they found — as we all still find — that the necessary data for economic planning, whether for input or output, were and are notoriously lacking. The Planning Councils could only concern themselves with the consequences of economic (and social) policies as reflected in physical development and they sought, by reversing the process, to use physical development proposals, together with such little economic data as were available, to produce what were essentially physical plans to improve the well-being of their respective areas. All EPCs have produced at least one and frequently a series of 'strategies' for their respective regions.

The EPC strategies were basically physical and aroused the immediate animosity of the statutory local planning authorities. This was notably the case in the South East, where the planning authorities had associated themselves into a relatively powerful Standing Conference.[3] Initially this was to defend the Metropolitan green belt against pressure from London, but latterly it has become an effective machine for analysing and pro-

159

pounding solutions for the South East — with the Home Counties and others now working in close accord with the Greater London Council. In 1967 the South East Economic Planning Council produced its *Strategy for the South East* (SEEPC, 1967), at a time when the Standing Conference was working towards a parallel but possibly conflicting document. In 1968 this conflict was resolved by adoption of the 'Tripartite Principle', which brought central government, local government and the planning councils together to commission a joint study, by an independent team representative of all three, to formulate and test alternative strategies. The South East Joint Planning Team, directed by the Chief Planner of the then Ministry of Housing and Local Government, produced the *Strategic Plan for the South East* (SEJPT, 1970) in 1970, which was adopted with minor reservations by the newly created Secretary of State for the Environment, after general public consultation in 1971. This plan can fairly be said to be the logical successor to Abercrombie's Greater London Plan of 1944 which, having served well for twenty-five years, had become patently out of date.

Strategic plans for the English regions: the current position

From the 1947 Town and Country Planning Act onwards, a major problem for the relevant Minister had been the attempt to reconcile the conflicting policies and proposals of more than 150 county and county borough planning authorities. The regional strategies provided a means of reducing conflicts to manageable proportions by establishing a 'framework' of social, economic and physical policies within which the more detailed structure plans (themselves now 'packages' of relevant and interrelated *policies* rather than physical 'town' or 'county' maps) could be neatly fitted to form a comprehensive and detailed regional whole.

Following completion of the *Strategic Plan for the South East*, broadly similar regional plans have been produced in the West Midlands (1971), mainly by joint work by the local authorities and, recently, in the North West[5] (following the tripartite principle but with proposals ranging over a much wider field than in the South East). A tripartite strategy for East Anglia is due for completion in the near future and a further one for the North is about to start. The terms of reference for successive strategies have changed somewhat in the light of experience but those for the North West (see Appendix) are typical. Other English regions are not yet convinced of the need to promote joint exercises and rely upon the development of the strategies produced by their Planning Councils. In Scotland, a large-scale sub-regional study is being made of west-central Scotland.

160

The regional strategies cover matters of regional planning concern — matters of a scale and significance warranting intervention at the regional level. These include the regional aspects of national policies (which may appear to be too general to apply at the local level) and the sum of certain local aspects and problems which often aggregate to a major problem at the regional level, which justifies intervention by central government. Such aspects include, for example, regional trends of population change and migration; movements of workers and employment; conflicts between locally and nationally selected growth areas; duplication of special provisions (shopping, airports, regional recreation provisions, etc.), the conservation of regionally valuable amenities and the treatment or clearance of frequently recurring eyesores which may appear of little significance locally but aggregate to a very serious problem at regional level — or even at a sub-regional level which involves several of the new county planning authorities. Thus derelict land, pollution and obsolescent industrial premises combine with other physical, social and economic factors to produce a sub-regional problem of impoverished urban environment throughout the Mersey Belt of the North West, which concerns the new counties of Merseyside, Greater Manchester and Cheshire and whose solution must have inevitable repercussions on the new Lancashire.

Lessons from the South East

The South East plan is aimed primarily at the co-ordination of twenty-four separate local planning authorities. It is doing this in the context of an almost certain continuing growth situation, whether expressed in economic or population terms.

When the work on the plan started there were question marks about the third generation of New Towns: Milton Keynes, Peterborough and Ipswich (though the last was subsequently dropped). Was there a sufficient mobility of employment to man them up? The view, developed all the more strongly by experience in the North West, is that the concept of footloose employers is very largely a myth and that what industrial policy *within* the regions has been doing has been an attempt to steer incremental growth, whether in the manufacturing field or in the service field.

There were difficulties in the South East which emphasise the problem of using an IDC policy to steer industry within the region; a problem which has given rise to doubts on the feasibility of all the Mark III new towns. For example, there are an estimated 11 million square feet of vacant industrial space within Greater London. There is also the highest

161

numerical pool of unemployed in the country, maybe only transitional and temporary and mainly semi-skilled and unskilled, concentrated in Central London. At the same time, London invariably has the highest number of job vacancies which, of course, do not match up with the skills of the unemployed labour force available. There is, therefore, an overheating of the economy which leads through to the social problems of the under-privileged; but all these factors — and others — added together produce a situation in which there is a lack of mobility of jobs and a lack of mobility of labour.

In fact, 65 per cent of moves which took place between 1945 and 1968 in the South East were moves of less than fifteen miles. The situation in the North West is more dramatic. According to the DTI, 90 per cent of all moves of manufacturing industry in that region have been of less than ten miles, 75 per cent less than five miles. This is not surprising when one weaves together the threads of job and labour mobility and the social threads of family ties and the uprooting of families. In London, the willingness of the semi-skilled and unskilled part of the labour force to move, along with their employers, falls from something like 50 or 60 per cent who are prepared to move up to ten miles to only 8 per cent who are prepared to move sixty miles. Higher paid and salaried workers, and those with a stake in the firm (such as pension schemes), are prepared to move in much higher proportion whatever the distance.

In the South East, then, the problem is one of controlling the snowball growth of Greater London and the metropolitan region which surrounds it. The line taken in the plan was to optimise the labour market by *concentrated decentralisation* within a realistic market-demand pattern and market area. That is, as far as further growth is concerned, the increment of growth of some 4 million people projected in the South East by the end of the century should take the form of sector development, particularly into the areas east and west of London, along the Thames Valley. Taking realistic account of the available mobility, the plan requires an attempt to get firms to move from the centre successively outwards in a sectoral pattern — each over a relatively short distance. Then, having moved firms, say, from London to Luton, it would be possible to provide employment for new towns like Milton Keynes, not so much from central London (except for special projects like the Open University, and new office and service growth) but from Luton and similar places on the fringe of London and its metropolitan region. The aim was to get the maximum possible movement and thereby release pressure on Greater London.

Because the Greater London Development Plan was under way at the time (leaving a rather gaping hole in the middle of the South East Strategic Plan), the plan did not give sufficient attention to the social problems of the under-privileged in the inner city. But it did weave together, in a rather primitive way, the social and economic threads of the London metropolitan region.

Problems of the North West

In the North West we have the second largest metropolitan region in the country, comprising Lancashire and Cheshire, plus the High Peak of Derbyshire, with a population of 6·7 million. Eighty-five per cent of this is in urbanised Lancashire and the northern fringe of Cheshire, extending from the coast of the Fylde, Preston and North East Lancashire, southwards to include the bi-polar conurbation of the Mersey Belt from Liverpool through Manchester to the Pennines. This was the first conurban development in the UK and perhaps the only true 'conurbation', i.e. a growing together of towns, that we have in this country — the first product of the industrial revolution of the last century. Twenty-six per cent of the land of the North West is in urban use and that percentage is bound to increase as densities are lowered from their present levels of up to fifty persons per hectare gross.

The results of industrial growth in the last century and the economic, social and environmental problems which it has produced, can be described as follows. Having examined, for all the regions for which comparable data are available, a number of indicators which are susceptible of action in the public sector, we find that the North West has the worst river pollution in the country measured in terms of the chemical classification of river water; the highest incidence of derelict land; the highest general standardised mortality rates; the highest infant mortality rates. The inter-relationship between some of those is immediately apparent. It has the lowest proportion of doctors to population — in spite of the need. It has the highest ratio of pupils to teachers anywhere in the country and the lowest availability of open country for recreation. The last item may appear strange and is not an indicator on which a lot of significance can be placed because the artificiality of the regional boundary in an area which is almost completely surrounded by national parks or very fine country-side is a matter that must be taken into account. But — and the qualification is important — that open countryside is only available to some, i.e. those with cars who can reach it, and not to all of the population. This is one aspect of the socially under-privileged problem which affects the Mersey Belt in particular. The North West is also near worst, not only in the areas which have been declared 'black areas' under the Clean Air Act (1956) but are not yet subject to smoke-control orders, but also in the ratios of footpaths and linear recreation features and urban open space per head of population.

As regards the economy, this is a region struggling to hold its own and slipping, with Merseyside sticking out like a sore thumb with a vast investment since the war which has not materially lowered the unemployment problem, in spite of very little change in the total population, because investment has been in capital-intensive and not labour-intensive industry. Yet there have been great successes since the war in reorientating the structure of industry in the North West. Textiles, coal and the ports have been successfully contracted without serious labour troubles (this is a good example of planning for decline) and at present we find that structurally, at least, the North West is not badly placed. It is not far different from the national industrial composition.

Where, then, are the faults? These are not easily identifiable but at least the performance of industry in the North West is worthy of further investigation and research, giving attention to a number of items: management and entrepreneurial activity; the efficiency of labour; productivity; the nature and quality of the products; the customer—supplier linkages; the dependence on external decision-makers (that is, branch firms with headquarters elsewhere); the expectation of firms thinking of moving into the region; their relative profitability; industrial relations; the relative geographical situation of the region in relation to markets and other sources of supply; and the general communications pattern. Finally, and in a separate category altogether, is the environment and its effect on the North West image; and it is on the state of the urban environment in particular that the strategy's proposals mainly concentrate.

There is a lack of appreciation of economic problems at the local planning authority level. The big counties may have the resources to do the necessary research. But in the case of the county boroughs (and particularly the small county boroughs), of which there are twenty-one in the North West, it is a waste of national resources to duplicate the research effort on matters of economic and social significance. On the other hand, a regional strategy can break down the content of national investment and similar plans to the manageable proportions of the eight English Economic Planning Regions and provide a framework for the structure planning carried out by the local authorities. At the same time, the strategic plan can aggregate from the local authority level and put into new perspectives local problems as they appear at the regional scale — perspectives which central government itself may not appreciate, at least in their full intensity. Thus there is a national input into structure plans, via a regional analysis and breakdown of them. Indeed, in the North West this has been carried further to an analysis of the eight sub-divisions of the region. Moreover, it has also been necessary to take account of the development of regional plans within a Common Market regional policy framework which imposes a need to keep the proposals open-ended.

In the North West, any analysis of national problems at regional level reveals in particular the poverty of the environment. The local authorities know that they themselves are poor but they do not appreciate how poor they are as a regional entity in comparison with the rest of the country. Hitherto, figures have not been put on this factor and, without doing the national research, it has proved impossible to evaluate the problem in full. However, the strategic plan shows, for example, that in the field of local authority finance, the bulk of the authorities in the North West are in receipt of rate-support grant. The rate-support grant (which brings the level of rateable income throughout the country up to the national average) offers no financial incentive to most local authorities in the North West to try to attract additional industrial rateable value. All that that does is to offset such new rateable value against the Government contribution in the rate-support grant. Liverpool, for example, would be no better off financially and is so far below the national average that it would have little chance of becoming so. The effect, therefore, is that the rich parts of the country are getting richer and the poor parts are getting poorer in resources available for environmental improvement. Moreover, we find that the North West seems to pay more in rates and taxes into the national kitty than it gets back and that the South East and the South West regions get back more than they pay in. This does not seem to be the equitable situation one would expect.

Prospects for the North West

What does the strategic plan propose to remedy the problems of the North West? First, it recognises the need to use existing social capital and to 'bend' trends within the limits of reality. While the region as a whole in the last decade increased in population by 160,000 people, the cities of Manchester and Liverpool each *lost* one-fifth of their population. Admittedly this was a period when over-spill schemes were at their height, particularly in the early years. The geographical county of Lancashire (including its county boroughs) lost for the first time in its history 23,000 people; a small loss proportionately but a loss nevertheless; whereas

Cheshire gained 13 per cent over its 1961 level – an increase of 175,000. The basic reason for the relatively low regional increase was a migration figure currently running at something like 16,000 people a year. Examined in detail, this means an expansion of the metropolitan area of the Mersey Belt and further development around existing built-up areas in an incremental growth of what is there already. This is partly served by the development of new motorways, 175 miles of which were built within the North West during the 1960s and the early 1970s. This produces a chicken and egg situation which attracts still more growth and still more urban development.

On future growth, the strategic plan has been unable to make firm forecasts. Growth could conceivably range, on various estimates, from nil to something like 1·8 million between 1971 and 2000. It is not possible to plan to the end of the century on that sort of basis. But the strategy has taken what can be called an 'indicative projection' of a half a million increase in population by the end of the century as a basis for a plan which it sees as a flexible instrument. This is perhaps the most important point of all: *that the planning process is much more important than the plan itself.* The strategy has therefore woven together a number of threads – social, economic and inter-city problems; the industrial and office-location problems; and the same kind of urban-sectoral development as was proposed and accepted for the South East. These have produced a fabric for a new North West which emphasises the important part (in complete contrast to the South East plan) that must be played by central government, not in providing money to a group of North West beggars but in ensuring that the region gets at least its just deserts and that some of the ravages of the industrial revolution are put right so that the region can itself proceed to develop a self-sustaining economy. Secondly, the strategy has been given a physical expression in an amalgamation of the social and economic needs and the realities of existing restraints in a Mersey Belt concentration in which renewal and renovation are combined. Use has been made of public transport corridors, with a view to reducing the volume of private transport – particularly by the development of transport interchanges from the private to the public sector within urban sectors along the spines of the railway network. Proposals have been put forward for improving the urban environment by anti-pollution measures, new social and cultural facilities, urban open spaces and recreation. In particular, emphasis has been put on the need for the new metropolitan complex of Greater Manchester and Merseyside to seize the great opportunities which exist in the very scale of the problem of obsolescence, to remedy the impoverishment of the environment by means of good design

— an aspect which appears to have been lost in much of British planning over the last quarter of a century.

Some of those factors have been costed, with results that do not give cause for optimism: for example, an experiment on combating pollution has led to the realisation that, whatever good intentions may have been expressed in respect of cleaning the rivers and the air and clearing derelict land in the next decade, the cost will be at least two and a half times the existing annual level if those programmes are going to be achieved. Bearing in mind the investment in the South East in Maplin and the Channel Tunnel, at least the North West deserves its share of additional national investment for the improvement of its environment. The estimated cost of the Channel Tunnel is of the order of £800 million; the North West requires some £50—£75 million to link, by means of a multi-purpose underground rail system, two quite separate railway networks, one extending northwards from Manchester Victoria, one extending south-wards from Manchester Piccadilly — thereby providing an effective London Transport-type system for the whole of Greater Manchester. Yet at the moment, this valuable asset is held up for want of approval of sanction to borrow the necessary capital.

Only by a comprehensive approach on all fronts, that is, by corporate planning, can there be any hope of solving the daunting problems, produc-ing a self-sustaining economy for the North West and providing a reason-able quality of life for its people. Revival in the North West would, of course, contribute to a reduction of the pressures and congestion costs in the South East, where they are already beginning to be felt by both the employer and the man in the street to be real deterrents to the quality of life in London itself.

We have heard of a five-year period for economic planning; and of a three- or four-decade period for development of the EEC regional policy. When one is thinking of thirty or forty years, one is thinking in terms of continuous planning and this is perhaps the most important issue of all. A continuous regional planning process should be established in the North West and elsewhere. This should not simply take the form of monitoring. Monitoring, in the words of the South East Strategy, is much more likely to represent a monitoring of the decay of a plan than if a continuous and flexible approach is adopted as part of a system which alters the plan to meet changing circumstances.

Conclusion

1 Regional strategies as a cohesive package of policies affecting both local and central government, with some expression of their effects in physical terms (which may be only part and not necessarily the most important part of the total strategy), should become a recognised part of the planning hierarchy. In spite of their importance, they have no statutory basis at present.

2 The generation of regional strategies has been piecemeal and experimental. Their value is not yet fully proven or accepted.

3 They should generate a regional consciousness which does not exist at present, so that the normal participation and inquiry procedures can be instituted to test formally public reaction and approval.

4 Above all, regional strategies should not be regarded as blueprints or master plans, but need to be kept flexible by a process of continuous planning and adjustment. They provide the framework and guidelines for sub-regional and structure plans, but equally they are themselves tested by, and should be open to, adjustment as a result of the more detailed studies involved at the structure and local plan levels. Continuity of the process is more important than the plans — whether regional, sub-regional or local.

APPENDIX

Terms of reference of the strategic plan for the North West

1 The planning team is to consider and report with recommendations on patterns of development for the North West region, taking account of the strategy proposals of the North West Economic Planning Council and of the planning work (carried out individually or jointly) of the local planning authorities and of other public authorities with relevant responsibilities. It must also take account of government policies and decisions, with the object of providing a regional framework plan serving to guide.

(a) the local planning authorities and other public authorities in carrying out their planning responsibilities, including, in particular, the preparation of structure plans under the Town and Country Planning Act 1968; and

(b)   Government decisions on public expenditure and economic and social policies relating to the region's development.

2   The framework must indicate a desired future pattern of social, environmental and economic development for the region, aiming at the proper use and conservation of regional assets and at establishing and maintaining in the North West region a quality of life in balance with that of the remainder of the country. In so doing, the framework plan should suggest policies for the solution of major, long standing, physical planning issues of regional significance, and throw light on the areas for which the joint submission of structure plans may be appropriate.

3   The work must proceed by the early submission to the commissioning body of a short issues report appraising the situation in the region and showing the planning team's proposals for tackling it. The main content of this report is to be

(a)   the team's identification of the main problems at regional level of the area to be planned;
(b)   the team's proposed method of dealing with these problems — a discussion of objectives and a suggestion of alternative strategies, with a description of the intended process of evaluating strategic proposals for the purpose of choosing between them;
(c)   recommendations about the form of a continuous planning process for the region after completion of the Study.

4   The issues report, described in the foregoing paragraph, should be received by the commissioning body within six months from the starting date of the work. The study as a whole should be completed in not more than a further eighteen months after the views of the commissioning body are known.

[These terms of reference were approved by the Commissioning Body on 11 March 1971.]

Notes

[1]   The views expressed in this paper are those of the author and are not necessarily shared by the Department of the Environment or the commissioning authorities of the strategic plan for the North West.
[2]   For example, see Andrew Thorburn, Town and Country Planning Summer School, York, as reported in *The Times* (8 September 1973).

[3] Now the Standing Conference on London and South East Regional Planning, including all planning authorities in the South East planning region.

[4] 'A Framework for Regional Planning in South East England' was produced by the Standing Conference in 1968 but not published.

[5] At the time of writing the report was awaiting publication as *Strategic Plan for the North West.*

References

Cmnd 6386, *Expert Committee on Compensation and Betterment* (Uthwatt Report), HMSO (1942).

Planning Advisory Group, *The Future of Development Plans,* HMSO (1965).

South East Economic Planning Council, *A Strategy for the South East,* HMSO (1967).

South East Joint Planning Team, *Strategic Plan for the South East,* HMSO (1970).

West Midlands Regional Study, *A Developing Strategy for the West Midlands,* Birmingham (1971).

8 Regional Policy and Sub-Regional Planning : the Confused State

L. S. Jay

Introduction

The purpose of this paper — against the background of the *Strategic Plan for the South East* — is to consider the administrative and political processes that operate within a region; to consider some of the current problems of present intraregional structure planning and the simulation of projects of a strategic and regional nature; and finally to consider some possible improvements to the system.

The existing administrative and political system

The local government system

Local government at the moment is in the process of change from an old and, it is said, outworn system to a new local government structure. Both the old and the new systems, however, comprise administrative and political control at county level and at a second tier. The emerging problem, as Peter Hall (1973) in reviewing a recent book has said, is the difficulty of establishing clear rules of relationship between one level of local government and the other. This, as Hall goes on to say, is particularly pertinent to planning, for which the new lower county district authority will command the unique effective power (in general) of sanctioning or refusing real developments on the ground — no matter how competent and well informed the new county planning authority may prove to be.

Within this framework, however, political control is exercised, together — in the case of the planning process — with public participation and involvement. This involvement of the public in the planning process — and in that process only — is a statutory obligation which adheres most strongly to the new counties, to the new county districts less strongly and to regions not at all. Even when it does adhere most strongly, it is difficult to

171

decide where the initiative should lie as recent issues concerning London's third airport and the growth implications flowing from it, begin to show. There the government have issued consultative documents (Department of the Environment, 1973A) and it is interesting to speculate as to where next, and at what stage in the planning process, similar interventions may be anticipated. Public involvement, however, is more developed and is more articulate at local levels and only now is it being exercised at sub-regional levels. At the regional level there has been no real involvement with the public.

In the case of the Crawley–Gatwick sub-regional study, which is not unconnected with the problem of London's airports, three counties – Surrey, and East and West Sussex – have been involved and have initiated the process which has to be carried into the formal structure plan procedure and accounted for at the final 'Examination in Public' (Department of the Environment, 1973B). At such hearings the participation process will have to be shown to have been carried out and the public will presumably be eligible to be heard on this point. Eligibility, however, seems now to be a lottery, since the Secretary of State can select those he wishes to hear. Whether or not this participation process works with respect to existing commitment, and whether or not it will or can be made to work with respect to new commitments, is a matter of debate; what matters is that the philosophy of the process exists.

The standing conference on London and South East regional planning

At present, and in the foreseeable future, the local government system of administration, management and political control breaks off at county level and does not reach regional level at all. As early as the mid-1950s local planning authorities in the South East were facing serious problems with respect to scale and the distribution of the changes in population and employment. The necessity to work jointly was seen and in December 1962 a standing conference of local planning authorities was inaugurated, membership at that time being related to the area covered by the Greater London Plan (1944). Membership was later extended to take in the London commuter area. Establishment of regional economic planning machinery then saw further expansion of the conference to cover the whole of the South East region. This latter extension was important as it provided for the first time a mechanism by which the views of local planning authorities on the problems affecting the newly defined region could be formulated.

The standing conference on London and South East regional planning was originally established to keep under review the principal planning issues affecting the area and to disseminate planning information; to make recommendations to the membership with a view to the formulation of joint policy; to co-ordinate subsequent action and, for these proposals, to consult appropriate government departments and other authorities and bodies concerned.

The constitution provides for a conference of nominated members of constituent authorities and a full-time secretariat. These are supported by an administrative panel of clerks of the member authorities and a technical panel of their planning officers with power to set up sub-panels and to consult other specialist officers. This association of local planning authorities can, perhaps, be regarded as a sophisticated organisation as far as it goes but it falls a long way short of regional power with executive control over regional finance, the provision of services and the means to organise the structure planning and transportation processes within the region. Based on this model, however, it seems reasonable to expect a similar organisation for the North West now that *Strategic Plan for the North West* has been published. Can the future of these associations, however, be regarded with certainty? Are they, and will they, ever be anything other than talking shops which, by their very nature, exclude political representation and cannot in any way become involved in or promote public participation?

Credit must, however, be given to the London and South East planning conference for being one of the three parties to the production by a joint team of *Strategic Plan for the South East* (SEJPT, 1970). The other two parties were the government and the government-appointed Regional Economic Council, with which last named body the local planning authorities have no links and of whose deliberations they are kept in ignorance.

The Strategic Plan for the South East

What then did this plan comprise? Really very little. It was developed from the 1981 base date, assessed on land availability for the region, and examined only two strategies: one previously developed by the South East Economic Planning Council and one developed by the joint team. The final strategy was a mixture of these two and there was not even time to do a transport evaluation on this hybrid (Figure 8.1). It gave, with 1981 as the base date, indicative populations rather than design populations for planning areas. But these planning areas were developed for statistical convenience — not necessarily for planning suitability — and it is doubtful that with the reorganisation of local government these areas are convenient even for statistical purposes — if indeed they ever were. It also gave

173

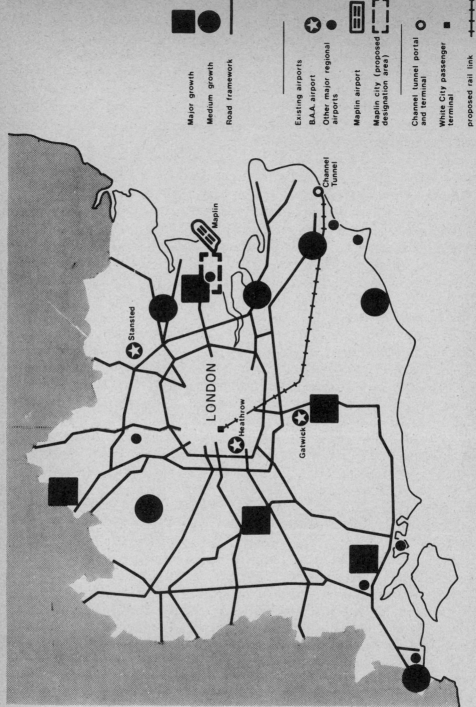

Major growth

Medium growth

Road framework

Existing airports

B.A.A. airport

Other major regional airports

Maplin airport

Maplin city (proposed designation area)

Channel tunnel portal and terminal

White City passenger terminal

proposed rail link

Channel Tunnel

Maplin

Stansted

LONDON

Heathrow

Gatwick

Fig. 8.1   The strategic plan for the South East, 1971

174

some indication of broad land-use zoning of agricultural land in environmental zones (Figure 8.2). Economic criteria were taken into account but no real justification emerged for concentrations of employment and population. These economic criteria led to the naming of 'major' and 'medium' growth areas. In their earlier report (1967, p. 12), on the *Strategic Plan for the South East* the South East Economic Planning Council urged caution over expansion within two of these growth areas: Crawley–Gatwick and Bishops Stortford–Harlow.

The government's statement on the plan in October 1972 endorsed the recommended growth areas with the exception of Bishops Stortford–Harlow, but Crawley–Gatwick was left in as a major growth area.

The structure plan exercises with which local planning authorities are presently engaged are the testing of this chosen strategy including the social, economic and land-use elements of it. Is this a logical approach? Why have a regional strategy at all if it requires validity at the structure plan level? If, on the other hand, it is argued that the strategy can be developed in a crude enough form to be useful, then is structure planning itself a valid exercise?

The issue also strikes at the problem of whether the government is wishing to arbitrate in a national context on the potential power and development – and hence on the demand on national resources which each region has – or whether it is merely adopting a 'normative' approach in its regional policy, treating each regional plan as a 'one-off' affair which can be validated by structure plans, to which all local planning authorities subscribe and which does not interfere with normative economic policies of government. This dilemma accounts in part for the chicken-and-egg situation which exists regarding regional economic and physical planning and – using the expression in its loosest context – sub-regional economic and physical planning. Well aware of the difficulties of defining a region for these purposes the plan for the South East did nothing to examine the existence of socio-economic sub-regions within its arbitrarily chosen boundaries nor did it do anything to suggest viable sub-regions for planning purposes within the framework of its strategy. All it did was to choose general locations for growth and for obscure statistical reasons, which seem to have little or no basis for subsequent monitoring and statistical analysis, defined a set of arbitrary planning areas. As a result the expression 'sub-region' has already come to mean a structure-planning area, whether created geographically by several planning authorities or related solely to a county administrative area or some 'start area' within it. How sub-regions or structure plan areas, arbitrarily chosen, spasmodic in their starting dates and proceeding independently of each other with no

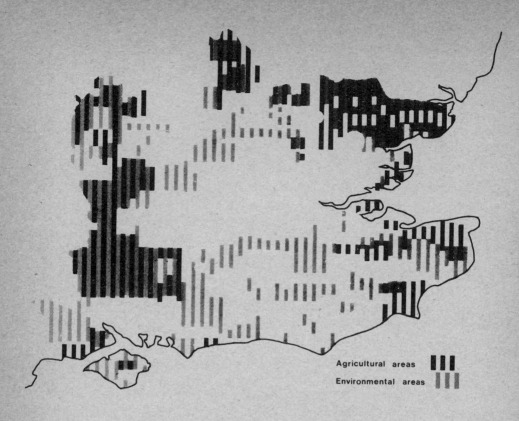

Fig. 8.2   Agricultural and environmental areas in the South East

centre for intraregional discussion can come to validate or confute the chosen strategy for the region is unanswerable. Notwithstanding that some monitoring of the region is in hand at government level, the joint team charged with the preparation of the strategy has been disbanded and there is little or no contact between the local planning authorities and the regional economic council.

Inherent problems of existing intra-regional planning

Local government reorganisation

Apart from present traumas within the structure planning process itself, local government reorganisation, as already mentioned, adds to the difficulties. Whether a two-tier system will work or whether a unitary system would work better has little relevance to the fact that the new boundaries for county councils as structure plan authorities is far from ideal. This is especially true in metropolitan areas where boundaries were drawn too tight but is also the case when absorption of county boroughs has taken place along county boundaries adjusted, it would seem, simply to ensure that existing populations and rateable values would appear to be in reasonable balance after reorganisation. For example, the Brighton urban structure plan (Figure 8.3a), which roughly conforms to the planning area shown in the strategic plan for the South East is divided under reorganisation, not at the local boundary formed by the river Adur but further to the east at the existing and indiscernible boundary between Portslade and Shoreham-by-Sea — notwithstanding the fact that Shoreham Harbour straddles the boundary (Figure 8.3b)! It is also true, for example, that the Crawley—Gatwick sub-region will fall dominantly in the new West Sussex with an important part in Surrey. Notwithstanding the existence (before reorganisation) of a joint advisory committee comprised of members of the three counties (East and West Sussex and Surrey) the structure plan process is to be in two parts — one prepared by West Sussex and one by Surrey. The sub-region is totally severed from the geographically constrained Brighton area, the structure plan for which is in an advanced state of preparation.

The Crawley—Gatwick sub-region

If we refer back to the chicken-and-egg situation of sub-regional and regional planning, Crawley—Gatwick seems a first-class example.

Crawley, a new town, buoyant economically but probably badly sited socio-geographically from the beginning, has further growth problems superimposed upon it by Gatwick Airport. This airport, originally chosen on the basis of unconvincing meteorological evidence — it was said to be relatively free from ground fog over an encouraging time-continuum on all occasions when Heathrow was fog enclosed — as London's alternative airport has crept in, as it were, as London's second airport. The South East Economic Planning Council in its published statement urged caution over the effect of growth in the Crawley—Burgess Hill area on the environment but the government statement on the strategic plan accepts it as a major growth area notwithstanding. In terms of growth implications, phasing meant that growth could take place fairly imminently and that being in the Outer Metropolitan Area it would attract people willing to move only short distances to new employment who do not wish to, or cannot move far from London. It is perhaps interesting here to note that in this connection only, so far as can be discerned, the South East's plan indicated

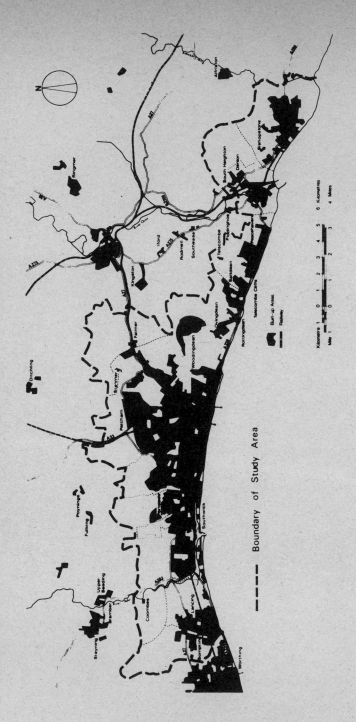

Fig. 8.3(a)   The Brighton urban structure plan area: built-up areas

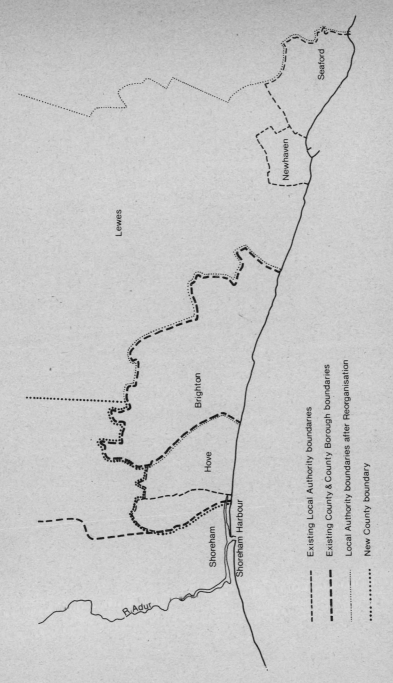

Fig. 8.3(b)   The Brighton urban structure plan area: local government boundaries

an ordering in the development of its chosen strategy by indicating that the minor growth area centred on Eastbourne—Hastings should not commence until the major growth area centred on Crawley was complete. The implications of a Hastings — Greater London town development scheme (already approved and presently in hand) together with the conclusions being drawn from the study of the Brighton and the Crawley areas indicate that this ordering may be difficult, if not impossible, to justify or to achieve.

A sub-regional study of the Crawley—Gatwick area (Figure 8.4) has been carried out by West Sussex in association with its neighbouring counties and alternative strategies for growth have been developed and publicly discussed. These studies indicate that it will be all the area can do to cope with its internally over-heated economy and growth at Gatwick with one runway let alone offer relief to the congested Brighton area. The *Strategic Plan for the South East* would seem to fail in this instance in terms of short-move employment bases because there is no room. The strategy would also seem to fail in terms of phasing, as office pressure is mounting some eight years before the strategic plan is due to start.

Strategic projects

A further question arises as to whether the plan fails also with respect to two strategic projects of immense importance: the Channel Tunnel and Maplin. Both have national and international implications and present weighty problems of local importance, and implications environmentally, socially and economically. The *Strategic Plan for the South East*, in an appendix, dealt with the various sites for London's third airport and their implications on the recommended strategy. With reference to Maplin it there stated:

> Although employment growth in south Essex is desirable and needs to be stimulated, it will be necessary, if Foulness [i.e. Maplin, ed.] is chosen, to make a detailed assessment of the area's capacity and of the transport and related environmental problems likely to be posed by a very large scale growth, and also to examine the extent to which the third London airport and the other possible alternatives might help in solving the social problem of the less privileged in Greater London.

With respect to south-east Kent the plan, again in an appendix that deals with planning areas, simply states 'the future of this area and particularly of Dover and Folkestone will remain uncertain until a decision on the Channel Tunnel is taken.'

180

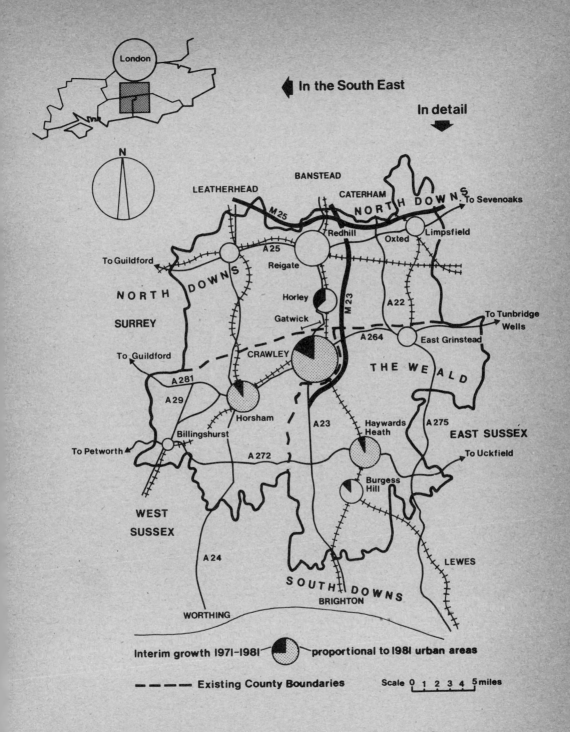

Fig. 8.4   Crawley–Gatwick sub-regional study area

181

These quotations are not used necessarily as a criticism of the plan but they are very illustrative of the scale of the chicken-and-egg situation which develops when producing a regional plan in a vacuum and in a hurry.

The result is that the plan offers no guidance in these matters and national controversy rages whilst local government is kept in comparative darkness. Local government, however, wishes to see participation at the local government level and that process is being carried out by central government with respect to Maplin via their consultative document entitled *The Maplin Project: designation area for the new town*, and the argument for this is that, far from being a local or even regional issue, it is one of national moment. This is equally true of the Channel Tunnel.

Is there then a cut-off point between local environmental issues and the national economic and political strategic decision? It may well be that this is never possible and the inhabitants of south-east Essex will have their future decided over Maplin by clamour raised in, say, the North East over inter-regional allocations of national resoures. Equally the fate of the inhabitants of Dover and Folkestone may be decided on the international scale by a hybrid of central government and multi-national financial interests. Where does local government stand in these situations? Should it stand aside or should it become parochial and defensive? And how then, in the structure-plan process, does it carry on a meaningful dialogue with the public and validate the strategic plan?

Possible improvements to the system

The statutory planning process

Apart from the need for improvement in our knowledge of the management of resources and of the effectiveness of existing policies, both inter- and intra-regionally, there is an obvious need for improvement in all lines of communication. The government (Secretary of State, 1971), in accepting the *Strategic Plan for the South East* said in paragraph 4:

> ... the strategy is flexible and will be kept under continual review in the light not only of national and regional trends as a whole, but also of specific problems thrown up at the local level in the course of implementation.

and, paragraph 15:

> The Government regard it as of the utmost importance that effective

arrangements should be made for its continuous monitoring and review.

But what are the arrangements for its review? The original team has been disbanded and there are none known to local government who have to struggle with the structure plan process.

Many of the future problems of attempting to relate structure plans intraregionally may well emanate from what some might criticise as an over-complex, over-ambitious structure planning system and it is a matter of opinion and interpretation as to how deeply the structure planning process should seek to influence social and economic elements — but the local planning authorities are charged under the relevant Act so to do.

The report of the panel of inquiry (Layfield, 1973) into the Greater London development plan under the chairmanship of Mr Frank Layfield, QC is relevant here. There is a difference, of course, between the Greater London development plan and structure planning in general. Nevertheless the panel felt that a number of lessons were to be drawn for other authorities.

One of the six defects identified by the panel was *over-ambition* — exemplified by the assumption that the plan could alter settled population trends: 'No policies by a local authority can effectively alter settled population trends in the short term, and the Greater London Council had neither the information to make employment forecasts nor the ability to relate them to floor space.'

Of equal significance is the fact that the Department of the Environment will be promulgating formally the more important draft modifications proposed by government after looking at the Layfield Report and that the Secretary of State has the right to make use, if necessary, of his power to approve the plan in stages.

To these new attitudes can be added thoughts expressed by the standing conference on London and South East regional planning in March 1973, concerning the necessity to get some form of structure plan approved, whether it be of broad brush, of limited policy involvement, or of a two-part nature. Could they be leading to a very different concept of structure planning, certainly not envisaged by the planning advisory group in their report (1965) or 1971/72 Planning Acts?

It seems certain that local government authorities, singly or in association, must give serious thought to these matters and it may well be that by so doing a key will be found for an easier approach to intraregional structure planning — perhaps on the basis of the region or of meaningful sub-regions related to the overall strategy.

It is not a positive thing to say, perhaps — but it needs to be said nonetheless — that planners have only limited confidence in the new system. The division of the development plan process and development control, together with such essential keys to the social element of planning as housing, augurs badly. At the same time as this divisive county and district system is being introduced, water, sewage and health authorities are moving in the opposite direction to the regional or sub-regional levels and there seems, for many facets of regional planning — including European regional planning — a movement towards a build-up of a regional institution.

Much will depend on the build-up of power at the district level but it is possible to imagine the squeezing-out of counties as effective bodies. They may have fallen between two stools of local and regional planning, both in terms of executive management of services and of political opinion and climate. It may well be that improvements will not be possible until a new regional and sub-regional institution, which will act as a strong guide to structure planning, is set up.

Currently work of a political nature is achieved by *ad hoc* arrangements with the standing conference and joint steering committees to develop structure plans over common areas of concern but there is clear ground for conflict in these arrangements as the several component authorities each move towards the corporate policies that their newly established managements will require. Perhaps a reflection on this can be seen in the comments in the *Architects' Journal* of 29 August 1973 on the City of Coventry structure plan:

> The investment and programming proposals, especially in the critical fields of social and welfare policies, are lifted from the comprehensive ten-year Local Policy Plan which has just issued from the City's noted corporate planning system [and] the comprehensiveness of this corporate plan calls even more into question the value of the official structure plan.

By far the greatest problem, however, is at regional level in coordinating intraregionally the structure plans and testing the *Strategic Plan for the South East*. Perhaps, however, the greatest opportunity also exists in that the standing conference on London and South East regional planning will itself require reorganisation after 1974 to fit the needs of the new local government structure with its divided planning functions. One important issue will be the administrative and political integration of transportation into a newly-constituted conference so that their consultative, advisory and coordinating role would extend from purely planning to embrace transport questions.

Other issues exist: for example, representation of new Districts at the standing conference. If districts cannot be represented in bulk then opportunities should exist for more manageable groups, perhaps, one hopes, on the basis of meaningful sub-regions and the setting up of *ad hoc* groups for dealing with specific subjects.

This would aid intraregional planning and the setting-up of regional objectives and then monitoring. It would also ease the design problems of local authority and regional information systems and make public participation in regional and sub-regional issues a more objective and meaningful exercise.

Conclusion

The message is perhaps not a terribly clear one because of reorganisation, because of the newness and lack of experience both in regional, sub-regional and in structure planning, and because of uncertainties over national and European regional institutions.

Hence it is necessary to sound a note of caution and perhaps of cynicism. The *Strategic Plan for the South East*, despite its brief references to the central metropolitan area, has a gaping great hole in the middle that the Greater London Development Plan and the Layfield panel of inquiry have begun to explore. All the diagrams to illustrate that strategy bear witness to this. The plan for the South East – and to some extent the new development-plan system – has by its very nature been set up for the guidance of growth and development. The population concerned with housing and employment problems in new growth areas, however, is but a small percentage of the whole. Exercises to involve the public by local participation in the problems of growth areas suffer as a result because the relevant populations are not there and, in so far as they do exist within or without the region, they do not know or anticipate that they will be involved and cannot be found.

Systems, both the structure planning and the new local government system and regional systems, take time to settle down and work. By the time they are settled and working, it may well be that the very nature of growth as we now define it will be called in question. Instead the equilibrium in the economy and in population may depend more on planning for decline in some areas. Some would say that this last aspect has been avoided for too long. Emphasis in planning will then be much more on management and improvement of existing urban systems and political choice concerned less with the allocation of resources to growth areas. The Layfield panel of inquiry issued a warning about the scarcity of resources, particularly in terms of skilled manpower, which could hinder the preparation of adequate structure plans, and this is, indeed, a matter for concern. Layfield also placed emphasis on the need to distinguish between strategic plan material and local plan material. Layfield's own attempt at a definition may not take this matter much further but there can be no doubt that he has identified an area of uncertainty which is also a source of difficulty. Resolution of this point may come out of experience, as structure plans are prepared and approved, but the likely time-scale and the lag in the systems militate against this. Debate on the function and nature of development plans continues and moves in a direction which suggests that the issues may be resolved only after a widely-based national study. In the *Strategic Plan for the South East* what are the implications of Greater London for the settlement pattern of the whole region? Are they likely to imply policies consistent with those hitherto pursued in the South East — for example, over the control of the location of industry and offices? Or with those posed in the strategic plan? If they are not, what sort of machinery will be devised for the review of that strategy? And will the new development plan system prove flexible enough to adjust rapidly to a shift in emphasis? It is important that these matters be considered.

References

Department of the Environment, *The Maplin Airport Surface Corridor*, HMSO (1973A).

Department of the Environment, *The Maplin project: Designation Area for the New Town*, HMSO (1973B).

Department of the Environment, *Structure plans, examination in public*, Circular 36/78 (Welsh Office Circular 74/73), HMSO (1973).

Hall P. G., 'Review', *Regional Studies*, 7 (1970), p. 235.

Layfield F., *Report of the Panel of Inquiry into the Greater London Development plan* (The Layfield Report), HMSO (1973).

Planning Advisory Group, *The Future of Development Plans*, HMSO (1965).

Secretary of State for the Environment, *Statement on the Strategic Plan for the South East*, HMSO (1971).

South East Economic Planning Council, *A Strategy for the South East*,
    HMSO (1967).
South East Joint Planning Team, *Strategic Plan for the South East*, HMSO
    (1970).

9 Regional Policies and Regional Government

David Donnison

What are British regional policies for and what political institutions are required for these purposes? For many years our regional policies were mainly economic, producing few political innovations. More is now heard of political regionalism but too often the proposed regions lack firm economic foundations. In this paper I shall try to reconnect discussion of these two aspects of Britain's regional problems.

What are we trying to achieve?

During the last century, social reformers such as Charles Booth — and before him, Thomas Chalmers — were concerned about small, inner urban areas and the problems of public health, poverty and disorder which afflicted the communities living in them. Such spatially oriented policies as there were tended to focus on small neighbourhoods of this kind. Things were transformed by the decline of Britain's basic industries which set in at about the turn of the century. The tide of migrations which had drawn people to the centres of these older industries turned. Areas like South Wales, which had steadily gained migrants for years (Friedlander and Roshier, 1966), began to suffer continuing net losses. By the inter-war years the problems posed by their industrial decline and its social repercussions were high among the priorities of every British government.

Policies for the 'depressed areas' were a central feature of the broad consensus on which the post-war town and country planning legislation was launched. The public health movement, originating in the nineteenth century, the conservationists, the Labour movement with the memories of the hunger marchers, those concerned about congestion in the growing conurbations or about the target offered to bombers by the concentration of productive capacity in the south-eastern corner of the country — all agreed that the burgeoning, sprawling prosperity of the wealthiest regions must be reined in, and that the industries of the depressed regions must be revived and their decayed urban structure renewed. Regional policies were strongly industrial and physical, calling first for new jobs and new houses.

To these concerns were added, by the early 1960s, growing anxiety about economic stagnation and Britain's failure to keep pace with her continental neighbours. When Labour was returned to power with the crucial support of Scottish, Welsh and North of England votes, regional policies were expected to play a central part in the programme that would enable Britain to escape from the cycle of 'stop–go–stop', a cycle that was itself due to the recurring need to halt expansion whenever full employment began to over-heat the economy by driving up wages in the prosperous midland and south-eastern regions. The problems of the depressed and the prosperous regions came to be regarded as opposite symptoms of the same fundamental disorders.

Next, it looked as if this essentially economic formulation of regional problems was to be given a more explicitly political dimension. The tentative innovation of setting up nominated regional planning councils in 1965 was carried further when the Crowther (later Kilbrandon) Commission was appointed in 1969 to consider the possibility of bolder constitutional changes. When it reported in 1973 the commission (Cmnd 5460) was still doubtful about the strength and the significance of regional nationalisms. But with the Scottish National Party capturing a Labour stronghold a few weeks later it became clear that such loyalties are not a negligible force. Nationalist passions may not be the prime mover in such electoral upsets, however. They may result from more deeply rooted economic and social grievances. The Royal Commission implicitly acknowledged this possibility. Its own research called for hour-long interviews with the public about dissatisfaction with government in which 'the only specific "solution" put to those being interviewed was some kind of devolution ... It must be recognised, however, that if a person is dissatisfied, and he is presented with only one suggested remedy, then he may be expected to take a generally favourable view of that remedy, whatever it is, even if he has given no previous thought to it.' (Cmnd 5460, para. 268). Yet despite these doubts the commissioners went on to recommend bold (though diverse and conflicting) devolutions of power to regional assemblies of various kinds.

Nevertheless, regional policies in Britain (and, till 1968, in Northern Ireland) remain predominantly economic. They are designed, as they always have been, to reduce the differentially high rates of unemployment in the ailing regions — both for the sake of these regions, and for the sake of the general development of the whole economy. Only in Northern Ireland are Westminster policies directed primarily to political questions of civil rights, power-sharing and public order.

Strategies for the future

We have achieved considerable success in bringing work to the poorer regions and promoting industry there. In many respects, South Wales, Yorkshire and Humberside, and more recently the Scottish Highlands, have begun to catch up with the rest of the country. Merely to prevent further decline of areas depending so heavily on declining or slowly growing industries might be acclaimed a success. Yet, even in the more successful of the depressed regions, we have failed to generate the self-sustaining growth which would enable them to dispense with continuing support from central government and its regional policies. That does not mean these policies are merely a drag upon the economy: they benefit the prosperous regions too. Nevertheless, they have failed to attain their objectives. What more must we do?

The government's aim is to give people more and better opportunities in an expanding economy. To achieve that we must attend to the whole complex, social and economic 'mesh' of the society we live in. The human race can survive incredible hardships, but tolerates very little disappointment. Indeed it is a mark of the intelligent that they switch, quicker than most, from activities which are unsatisfying to those which seem likely to be more satisfying. That means we must try to ensure, in each activity, that more rewarding opportunities are within easy reach, financially, spatially and culturally. The rungs in the ladder must be placed closer together. Moreover, each ladder of opportunities must be sustained by others in neighbouring sectors of the economy. Why should we expect children to sacrifice opportunities for earning, to stay on at school and take their education further, unless they are convinced by the experience of their families, friends and neighbours, that by so doing they can get better jobs? Why should young people do the extra work, take the extra training and assume the extra responsibilities which bring promotion unless they believe that this will open up new opportunities and earn them more money? Why should they bother to earn more unless they can see — again within easy reach — better houses and other goods and services which they could buy for their families? Often people do achieve these things despite adverse circumstances; but the achievement must have been harder, and a price — such as migration to more prosperous regions — will often have been paid for it.

If this over-simplified psychology is fundamentally sound, it suggests that we must beware of discontinuities, where the rungs of a ladder are missing or lead nowhere, and disjunctions, where neighbouring ladders are not available to provide mutually supporting opportunities. The poorer regions appear to have more than their share of these discontinuities and disjunctions. Some are the result of long-term changes in the pace and direction of their economic and social development. Some have been exacerbated by clumsy public intervention in the region's affairs.

Where are the lowest council rents, and where — after the South East — are the most expensive owner-occupied houses? Both are generally to be found in Scotland. There the middle rungs of the housing market are often missing, making it unusually difficult for people to secure a better or more conveniently located house. This must reduce incentives to earn the money which could secure a better home and must encourage enterprising people to move elsewhere.

Where is the highest educational attainment to be found — the largest proportions of seventeen-year-olds still in school, and the largest proportions securing advanced level examination successes and moving on to higher education? Wales usually comes at or near the top of these lists. In this case the ladder works well, but because in many parts of Wales the neighbouring ladders are often missing — there are too few jobs for well-qualified young people and too few houses of the sort they later want to buy — the most able often have to leave the region, or remain there as underemployed workers and housewives. Meanwhile, people who do want to set up new industries in underemployed regions may be deterred from doing so by other disjunctions such as the lack of skilled workers, managerial talent, sub-contractors, merchant banks and risk-taking lenders.

Too often regional policies have tended to exacerbate these disjunctions and discontinuities, rather than to diversify and enrich opportunities. The aluminium smelter, a typical show-piece of such policies, employs very few people in relation to the capital invested in it or the subsidy it demands and many of those employed are either routine workers with few opportunities for promotion, or highly qualified outsiders with few roots in the area. Thus new discontinuities are added to those already afflicting the region. Meanwhile the arrival of the smelter may discourage tourism and halt the development of the holiday and retirement cottages, which are built, provisioned and repaired by local people in small local firms.

This analysis suggests the ailing regions should in future look for more work that is both skilled and labour-intensive, more service industries (including tourist services), more training and more managerial and professional opportunities. They should rely less on costly subsidies for investment in capital-intensive, manufacturing industries offering few opportunities for training and advancement and they should be cautious about recruiting branch plants which bring few managers and no headquarters staff with them.

There is nothing new about these ideas. Many politicians and their advisors are well aware of the inadequacy of current strategies. They know that manufacturing industry employs a continually declining proportion of the labour force in advanced economies and thus offers less and less leverage as an instrument of regional policies. They know, too, that some of the country's biggest employers who set up new works in underemployed regions during the past decade have had their fingers burnt and are reluctant to repeat the experience, while others have been tempted to leave once the temporary advantage conferred by generous depreciation allowances is exhausted. Recent research shows that even when such enterprises succeed, their multiplier effects rapidly 'leak' to other regions — often the more prosperous ones — and generate little further local growth. It might be expected that new initiatives in regional policy would be designed to cope more successfully with these problems.

But, commonplace though they are, these are not the ideas currently advanced by advocates of constitutional reform and the devolution of powers to regional government. The Kilbrandon Commission's Report and its accompanying Memorandum of Dissent have a different starting point. They say very little about the economic and social structure of the regions or the opportunities they offer to their people. 'The defects to be remedied', according to the majority, are 'centralisation', the weakening of 'democracy', and the failure to recognise 'national feeling'. (Cmnd 5460, Ch. 23) The minority report tells the same story:

> The essential objectives of any scheme of constitutional reform must be:
> (a) to reduce the present excessive burdens on the institutions of central government;
> (b) to increase the influence on decision-making of the elected representatives of the people;
> (c) to provide the people generally with more scope for sharing in, and influencing, governmental decision-making at all levels;
> (d) to provide adequate means for the redress of individual grievances. (Cmnd 5460–1, p. xiv)

This is a middle-class — indeed a donnish — formulation of regional problems. The questions posed are important enough but anyone who has seen Govan, in Glasgow, the seat which a Scottish Nationalist captured from Labour in 1973, can envisage the more pressing and practical deprivations which are likely to motivate its electors; and those electors are not so naive as to believe that 'the redress of grievances' can be brought about by reducing the 'burdens on ... central government' — quite the contrary. Their grievances about unemployment, bad housing, poverty and the politicians who fail to remedy these things, could be explained without reference to 'national feeling', and are unlikely to be satisfied even by the most generous recognition of nationalist aspirations.

Institutions

Although some may conclude that the commissioners' proposals are a colossal *non sequitur*, that should not obscure the need for a more relevant reorganisation of regional government. The planning strategies which I have outlined may be widely accepted but they amount to little more than a useful metaphor. The procedures for implementing them are much less clear. We need regional authorities capable of gathering and relating information about the different 'ladders of opportunity' and monitoring the economic and social development of their regions. For a start the boundaries of existing regional authorities — for health, employment, education, social security and many other services — should be reconciled. They cannot talk to each other till they are talking about the same areas. Related to this administrative system, we need political assemblies capable of providing a forum for debate about trends and policies, particularly in the more vulnerable regions. That may call for stronger regional offices of central government, more representative planning councils and some further devolution of powers to both; but it would fall a long way short of the wholesale legislative devolution to 'democratic assemblies' throughout the country which some of the Kilbrandon commissioners call for.

Does this country have room for another layer of government? Britain is a small place, similar in size and output to the state of California. Its population is about twice the size of California's but has less ethnic, linguistic and cultural diversity. Britain's industrial, commercial, cultural and political life is centred on one urban region, California's on two — neither of which is the state's political capital. In comparison with many other countries, Britain has a strong central government and a vigorous local government which is currently being recast to produce fewer and stronger units to which more powers are to be devolved from the centre. (That, at any rate, has been the continuing theme of more than fifteen years of debate about this reorganisation, and the government's case for the current reforms.)

Meanwhile an increasingly vigorous under-layer of 'micro-politics' has been developing. Repeated studies (Baker and Young, 1971; Boal, 1969;

Cmnd 4040, 1969) have shown that local loyalties in this country tend to focus most intensely on small areas, often about 5,000 to 20,000 people. It is this sort of localism which has helped to create the neighbourhood councils, community-action projects, legal-advice centres, tenants' associations, amenity societies and local pressure groups concerned with civil rights, education, conservation and many other matters. Meanwhile it is often forgotten that within the conventional system of local government it is the parish councils – the smallest units of all – which have been expanding their activities most rapidly over recent years (Cmnd 4040). We are witnessing, in new forms, a revival of spatially-oriented programmes dealing with areas similar in scale to those which concerned Charles Booth and his nineteenth-century contemporaries (Donnison and Eversley, 1973).

To justify the insertion of a new layer of regional government into this system it must be shown that government has to make a range of decisions which are important, related to each other, too large in scale to be given to the enlarged local authorities of the future and too small in scale to be left with the central government. In Northern Ireland there would be an unanswerable case for strong regional government, quite apart from the arguments derived from current conflicts, because local government has been virtually destroyed. The new district authorities have practically no powers over housing, education, social services, police or any of the other things which make local government in Britain a reality. Without an effective regional government there will be no means of coordinating these different powers of formulating policies for the development of the province.

How about Britain? Decisions to open a major new museum, a nature reserve, a large sports centre or a hypermarket might fall into the category (i.e. too large for a local authority but too small for central government). But consider more important decisions such as the closure of a major pit or shipyard, a twenty-mile extension of a motorway, or the founding of a new university or teaching hospital. These would benefit from better evidence about regional needs and from debate in more effective regional forums of various kinds. But if spokesmen of the major interests at stake (such as the National Union of Mineworkers, Vickers, the University Grants Committee, or the Association of Municipal Corporations – all with their headquarters in London) were aggrieved at the outcome, each could secure an interview with the relevant minister within a week, no matter how formidable a layer of regional institutions were interpolated below him – and that is not because people enjoy talking to ministers but because the resources of money and power required to implement decisions of this kind come from the centre. And no one insists more vociferously that the national taxpayer and his government should continue to provide those resources than the spokesmen of the most deprived regions.

The Kilbrandon commissioners aim to cull the powers of a strengthened regional government from the centre, which poses contradictions for anyone attempting to equalise opportunities and living standards among the regions. For equalising policies call for a distribution of resources that will benefit the regions which need help most — and that implies restriction of growth in the more prosperous regions, at least in the short term. Thus the central government could not give much autonomy to governments of the more prosperous regions if they used their powers to grab more growth for themselves. But the electors would not take much interest in — or continue to re-elect — politicians who consistently subordinated their interests to those of voters in other regions. The majority of the Kilbrandon Commission recognise this dilemma and propose a legislative devolution of powers only for Scotland and Wales.

England, too, has its regional problems and needs more effective administrative and political institutions to handle them. Current trends in employment, transport and the location of jobs and housing are creating, over much of the country, a continuous low-density urban system linked by a network of predominantly car-borne communications between homes, work, shopping, education, recreation and other activities. The urban patterns now taking shape in England are less 'regional' in the old-fashioned sense. People no longer look to a regional capital for so many of the goods and services they need: they travel longer distances, and in different directions for different purposes. The centres of some of the biggest cities — London, Manchester and Liverpool, for example — are being deserted by industry and people at such a rate that some planners fear it will become increasingly difficult to rescue them from urban decay, municipal impoverishment and social disorder. It is much too soon to say that this American-style crisis of the cities is upon us, but such dangers are not to be dismissed. It is often forgotten that some half-dozen boroughs in the middle of London have lower incomes per head and higher percentages of their labour force unemployed than the British average.

Such problems must be tackled on a regional scale, since their solution calls for policies for the location and mix of employment, the building and allocation of housing and the development of public and private transport which extend beyond the territory, powers and resources of local government. Since the problems to be resolved arise partly from conflicts between the interests of city and suburban authorities, they will probably require a central arbiter. This amounts once again to a case for institutions capable of gathering and analysing regional data, formulating regional plans and creating a forum in which they can be debated — a strengthening of the institutions we already have, rather than the creation of autonomous regional authorities.

Steps to strengthen regional government will probably be taken after the next general election. But what bearing will they have on regional policies and problems? Will they make it easier or harder to enrich and diversify the opportunities which life offers to the people in the more deprived regions — or in the deprived parts of prosperous regions? To achieve that we need development agencies of various kinds, armed with information and money and working in close collaboration with central government, the nationalised industries and local authorities. They should be staffed by people with a flair for picking and backing entrepreneurs in the public and the private sector. Such agencies need regional focal points for the interchange of information and formulation of plans but there is no reason to cram them all into a regional mould. Some will deal with parts of a region such as the Highlands and Islands or particular centres of growth or redevelopment such as the London Docks or (in Ireland) the Shannon Free Airport. Others will deal with particular industries, such as tourism, on a nationwide basis. Their relationship to the political system is vital, but delicate.

The successful development agency must be innovative rather than defensive, seeking new talents and fostering new enterprises, wherever they are to be found. It must select, discriminate, and back success rather than failure. Elected authorities do not do these things well. Politicians are necessarily and properly obliged to look after the largest and most vulnerable groups in their constituencies — which in failing economies means the long-established, failing industries and communities. They have to be chauvinistic, preferring their own people to newcomers and outsiders. They give priority to the poorest group — provided they are large enough to count electorally — and they tend to spread resources thinly and allocate them according to rather rigid, publicly defensible rules. All of that is good politics but very bad development policy. In the ailing regions of the United Kingdom it tends to be one-party politics too, for opposition is weak in these areas. That makes things worse still. In Northern Ireland fifty years of one-party government ultimately provoked conflicts that destroyed all the gains which economic planners were beginning to achieve. In this context there is irony in hearing of the devolution of powers to Scottish and Welsh legislatures — in which opposition is likely to be even weaker than it was at Stormont — advocated as a means 'to enlarge democratic accountability' (Cmnd 5460, para. 122).

The institutions we need to formulate regional policies and put them into practice must be demonstrably accountable, because they will have to wield too much money and power to survive for long if they are not. But the regional assemblies to which they should account must be no more than vigilant shareholders in these development agencies — prepared to withdraw their support if progress towards the general objectives of enlarging and diversifying opportunities is not made. Such progress is unlikely to be made if regional planning becomes the direct responsibility of elected regional legislatures.

Conclusion

As this country develops its regional institutions and devolves more power to them we must not lose sight of the real human character of regional problems or allow political aspirations unrelated to these problems to make the difficult task of solving them any harder than it already is. Hitherto, Britain's regional policies have been directed to simple but pressing needs — particularly for work and wages. Clumsy though these policies have too often been, they have not been wholly ineffectual. In future we need more discriminating regional policies based on a wiser understanding of the social and economic processes which enlarge or restrict people's opportunities. The right kind of regional political and administrative institutions can help to formulate these policies. But if a political rhetoric, flimsily rooted in economic and social realities, leads to wholesale devolution of powers from the centre to a countrywide system of elected regional assemblies, the outcome could be disastrously inegalitarian and conservative. Between regions it would provoke conflict, strengthening the hands of the most prosperous, and making it harder for the poorest to secure the help they need. Within regions it would strengthen the hands of all the most defensive, conservative forces making innovation and the expansion of opportunities harder than ever.

References

Baker J. and Young M., *The Hornsey Plan,* The Association for Neighbourhood Councils (1971).

Boal F.W., 'Territoriality in the Shankhill—Falls divide' *Irish Geography*, 6 (1969), pp. 30—50.

Cmnd 4040, *Report of the Royal Commission on Local Government in England, 1966—1969*, vol. 3, Appendix, 7 HMSO (1969).

Cmnd 5460, *Royal Commission on the Constitution, 1969–1973,* vol. 1: *Report*; vol. 2: *Memorandum of Dissent*, HMSO (1973).

Donnison D. and Eversley D. (eds), *London: Urban Patterns, Problems and Policies* (1973).

Friedlander D. and Roshier R.J., 'Internal migration in England and Wales'; Part I; 'Geographical patterns of internal migration, 1851–1951' *Population Studies*, 19 (1966), pp. 239–80.

10   Centre and Region in Regional Policy

Maxwell Gaskin

The aim of this paper is to explore the centre—region relation in regional policy. The two main questions to be discussed concern the nature of the regional 'input' in regional policy; what it is in fact; what it should be. At this point, though not later, 'regional policy' is used in a broad sense to embrace all the measures, machinery and decisions which the central government directs towards, or devolves upon, the regions over which it governs; and the national context of the discussion is exclusively British. This context is not too confining as far as the generalities of the matter are concerned; but the distribution of political power between centre and periphery — a spectrum in which Britain occupies a fairly extreme position — greatly affects the facts and the possibilities of regional initiative. There is one other preliminary qualification and it is about the use of that ambiguous concept, 'region'. Here the terms 'region' and 'regional' will appear with a variety of meanings: at some points they will refer to sub-national areas subject to existing local government authorities; elsewhere, they will denote other geographical divisions, actual or projected, or even simply posed for some particular purpose. For brevity, the context must be relied upon to establish the sense in which the terms are being used in any one place.

The importance of the questions we are asking is self-evident. But it may clarify the direction of the discussion to refer, at the outset, to some of the views that are expressed on the issues involved. The common thesis advanced is that the regions, as the subjects of regional policy, should themselves have greater influence in determining its application to — and hence impact on — them. 'Greater influence' may be interpreted in various ways but some freedom to vary the terms or direction of regional inducements is a measure frequently envisaged. Thus, Professor Peter Hall (1970, p. 81), discussing the relationship between central and local planning, says:

> You could theoretically create regional provincial governments which were responsible for drawing up physical structure plans, that is the regional local planning, which could perhaps then be carried out in more detail by lower tier authorities; but these provinces could simul-

taneously, I think, do quite a lot of regional economic planning themselves, because they could be empowered to offer different sorts of incentives for instance to industrialists.

Hall is here talking about regional planning which, on the distinctions to be drawn here, is not coterminous with regional policy; but the reference to incentives brings in regional policy and what he suggests is greater freedom for the regions, under a reformed structure of authority, in the application of such policy. This is an explicit statement of the matter; elsewhere, the viewpoint is implicit in criticisms of the state of regional policy in recent years. For example, some accusations of neglect or inequity towards particular regions could be taken in this sense, particularly when these regions are themselves the disappointed originators of development proposals (Clements, 1971).

Types of regional action

What is the local input in regional policy in Britain today? To answer this we must depart from our broad usage of 'regional policy', and confine the term to one of three components of what may be called 'regional action', the other two being 'regional planning' and 'regional development'. As will appear, these are far from being separate compartments of regional action but it helps to make certain distinctions between them.

For present purposes 'regional policy' denotes a set of predominantly economic measures, determined by a superior authority with the purpose of changing the course of events — especially, but not exclusively, economic events — in the various regions into which its jurisdictional area is divided. Regional policy, as so defined, forms a framework of policy within which the authorities at regional or other sub-national levels must operate. The nature and scale of the operators varies with the system: a federal state, for example, can present a more complicated picture than a unitary system (Brewis, 1969). In Britain the central government is clearly the 'superior authority' and the lower authorities are those of local government (as rearranged and relayered in 1974). There is no need here to recite the measures of regional policy in Britain: let us simply say that they are a mixed bag of financial assistance or inducements to industry, financial assistance to local government and statutory controls over certain kinds of industrial development in certain areas.

In contrast, 'regional planning' and 'regional development' denote types of action which are undertaken primarily at local or other sub-national levels. The borderline between the two is blurred indeed, but there is a distinction worth making. 'Regional development' here means action designed to expand or change the economic structure of an area, by attracting new industries or by assisting traditional ones to expand or adapt themselves to changing conditions. Regional development is normally regarded as forming part of 'regional planning' but as an activity it is frequently conducted independently by bodies which are themselves separate from the formal organs of regional or local planning. Such bodies are usually set up by groups of neighbouring local authorities: the North East Development Council, the Mid-Wales Development Association and the recently formed Yorkshire and Humberside Development Authority are examples of this. But there is one statutory agency in the field, the Highlands and Islands Development Board, with its own powers and finance and with no formal connection with local planning authorities. In addition to these, many local authorities have development officers and departments, separate from their planning counterparts, who also operate in this sphere.

'Regional planning' is used here, as commonly, to denote a process embracing a much wider set of activities, almost invariably including regional development, as just defined, but much else besides. It includes the assessment and analysis of potential changes in an area and the relating of them to stated objectives; the forecasting of resource requirements to facilitate, or simply consequent on, such changes; the formulation of plans for necessary infrastructure; the projection of land use; and, where the planning agency has the powers to do so, the reservation or 'zoning' of land for uses consistent with the objectives. Where the 'plans' which emerge from this process have objectives that depend on economic expansion (and they usually do) regional development will be necessary to their implementation. It will hardly need saying that the objectives of planning in any one region, and the resources to be allocated to achieve them, cannot be determined in isolation from what is happening in other regions. Problems of coordination and allocation are posed which must be resolved at the centre. This is one point among others at which central and local responsibilities make contact with each other

Recent developments in regional action in the UK

These are very summary statements. For some, the distinctions will have been drawn too sharply. It may even be argued that in a country such as Britain where, in principle, all power resides with the central government and sub-national bodies act only with devolved authority, the very existence and shape of regional planning or regional development must be regarded as aspects of regional policy. But this would be to quibble over words: no more is claimed for the distinctions made here than that they have some basis in reality and offer a useful point of departure for this discussion. There are qualifications to be made, some of which bear importantly on the dichotomy suggested here between 'policy' as the responsibility of the centre and 'planning' as a function of the regional or local level. But these will come out in the course of what follows.

The last fifteen years have seen a marked intensification of regional action of all three kinds. Regional policy originated in the pre-war conditions of extreme depression and structural decline in old industrial areas of Northern England, Central Scotland and South Wales. It produced a spate of activity in the immediate post-war years, was applied with notably less energy in the 1950s, but has been a prominent concern of all governments since the final years of that decade. It has been, and still is, overwhelmingly centred on industrial location and most of the varying collection of measures have been directed to this end. The motivation of the policy has been more complex. Originally, and during its early phase, the mitigation of the social ills stemming from high regional levels of unemployment was the dominating objective – and it remains a continuing concern. But in the 1960s the improvement of economic performance in the lagging regions came to be viewed also as an essential ingredient in a policy of improving the rate of growth of the national economy, notably by permitting a fuller use of manpower resources and, through a more even spread of demand, by lessening the inflationary pressure associated with any given level of national activity.

But the 1960s have seen a further development in regional action which is very relevant to an elucidation of the centre–region relationship. This is the beginnings of a confluence of the three streams of regional action: policy, planning and development. This process, which is very far from complete, has been clearly analysed by others (Self, 1969), and will be only summarily described here. Briefly, regional planning was, in origin, a narrower activity than we have defined it. It grew out of 'town and country planning', the planning of land use and urban development. At its regionally most ambitious, for example in Abercrombie's plans for London and Clydeside, it was pre-eminently concerned with the problems of great conurbations, the solution propounded being the planned dispersal of population to new or expanded towns. It was really only in the 1960s that regional planning came firmly to be viewed as inevitably involving economic planning of some kind. Under the influence of certain key documents,

204

notably the 1963 White Papers on North East England (Cmnd 2188, 1963) and Central Scotland (Cmnd 2206, 1963), it was recognised that an adequate attack on the problems of the lagging regions demanded strategies that combined the concerns of planning, in the earlier sense of control of land use and the shaping of urban development, and of regional economic policy. The clearest product of this union was the emphasis on the concept of growth centres or growth zones: sub-regional areas selected for their presumed capacity for industrial and urban expansion and where, at least in formulated plans, a planned concentration of economic growth both supports and is supported by planned development of housing and other infrastructure.

Under the Labour administrations of 1964–70 regional economic planning, as a conception, moved strongly into the ascendant, with designation of planning regions covering the whole country and the setting up of the structure of regional economic planning boards, composed of regional officers or representatives of the government departments directly concerned, and regional economic councils with a membership drawn mainly from local government, industry, the trade unions and the universities. This development, of course, reflected a strong swing to economic planning at the national level which culminated in the National Plan of 1966. The regional structure, like the parallel structure of economic development councils in industry, survived the demise of that venture; it is still with us, though its future in England is clouded with uncertainty about the degree and shape of regional planning under local government reorganisation.

Outcomes and other developments of the 1960s

One of the more obvious products of this phase of regional planning has been the clutch of 'studies' or 'strategies' which all the planning regions produced between 1965 and 1967. Only one of the regional documents, the White Paper, *The Scottish Economy 1965–70* was a 'plan' in the sense of specifying economic targets to be achieved and having some degree of government commitment (McCrone, 1969).[1] But Scotland was exceptional in another way that bears upon this phase of regionalism in British economic policy. With the partial exception of Wales, only Scotland among the planning regions had — and has — a continuing administrative structure of its own, capable of implementing major elements of a plan relating to the whole geographical area covered by its regional institutions. The regional boards and councils as such were advisory only; in England the power to make and to implement many of the decisions relevant to regional planning – land-use control, extension of infrastructure – has lain, and still lies, with local government authorities which (if we except London) cover much more limited areas. For this and other reasons it is easy to exaggerate the extent to which, over the last decade, regional economic development and physical planning have been synthesised into a more comprehensive regional planning process. It is not simply that one may be tempted to dismiss the achievements of the economic councils, as many do, as so many informative documents issuing in no effective action. It is also the case that even where the power lies, the harnessing of physical planning to economic objectives has been very partial.

Nevertheless, despite the incompleteness of this development, during the last decade the regional planning scene has unquestionably changed in ways that bear importantly on the centre–region relation. There has, for example, been a much increased local concern with regional development. However imperfect the union between traditional physical planning and economic development, at the regional or local level there has undoubtedly been growing consciousness on the planning side of the place of the economic component in regional change. Furthermore, in consequence of the nationally comprehensive nature of the regional planning structure established in the 1960s, this consciousness has spread far more widely than formerly, and has channels of expression, and means of exerting pressure, which did not exist before.

But there have been other developments in regional action, some administrative, some in the nature of policy, which have influenced regional planning during this decade. They are especially noteworthy here in that among the tendencies promoted by them have been, on the one hand, a strengthening of the economic element in regional planning and, on the other, a qualifying of the dichotomy suggested earlier between regional policy as the province of central government and regional planning as the function of sub-national authorities. The provision of resources for regional economic development has played a major part in these developments. It hardly needs saying that if regional planning is to mean anything, in the sense of changing the course of events within a region, it usually requires resources – to put it simply, money. A large element in regional planning, especially in regions where there is a deficiency of economic expansion, consists of improvements or additions to infrastructure, so much so that in many situations planning without resources becomes an exercise in hypothetical strategy. But the use of resources for purposes of regional development depends on national decisions about resource allocation. At this level 'policy' in the fullest sense is involved since here choices must be

206

made between major fields of public action. Such decisions on the global allocation of resources have to take account of the specific regional purposes to which resources will be put. This fact, coupled with a greatly increased amount of central resources devoted to regional purposes during the 1960s, has brought the central government into ever-closer contact with the purposes and content of regional planning. In Britain, the government has exercised discrimination in the roads programme; it has assigned resources for new town development; it has provided supporting infrastructure for major industrial developments in many areas — all in the interests of regional economic (and social) development. Such action has inevitably brought government into close contact with local planners. In specific cases it has taken an initiatory role in broad schemes of regional planning. A major example of this was the 'Hailsham Plan' for the North East, launched in 1963. Among the components of this were a large public investment programme in which priority was given to a selected growth zone and the setting-up of an inter-departmental regional committee which foreshadowed the economic planning boards established by the Labour government (Smith, 1971). In Scotland there has been a more continuing close involvement of the Scottish Office — considered here as what it formally is, a regional arm of central government — in the planned deployment of public resources in the interest of development — and indeed in every aspect of regional economic planning.[2]

These developments clearly point to a blurring of the line which we drew earlier between 'policy' and 'planning'. But the blurring process is also aided, though in lesser degree, by action within the regions themselves, and not least in those that are not especially favoured in the allocation of public resources, nor benefited by that persuasive power which, within limits, the administrators of policy can bring to bear on mobile industry. For some areas, for example the remoter rural areas, what they can do for themselves in the way of planning measures, notably those designed to concentrate scattered populations into more viable labour markets, may be almost the only counter to the powerful attractions of more urbanised regions. The effect of planning measures on industrial location is an unknown quantity and one should not exaggerate its importance — certainly not in isolation from other factors; but everywhere, among the favoured and the unfavoured, improving the attractive power of regions by planning is one part of the strategy of regional development. It is important because, within the limits set by resource constraints, it is a field of action open to the regions themselves and one in which their actions may extend or modify the effects of central policy.

Regionalism and the objectives of regional policy

In the light of the developments outlined in this section — the extension of regionalism and the closer union of planning and economic development — one may fairly say that the area within which regional initiative can operate has been extended. The extension may not be much in practical terms and ever-present pressures on resources tend to create a feeling of constraint rather than of freedom. Nevertheless, however confined and imprecisely defined, an area of action has been opened up of which sub-national authorities were very imperfectly aware before 1960. Those who favour a thorough-going regionalism in economic and social policy will welcome this change, though no doubt regard it as inadequate. But there is another view which raises fundamental questions about ends and means in British regional policy. It has been argued, notably by the late Professor Donald Robertson (1965), that regional policy in Britain should concentrate on two sorts of region only: those which 'suffer from above average difficulties in labour recruitment and are short of land, and others... with higher than average unemployment rates, lower participation rates and lower income per head'. He regarded the South East and the Midlands as comprising the first class, and central Scotland, Northern Ireland, the North East and South Wales as the 'clear cut examples of the latter'. Pursuing this argument it could well be claimed that what Robertson called the 'fatal wish for comprehensiveness' in regional issues has tended to distract regional policy from its prime objectives of revitalising the older industrial regions. It has compounded the distraction by intensifying, even creating, competition between regions for what is proving to be an inadequate amount of mobile industry; it has led to the kind of frustrations and dissatisfaction that, for example, inform the criticisms of regional policy launched by the first chairman of the South West Regional Planning Board (Tress, 1969).[3]

Professor Robertson was writing at the very beginning of the phase of regionalism introduced by the Labour administration. In retrospect one might say that events have vindicated his position: there has not been enough development to go round and, above all, the problems of the more intensely 'problem' regions seem almost as far as ever from solution. But looking at it today, one can surely say that this is a clock that cannot now be put back. It is a fair question to ask how far the regional planning structure actually stimulated the well-nigh universal thirst for economic development. The probable answer is that the marriage of planning and economics, which the regionalism of the 1960s promoted, could have been postponed — but not indefinitely. It cannot now be argued away.

Regional policy and regional powers

Up to this point we have been concerned with what the regional — or at least, the local — input in regional action actually is. But in the paragraphs immediately above the question of what it appropriately should be has begun to raise its head and we must look it in the eye. This we shall do by considering the case for devolving greater powers on the regions to vary the operation of regional policy measures and the forms that such variations might take. But there is one preliminary issue to dispose of.

Any action to devolve wider powers in applying regional policy measures requires the existence of appropriate authorities to hand the powers to. If one were to look for bodies that could fairly be described as regional in scope, they do not exist in England. The economic planning councils as presently constituted are, of course, not executive bodies. With the doubtful exceptions of the six metropolitan authorities (seven if we include London), the new authorities proposed for England are too small and too numerous to be appropriate recipients of regional policy powers. As Professor Hall indicates in the passage quoted at the beginning, something like the 'provinces' of Redcliffe—Maud are called for; but these appear to have been ruled out in the new structure. Scotland and Wales are in a different position in that each has a measure of administrative devolution; in the Scottish case it is substantial and of long standing. Also, each has hitherto constituted a single planning region within the British frame (though this has been dictated by political, rather than economic, reasons). However, neither country has a supreme elected body to receive any regional policy powers that might be devolved upon them. Were the recommendations of the Kilbrandon Commission to be accepted, this gap would be filled but whether it would then be possible to make this particular devolution in the absence of parallel moves in England — where regional legislatures are not recommended — is open to doubt (Cmnd 5460, 1973).[4] These are not negligible problems and they have a very obvious bearing on the present subject. But they raise issues that cannot be pursued here and we turn now to the main questions of this section.

What form might greater policy power in the region take? The one most widely canvassed is probably that referred to by Hall (op. cit.): the power to exercise some selectivity in the encouragement of economic development. A region, it may be argued, would benefit from the ability to concentrate resources on certain types of development, either in the shape of activities already established within it, or new ones which it considers could suitably be promoted by attracting incoming firms. A choice of a different kind that might be left open to individual regions is the weight to be placed on financial inducements as against improvements in infrastructure. This form of selectivity raises some considerations which are different from those involved in the selective use of inducements.

Looking first at the arguments for such devolution, it can fairly be said that wider powers in the application of policy would bring greater interest and wider involvement within the regions themselves. One might think that such interest would hardly need stimulation, but concern with regional development is deficient in some surprising quarters — for example, in the trade unions. A bit of effective power might correct this, as well as inducing some other useful changes of attitude.

But a broadened scope of action at the regional level is principally supported on the ground that it would allow a greater trimming of policy to the needs of the individual regions concerned. [5] Regions, it is said, vary in their possibilities, in their economic structures, in the kinds of new or revitalised activities that can be appropriately promoted within them. Furthermore, one might add, the regions themselves are — at any rate potentially — the best judges in this matter, both through their knowledge of their own areas and because they can apply themselves individually to hard thought about their own predicaments. In some regions arguments of this kind are linked with the criticism that the present regional policy is too much geared to the needs of one type of region, the great industrial conurbations, and too little sensitive to the plight and needs of the others — for example the less urbanised regions. Under the 1972 Industry Act, notably in its provisions for selective financial assistance, policy has moved in a direction offering the prospect of greater powers of initiative for the regions in their own development. But before examining them we should look at the arguments against allowing the regions too much freedom in applying regional policy measures.

First, on the question of regions being selective in their development policies with the object of matching these to regional need, it is not difficult to be deeply sceptical of our capacity, with present understanding and methods, to specify what types of industrial development a region should try to encourage or attract. Indeed, one may well doubt the need for this capacity. For example, if we look at the large industrial conurbations, there are certainly some differences of economic structure among them, but it is questionable that they are such as to point to any credible differences in the kinds of new industrial development that each would wish to promote. But even attaching weight to the differences that exist, even if, for example, we have regard to the contrast between a region like central Scotland and, say, the West Riding of Yorkshire (assuming the woollen industry to enter an as yet unpredicted decline), are we really able confidently to distinguish differences of locational factors, such as would allow us to select between activities in ways optimal for all concerned? One doubts it. There are some distinctions to be made but they provide a very short list of rather obvious prescriptions — such as not trying to make heavy industrial boilers in remote inland areas. [6]

The position appears to be that most manufacturing industry can, in principle, be reasonably located in any of the major industrial regions of Britain; perhaps, for that matter, in any of the larger towns of otherwise rural regions like East Anglia and South West England. This being so, and if we add the equally powerful consideration that the prospective supply of mobile industry for the various development needs of the next decade or so is inadequate, it is hardly difficult to account for a state of affairs, such as we now have, in which all the major urbanised regions are eager to get every bit of mobile industry that offers itself. The situation does not only destroy much of the point of allowing initiative to the regions in the attraction of incoming industry; without careful controls at the centre it leads inexorably to the well-known trap of regional policy — the competitive escalation of inducements. There is enough of this at the international level to convince us of its reality and indeed the desire to control it is one powerful motive behind the present attempt of the EEC Commission to evolve some common principles of regional policy (the 20 per cent limit on 'transparent' aid is specifically directed to this problem). In Britain the present scope for inter-regional competition is confined to such matters as publicity, which offers problematical returns, and the degree of accommodation and co-operation in the provision of services and, above all, housing for key personnel which local authorities are prepared to offer. Such competition is no bad thing and, in any case, has definite limits.

Another possible area of choice that might be allowed to regions is the distribution of centrally allocated resources between inducements to industry and improvements of infrastructure. There is no evidence that the present bodies at local or regional level do hold different views on this choice, or disagree with the allocations made by central government (though they all want more resources for infrastructural expenditure). But it is one area of controversy in regional policy. The Confederation of British Industry, for example, has argued strongly for infrastructure and against inducements. As a choice to be left open to sub-national authorities it meets the formidable objection that the economic implications of expenditures on infrastructure can be quite different from those of financial inducements, so much so that the central government can hardly let them out of its grip. Regional financial assistance to industry may have little, if any, significance for the total balance of real demand in the national economy: the effects may simply be redistributive, diverting demand on resources from one area to another, and on national grounds this might actually be desirable. Expenditure on infrastructure, on the other hand, inevitably puts demands on real resources; substituting this for financial inducements could not decrease, and would normally increase, pressure on the national economy. The central government, responsible as it is for controlling the total pressure on resources, could not tolerate the un-predictability involved here. It must therefore retain overall control of such demands and this entails, at the very least, a drastic curtailment of the freedom of regions to make their own choices between these two types of measures.

Regional action, selectivity and the Industry Act

So far we have found nothing but difficulty in the idea of regionally determined selective action to promote economic development. Must the answer be entirely negative? That it need not be so, and one direction such action might take, is suggested by recent innovations in regional policy. With the Industry Act of 1972, a measure of selective financial assistance is now available to the development and intermediate areas. Indeed the formal powers conferred by the Act on the Secretary of State to provide financial assistance to individual firms to promote development, modernisation, efficiency and so on, are very wide indeed. In this matter he is advised by the Industrial Development Advisory Board and the policy is operated through the system of regional offices of the Department of Trade and Industry. In those planning regions which form the development and intermediate areas — Scotland, Wales, Northern England, Yorkshire and Humberside, the South West and the North West — there are regional industrial directors who, advised by regional industrial development boards composed of local industrialists and businessmen, will provide finance on varying terms to particular firms in their regions.

It is too early to judge how this system is working and in particular how much initiative the regional industrial directors and their staffs are taking in seeking opportunities for development. Recent encouraging reports on the numbers of firms that are approaching the regional industrial offices[7] are not in themselves reassuring. It is yet to be seen how far this represents a backlog of hitherto frustrated projects, or a reflection of a cyclical upsurge in activity. A more searching test of the system will come when the present cases have been worked off and much more depends on the imagination and initiative of the regional officers. What one looks for here —

what the wording of the Act encourages one to look for — is a series of regional reincarnations of the Industrial Reorganisation Corporation, perhaps without the more abrasive elements of that ill-advisedly condemned body. At least, the emphasis called for is on the stimulation of local industrial initiative and on measures to improve the efficiency and accelerate the adaptation of firms already established within the region. Compared with much previous discussion in this area the approach is management-centred rather than planning-centred — it puts the emphasis on entrepreneurial rather than location factors.[8] Its importance is underlined by the fact that, in spite of all that is (quite rightly) said about slow growth in the lagging regions, numerically speaking most of the new jobs coming forward at any time are in firms indigenous to these regions.

A major criticism to which this prescription is exposed is that its success depends very much on the people who run the system and whether or not one can reasonably, or fairly, expect this kind of approach from men drawn, as at present, from the administrative arm is a pertinent question. Another problem for any exercise of this kind which has its base in the public sector is that, in the very nature of things, the bodies concerned will make mistakes and will lose money. If they are to take proper initiatives this is unavoidable since they will be operating in an area of high risk — higher than such private institutions as merchant banks who tend to concentrate on the better risks among developable firms.

However, for many these points will be second-order matters beside the over-riding objection that the system set up under the Industry Act is an administrative structure and an extension of central government, without responsibility to any local or regional political authority. And while it is far from self-evident that such local responsibility is necessary, or even particularly conducive, to effective action on the lines opened up by the 1972 Act, it can fairly be claimed that this kind of arrangement does not extend regional or local powers in ways that people have in view when they argue for greater freedom of action at the regional level. This raises considerations of politics and devolution which lie outside the scope of this paper, but on more familiar ground there are strong reasons for establishing some link between selective industrial assistance and the organs of local or regional government.

One is the point made earlier that the involvement of local political bodies will increase interest in, and understanding of, the problems of regional development. There is an important educative function to be performed here and, whatever pattern of operation is devised for the offices or agencies concerned with selective assistance, there is a strong case for a close association with local or regional authorities. But this association will, in the end, be necessary for another group of reasons which were discussed in the first part of this paper. It has been argued above that an appropriate type of regional industrial development to be undertaken in the regions is one that is management-centred rather than one deriving from the kind of factors — location, industrial linkages and so on — usually emphasised in planning approaches. But this is not to say that such activity can be insulated from the concerns of planning. In the course of aiding industry to modernise or change, numerous considerations of infrastructure, of labour supply, of structure and change in the regional economy will arise — all of them vital concerns of the regional planner. The suggestion here, that regional initiative should place more emphasis on stimulating or assisting change in indigenous industry, could lead to a more practical and more fruitful role for the development component of regional planning than it has so far been able to fill.

Notes

[1] Northern Ireland was also, of course, an exception. A comprehensive plan for economic development, containing physical and economic components was accepted by the province in 1965. This was subsequently updated to produce the *Development Programme 1970—75* .

[2] Under the Labour government the Secretaries of State for both Scotland and Wales were responsible for formulating regional plans. Whether one regards them as 'central' or 'regional' in this connection will depend on what aspect of regionalism one is concerned with.

[3] See R. C. Tress (March 1969), pp. 3—30. Among other things Dr Tress criticises the concentration of financial inducements on the development areas. He sees this as a backward-looking policy, obstructive to the necessary development of the conurbations in the non-development areas; and he calls for 'a new locational appraisal' of where, in the longer term, industry and population should go.

[4] The majority recommendations of the commission on legislative devolution are summarised in pp. 484—7. In the *Memorandum of Dissent* which forms vol. 2 of the Report, Lord Crowther-Hunt and Professor Alan T. Peacock recommend a system of legislative devolution extending to England, divided into five regions, as well as to Scotland and Wales: see *Report* vol. 2 (Cmnd 5460—1), Ch. 6.

[5] Among the policy-making functions which Lord Crowther-Hunt and Professor Alan T. Peacock, the main dissentient members of the Kilbrandon Commission, foresee for their regional assemblies is '(to) decide on

the "right" ' balance of industry for their areas and so operate within 'the framework of the United Kingdom distribution of industry policy to attract and control the siting of the sort of mix of the different types of industry which they believe is in their interest.' They maintain that while the central government would have to prescribe uniform cash inducements for all regions 'this would still leave wide scope for Assembly policy-making'. See op. cit. vol. 2, para. 218(a), pp. 88—9.

6 Hopes used to be reposed, perhaps still are, in industrial-complex analysis and the concept of growth poles, especially as guides to planners of new major growth areas. But some ambitious attempts at this abroad, notably in Italy, have not been conspicuously successful and the sceptics remain unconvinced.

7 See 'Government aid to regions' *The Financial Times* (3 September 1973), p. 22.

8 The DTI's small firms information centres now established in the cities are an innovation worth mentioning. They offer help to firms with general management problems — for example, by putting them in touch with appropriate consultancy services. The initiative in approach is left to the firms themselves.

References

Brewis T.N., *Regional Economic Policies in Canada,* Toronto (1969).

Clements R.V., 'Economic planning machinery in the South West, 1965—1968' *Regional Studies Association Occasional Paper*, Series A, No. 5 (1971), pp. 46—7.

Cmnd 2188, *The North East: A Programme for Regional Development and Growth*, HMSO (1963).

Cmnd 2206, *Central Scotland: A Programme for Development and Growth*, HMSO (1963).

Cmnd 4040, *Royal Commission on Local Government in England and Wales*, HMSO (1969).

Cmnd 5460, *Royal Commission on the Constitution*, 1969—73, vol. 1 *Report*; vol. 2 *Memorandum of Dissent*, HMSO (1973).

Hall P.G., *Theory and Practice of Regional Planning* (1970).

McCrone G., *Regional Policy in Britain* (1969).

Robertson D.J., 'A nation of regions?' *Urban Studies* 2 (1965), p. 126.

Self P.J.O., 'Regional planning in Britain: analysis and evaluation' *Regional Studies* 1 (1967), pp. 3—10.

Smith T.D., 'Economic planning and the northern region of England' *Regional Planning and Regional Government in Europe*, E. Kalk (ed.), (1971).

Tress R.C., 'The next stage in regional policy' *The Three Banks Review*, no. 81 (1969), pp. 3–30.

11 The Long-Term Aim of Regional Policy

Derek Diamond

Introduction

The main aim of this contribution is to state the case for a changed outlook by government on regional policy. The essence of such a change is that government should take a longer-term view of the structural relationships between the regions and, as a consequence, recognise in a relatively explicit fashion that *rate* of structural change is the central focus of regional policy.

The case is argued in three stages. First the general conditions fostering a reappraisal of regional policy aims at this time are outlined followed by an identification of the salient characteristics associated with the evolution of regional policy to date. Finally an attempt is made to fulfil the identified future need, without disrupting too severely the existing trends which have conditioned the style and structure of regional policy in Britain.

Three sets of inter-related pressures make such a recasting or reformulation of regional policy aims appropriate at this time.

1   First is simply the historical fact that during the passage of the forty years since regional policy began to exist as an aim of government action, it has managed to gather to it multiple objectives of several kinds causing no little confusion in the minds of both policy-makers and policy-implementers. It is to be hoped that reformulation will result in greater clarity and an increased degree of understanding by all concerned. Indeed there are several indications that a reconsideration of regional policy aims has in fact already begun.

2   Without an attempt to reformulate the aims of regional policy it is reasonably certain that in the near future inter-regional dispute could increase to the point at which central government would regard regional policy as positively dangerous, threatening the cohesion and stability of the state, and would consequently attempt to suppress and ignore it. Mounting pressure by the 'management-by-objectives' school for explicit aims, operational objectives and monitored outcomes to be applied to regional policy can be seen as the major force leading to the likely de-

generation of a national policy for the regions into a regional 'pressure-group' conflict model. However, even if one regards such a scenario as somewhat unlikely in Britain (despite the evidence of Northern Ireland), there remains the point that a constituency-based political system will find the present ambiguities and short-term emphases in regional policy more difficult to handle as the demand for greater explicitness grows. *The Guardian* report (6 July 1973) describing the theme of the forthcoming regional strategy for the North West as a bid for a greater share of public expenditure together with headlines such as 'Regions fight for plums' on the issue of office dispersal, illustrates the nature of the problem clearly enough. Any recasting of aims which will help to mitigate this threat has real advantages therefore and these seem likely to apply with equal or greater force to the Commission in Brussels.

3   Thirdly, pressure for recasting arises from the existing difficulties in demonstrating the success or failure of recent regional policy measures. Given the strength of external influences on the economic and social structure of Britain and the length of time structural adaptation takes, it becomes increasingly difficult to convince the sceptics and the uninterested of the value of regional policy. When a short-term view is held it becomes difficult to maintain political commitment. It is not yet clear whether anti-regional arguments are dead or merely dormant. The possible backlash to government regional policy could clearly be more powerful and sustained than that of 1970, introduced as it was by a White Paper (1972) which began, '... the ending of regional imbalance has been an objective of successive Governments for nearly four decades. Much has been achieved but no solution is yet in sight ... It is clear that the accumulated measures of the years are not enough'.

With the need to produce a reformulation of regional policy to avoid or overcome these potential threats established, it seems sensible to examine the recent past in order to discover any significant trends in regional policy-making.

Evolution of current aims

Six reasonably broad and no doubt familiar objectives of regional policy can be identified as current today:

— relief of persistent and localised high unemployment
— restraint of expansion of employment in the congested conurbations
— fuller utilisation of national resources, notably labour

218

— reduction of inter-regional differences to assist with macro-economic management of the economy and control of inflationary pressure
— maintaining and strengthening of provincial cultures and identity
— assisting in achievement of a balance between population and environmental resources.

Associated with this very considerable width in the scope of the aims is a comparable diversity of instruments for implementation — ranging from financial inducements to physical planning strategies and from administrative controls to coordinated public expenditure on infrastructure. This complex of aims, embracing significant social, economic and environmental considerations and its related range of instruments has evolved since 1945 with altering emphases through time.

Nevertheless it seems worthwhile to try to identify the main characteristics of this evolution in the belief that they provide some guidance for the likely future trend of regional policy.

1   The recognition and adoption of each new aim has not involved the deletion of any previously held aim — the process has been entirely one of addition and not one of replacement. Despite this there has been very little attempt to assess the nature of the overall impact or even to recognise the multifarious ways in which the regional structure of the nation has been modified. Professor Chisholm (1971) has asked recently if in the light of this complex history it is not now time to attempt to produce some fresh and more comprehensive criteria to measure the outcomes of regional policy and offers as a possible starting point the question 'Which spatial distribution of city sizes optimises welfare, which might be defined as the maximum access to social and economic opportunity that can be obtained for a given volume of the gross national product?' Further it seems eminently reasonable to suppose that this process of a continuously extending content is likely to persist, particularly as a consequence of the reorganisation of local government and the growing use of regional offices by the Whitehall ministries.

2.   The comprehensiveness of regional-policy concerns thus seems well established in practice and thoroughly likely to persist. In reality, of course, the ramifications of government regional policy embrace wider issues than those included in official dialogue about the regions. Government intervention which is overtly regional cannot readily be separated from many other forms of social expenditure which discriminates between the different parts of Britain in its practical effects. Policies for industrial location are in a very real sense policies for the location of population. It is relevant to note in this context that the EEC Commission's green paper

of May 1973 argued that the case for a Community regional policy is based on moral, environmental and economic grounds. Thus it clearly accepts the comprehensive nature of this field of government endeavour.

3   The great scope of the objectives, together with the diversity of instruments for implementation of policy, has placed enormous burdens on the effective working of the administrative capacity to coordinate its activities among different levels and sectors. This is a problem which, perhaps inevitably, is compounded by the high degree of discretion (many would say secrecy) often given to the administrative machine in Britain. Many of the programmes of intervention associated with the aims of regional policy do not have the spatial explicitness that the designation of various types of 'assisted areas' provides. On the contrary, such programmes as the development of a network of freightliner depots, the expansion of retraining facilities and derelict land reclamation depend almost entirely on unseen administrative action to produce a sequence and pattern of development that is coherent with other aspects of regional policy. To use this powerful bureaucratic machine effectively requires that guidance on the overall objective is sufficiently clear to enable the proper coordination of the various parts of regional policy.

4   In the British situation the width of regional policy aims has proved helpful in providing scope to accommodate the shifting ideologies within our main political parties and, more importantly, in facilitating changes in government. Whether this is a classic example of Downs's (1957) theory of party convergence in two-party democracies or not, it seems a sufficiently significant trait that it should be possessed by any reformulated regional policy aims.

The foregoing assessment of the main attributes of regional policy development in Britain does suggest that any reformulation likely to obtain acceptance will almost certainly have to possess at least these same characteristics. It must be comprehensive in content, be capable of being added to, be understood by and operated through a bureaucratic administrative process and, if possible, possess sufficient generality to encompass the variations in political ideology found in Britain.

Now we are in a position to turn to the problem of matching future need (for a reformulation of regional policy) with existing trends (in the making of regional policy).

Future aims

The history of British regional policy shows that the evolution of its aims from a single traditional (reduction of unemployment in the development areas) objective to the multiple and comprehensive objectives of today has been largely in response to altering circumstances in world affairs and to changing political fashions at home — both often subtly supported by a lack of knowledge of the effects of past policies. In 1972 Mr John Davies (then Secretary of State for Trade and Industry) drew the all-too-obvious conclusion when he wrote, 'regional industrial problems can only be solved by long-term measures consistently and continuously applied.' Further, all the evidence (e.g. likely EEC influences and proposed transport technology changes) suggests that these external and internal pressures for changing the emphasis and procedures of regional policy will continue to exist and possibly even to intensify. This situation, while it clearly reinforces the validity of viewing regional policy in a long-term perspective, at the same time underlines the enormous practical difficulties that would arise in operating a regional policy without short-run aims. This is a major paradox within regional policy: while the logic of analysis and evaluation requires a long-term view, the practical needs of political decision-making require clear shorter-run policy guidance. Thus it only becomes feasible to adopt a longer-term perspective if a workable short-run aim can be devised.

With the regional structure being subjected to continuing, if irregular, impacts causing both shifts in the policy mix and the emergence of new policy issues then there must be available short-run guidance if there is to be any chance of avoiding confusion in the administrative machine and ameliorating, if not fully avoiding, inter-regional strife. Any such short-term aim must also be capable of being easily understood in relation to the long-term perspective and consequently it would be a real advantage if it were broad and comprehensive. Whether the problem in the short run is described as social, economic or environmental, all regional problems can be regarded as symptoms of insufficient adjustment to a changed set of circumstances. By presenting the issue as one in which the government seeks to influence the *rate of change* (either moderating or stimulating it) so as to minimise the social, economic or environmental 'stress' created by inadequate adjustment, it appears that a satisfactory short-run policy aim exists. Put rather blandly, the long-term perspective provides the *direction* of change which government intervention in regional structure seeks to achieve while, in the short term, issues are focused by considering what *rate* of change is desired. Such a formulation appears to meet the needs of the future as identified in my first section, without causing interruption to the underlying influences traced in the second section.

When regional policy explicitly recognises that the rate of change is its central focus in the short run then theoretically there should be no difficulty in achieving acceptability in the longer term for fundamental alterations in the regional structure of the country. By working in the short run to lessen people's fear of things changing too quickly it should be possible to establish such long-term outcomes as which regions will decline gracefully, which will renew themselves steadily and which will grow in a comfortable manner.

Considerable evidence exists (usually heavily disguised by technical jargon) in many recent regional planning studies — e.g. *Central Scotland* (1963), *Long Term Distribution of Population* (1971) — that just such a combined view of the long and short term is in fact already being put into practice. In political debate the situation is quite different and the purpose of regional policy is almost always explained as to reduce the disparities between the regions, which in practical terms leads to a situation which is aptly described as 'sanctification of the *status quo*'. As *The Times* put it in May 1972, 'Once again social or even electoral reasons will be at least as compelling as industrial reasons ... Once again everybody will be owed a living, whether he is efficient or productive or not and wherever he chooses to try to earn his living'. The reformulation of regional policy outlined here should enable political dialogue to escape from this dubious and unsatisfactory format and become more honest.

In conclusion, it must be pointed out that such a reformulation gives rise to a need to reassess the appropriateness of the tools for implementing regional policy and the effectiveness of the traditional criteria for evaluating success or failure. These issues are too extensive to develop here but two points have particular significance. Once the acceptability of long-term radical change in regional structure is established, the way is opened for a much more fruitful co-operation between the economic allocational aspects of regional policy with the physical (land-use) locational aspects, since both can now be treated more realistically in a dynamic rather than a static framework. A second major consequence is the greatly enhanced significance of the national settlement system as the basic frame of reference for regional policy. Nevertheless, before these essentially technical opportunities can be explored and developed, it would be wise to ensure that the fundamental assumption on which the above thesis rests is, in fact, valid. Will the population and their political representatives really accept long-term structural change in return for an explicit policy process of intervention with the rate of change in the short term?

References

Chisholm M., 'In search of a basis for location theory: micro-economics or welfare economics?' *Progress in Geography*, vol. 3, C. Board *et al.* (eds), (1971).

Cmnd 2206, *Central Scotland: A Programme for Development and Growth*, HMSO (1963).

Department of the Environment, *Long Term Population Distribution in Great Britain*, HMSO (1971).

Downs A., *An Economic Theory of Democracy*, New York (1957).

12 Objectives for Regional Policy: the View from Industry

J. Allan Stewart

Introduction

Over the past few years, efforts to influence businessmen to choose one location rather than another seem almost to have become a major new international industry. Even the wealthiest industrial nation sends literature and emissaries from some of its states to encourage inward investment from Europe. Many economists and most economic policy-makers now doubt the efficacy of competitive markets in allocating scarce resources but this has not prevented the emergence of vigorous competition in the business of influencing location decisions. Yorkshire and Humberside have now completed the list of major assisted areas with their own publicity machine to entice industrial investment. Every self-respecting town has its own industrial development officer.

The introductory section of this paper therefore briefly discusses the considerations which motivate businessmen to choose one particular new location rather than another. The second section looks from the factors which influence industry to industry's reactions to the objectives and methods of regional policy as they have developed in Britain. The final paragraphs look briefly at the future.

Individual location decisions

To give a thumb-nail sketch of a very complex field, early location theorists emphasised the influence of supply factors in location decisions. The optimum location was seen as that which minimised transport costs or, in more sophisticated versions, which minimised total costs, since costs other than transport could vary spatially. At a time when the major new industries which dominated the newly industrialised economies were such as mining, iron and steel and shipbuilding, this emphasis on supply factors corresponded to reality. With the growth of new and different industries, notably consumer durables, location theorists became increasingly sceptical of the assumption in earlier analyses that demand did not vary spatially.

225

The logical culmination has been models which determined profit-maximising location or, depending upon one's view of business behaviour, sales-maximising location.

In practice, it is often suggested that industrialists make location decisions on irrational grounds such as proximity to a good golf club or a shopping centre which conforms to the exacting standards of the chairman's wife. More specifically, businessmen in the South East and Midlands have been accused of harbouring ill-founded prejudices against the economic advantages and cultural delights of, say, Glasgow or Liverpool. It should be pointed out that giving weight to the social or recreational facilities available in particular places is compatible with any theory of location, including profit maximisation, since they may determine whether or not a firm will be able to recruit and retain key skilled and managerial staff.

But the major point is that in the real world it seems to be highly unlikely that the businessmen endeavour to maximise anything. Of course it is dangerous to apply any general statement to institutions as diverse as a giant multi-national corporation and one man in business on his own with a few workers. But both must make choices with limited resources, in limited time and in the face of uncertainty surrounding the major factors which will influence profitability in the future. A maximisation objective is therefore not usually realistic. Instead the rational aim is satisfactory levels of profits and growth. If we apply a satisficing hypothesis, the observed pattern of location decision-making becomes quite compatible with theory. A satisficing hypothesis, stressing uncertainty, would suggest that firms will be reluctant to take a relocation decision. Again, there is no sacrifice of business objectives if a managing director permits his personal preferences to determine the eventual choice among satisfactory locations.

It is also important to realise that the decision to move to or expand in a new location is usually two decisions, each of which is influenced by different considerations. First there is the decision to move, which will derive from the realisation that existing production facilities are unsatisfactory if the objectives of the enterprise are to be achieved. An existing site may be too limited to accommodate planned expansion of production, or penetration of a particular market may reach a point — or be planned to reach a point — at which it can no longer be most economically served by exports.

Many industries have individual characteristics which will predetermine their range of satisfactory locations. Thus a modern integrated steel works needs an ore terminal and for many large plants, such as oil refineries, site facilities will be all-important. There are relatively few sites suitable for the manufacture of production platforms for the offshore oil exploration industry, to take a topical example.

It is not the task of this paper to discuss in a systematic way the factors which will be important for a range of particular industries. As a general rule the major consideration in any location decision is availability of labour. This does not necessarily suggest that firms are particularly attached to areas with a large pool of unemployment and a low female activity rate, since these are compatible with shortages of the skills which may be necessary for a particular production process. Nor is it inevitable that firms will tend to look for a location in a large population centre. The counter-attractions of smaller communities with their typically lower rate of labour turnover can be considerable.

Policy objectives

If the key characteristic of those who make industrial location decisions is that they operate in conditions of uncertainty with limited resources, then policy will be more effective and more certain, the simpler its object-ives and methods are. It may be argued that what is important in success-fully influencing industrial decision-makers is certainty and simplicity in the means — that industrialists react in a certain way to the level of grants whatever the motivation for those grants.

But this is an over-simplified view. First, uncertainty concerning policy objectives tends to result in constant changes in the instruments of policy because they will be particularly vulnerable to short-term political pres-sures. Second, industrialists will have much greater confidence in the longevity of policies if their aims are clearly set out and accepted. Increas-ed confidence in a policy of those whom it is designed to influence must tend to enhance the effectiveness of that policy. Third, clarity of object-ives will presumably mean that they will be accepted by all parts of the machinery of government — both central and local.

It can fairly be argued that the objectives of the regional policies pur oued in Britain by successive governments have been clear only at the level of broad generality. For example, the 1972 White Paper on industrial and regional development (Cmnd 4942) states that 'the ending of regional imbalance has been an objective of successive governments in the United Kingdom for nearly four decades.' The White Paper defines the regional problem in terms of a high level of unemployment, net outward migra-tion, slow economic growth, derelict land, old and obsolete factory buildings and often a relatively low level of amenity. If one takes these statements at face value, among the aims of successive governments have been the equalisation of unemployment rates between regions and ending net migration between regions. Given the rapid rates of change in modern complex economies, such objectives are totally unattainable and there seems little point in pretending that they can be realistically pursued. Giving governments the benefit of the doubt by assuming that they have not believed their own rhetoric, what policy has in fact been aiming at is the reduction of regional disparities to undefined acceptable levels.

The clear definition of policy objectives is desirable not only for its effect on industrialists. Unless objectives are clearly defined, an accurate assessment of the effectiveness of a particular policy is impossible, and consequently a rational judgement on the deployment of resources between competing claims cannot be made. A particular complication, so far as regional policy is concerned, is provided by the explicit or implicit inclusion of policy aims additional to the traditional ones relating to employment and growth.

On occasion it seems regional policy is regarded as a branch of the welfare state and is justified in social-justice terms because it transfers resources from rich areas to poor areas. But at least in traditional welfare economics, the prosperity of an area is not a valid objective of policy – only the economic prosperity of people can apply (West, 1973). In some economics regional policy measures might be as effective a redistributive mechanism as any other but this cannot be true of Britain, where average incomes, except in Northern Ireland, vary only slightly between regions. There is no guarantee that the recipients of regional largesse will be the poorer sections of the community in Scotland, Wales or the North – indeed this is probably unlikely. On equity grounds there is no justification for discriminating in redistributive policy between the poor in one area and in another. Regional policy is therefore not an appropriate instrument.

The anti-congestion argument, stated at its simplest, is that it is desirable to move people from the congested, overcrowded South East, where they suffer external diseconomies, to the wide-open spaces of Scotland, Wales and the North. The fact is, however, that the South East outside London is not particularly congested. Congestion is about external diseconomies and these are very difficult to measure. But, other things being equal, congestion must be closely related to population density. The South East is less densely populated than many areas towards which industry is encouraged to move. Even excluding sparsely populated East Anglia, the South East contains 11,000 square miles. Apart from London, if we compare this 11,000 square miles with Lancashire outside the conurbations, we find that Lancashire is more densely populated. So also are Glamorgan, Durham and Renfrewshire. It is true that inhabitants of the South East may be particularly liable to suffer from the congestion created by the capital but the congestion argument is clearly much more complex than it might appear at first sight.

No doubt we shall hear more of it as concern with the quality of life and the environment grows. It is a subject to be discussed by the EEC's new regional development committee and the EEC's recent regional policy report gives it considerable emphasis (Commission, 1973), arguing that a Community regional policy '... is in the interests of those who live in the great conurbations with their increasing congestion. The physical poverty of the underprivileged regions is matched only by the mounting environmental poverty of the areas of concentration.' The fundamental difficulty with the congestion argument, even if it can be objectively defined, is that there are many uncongested areas other than problem regions to which it may be more convenient for people to move — witness London over-spill. In the context of the general theme of this paper, the point is that it adds another ill-stated aim to the existing confusion about what regional policy is actually trying to achieve.

If we accept that lack of clarity on aims must make the effectiveness of a policy difficult, if not impossible to evaluate, then regional policy may well be a classic case. The Expenditure Committee of the House of Commons recently argued:

> There must be few areas of government expenditure in which so much is spent but so little known about the success of the policy. The most our witnesses could say was that, although the imbalance persisted between assisted and non-assisted areas, they thought that the situation was better than it would have been without the incentives and controls of some sort of regional policy...we believe that it is unwise to forego the maximum use of existing research techniques to help in the formation of long-term policy in this most important field.

But no amount of academic research can compensate for the failure of policy-makers to set clear objectives. For political reasons it is unlikely that they will do so. Like most electorates, British voters are divided into geographical units for voting purposes. Because of our rigid two-party voting structure in the House of Commons the swing of a few marginal seats may determine who holds power for the ensuing four or five years. There is therefore a considerable temptation for the party in power to increase both the level and coverage of geographically selective expenditure in the hope that such evidence of goodwill will be translated into votes from the areas concerned. Similarly, there is a temptation for opposition parties to try to attract votes by outbidding the ruling party in what it offers to do for particular regions. Since the costs of regional expenditure are spread over the taxpayers as a whole — and the resource costs may of course be much less than the budgetary costs or even non-existent — they do not tend to lose votes. If this analysis is valid then it is hardly surprising if objectives remain less than crystal clear.

Finally, regional policy objectives may conflict with other policy aims, notably those concerning the environment. In Britain today almost any major new development will conflict with some interest or another. At present, this is most strikingly true in Scotland. The advent of the off-shore oil exploration industry has posed a very clear choice for particular communities in an area which officially wants more industry. In some cases it may be possible to make compatible, or reach an easy compromise between, employment and environmental aims. But in other cases this simply cannot be done and the options, which may become increasingly difficult, must be faced.

Policy instruments

Although policy conflicts and confusion will remain, this is not to argue that nothing can be done to improve the effectiveness of instruments of policy. Indeed the Conservative government accepted in principle the criticism from industry that the constant changes in both the form and coverage of the incentives offered by successive governments have undermined their effectiveness. Since 1966 we have had development areas, intermediate areas, special development areas, derelict land clearance areas — and a number of alterations in the coverage of the various categories. Tax reliefs were replaced by investment grants, followed by investment allowances and regional development grants. Operational grants have arrived, been altered and departed. Policy changes are often necessary because of changing needs or inevitable on the arrival in office of a new government. But what British regional policy now requires is a period of stability.

The government announced its attention to maintain the new system of incentives at least until the transitional period of entry to Europe is over (i.e. 1 January 1978). There is no doubt that this is helpful but there may well be additional measures which could be taken. Industrialists often undertake expansion projects with hopes but not firm commitments to

230

increase their scope. Certainty concerning the incentives available for subsequent development would undoubtedly enhance the attractiveness of expansion in the assisted areas. In order to give particular firms the certainty that the incentives on which they are basing decisions will remain, it would be possible to establish a system whereby firms receiving assistance could be guaranteed a certain level of aid for future expansion.

There are many examples of firms choosing one location rather than another solely on the basis of the enthusiasm and effectiveness of local officials. With time at a premium for the satisficing businessman it is perfectly logical for him to do so. It is helpful, perhaps particularly for an investor from abroad, if one contact man can take him through from start to finish in the many dealings with different arms of government which a major industrial investment will entail, shielding him as far as possible from conflicting official objectives. How far the operation of Adam Smith's invisible hand applies to those involved in attracting industry is not clear but there is certainly vigorous competition. In one small area of Scotland, there are operating, under the superstructure of the major government departments in Edinburgh, the Department of Trade and Industry, the Scottish Industrial Development Advisory Board in Glasgow, the Scottish Council (Development and Industry), a vigorous regional development authority, an active county council, a new town development corporation and two large boroughs — each with its own promotional campaign. As it happens, the area has been very successful in attracting industry, although it is not clear how far this is due to its natural advantages, the keen competition between the various authorities involved or their mutual co-operation.

All this activity is designed to influence the location of *manufacturing* industry. The realisation that this traditional approach to regional problems is too narrow and that service industries may have an important role to play is of relatively recent origin (Rhodes and Kan, 1971). Much service sector activity is locally generated — it is a function rather than a determinant of population and economic activity in other sectors. But much is nationally generated and, with expansion of service activity likely to continue, this will provide an important potential supply of employment. The new incentives for mobile office development are a step in the right direction but only experience will show whether or not they are sufficient to have the desired effect.

British policy also seems to be taking a more balanced view of the question of mobility of labour. The economic arguments are conflicting. Other things being equal, moving labour from under-employed to full-employed regions must give a net gain in efficiency terms since resources are

231

being moved from areas of surplus to areas of shortage. But other things may not be equal since, for example, the cost of providing infrastructure for the immigrants may be exceptionally high in areas of labour shortage. Despite the advantages to a person of maintaining established social contacts, there is a great deal of labour mobility, both intra-regionally and inter-regionally. Official policy now provides encouragement to those who wish to move to find employment in different areas. But housing policy remains a major disincentive. The continuation, over many decades, of rent control measures designed to meet temporary emergencies and the assistance given to other forms of housing are rapidly eliminating privately rented accommodation. The British workforce is increasingly split between owner-occupiers, who can move relatively easily, and local authority tenants, who find it extremely difficult to move since such housing is usually allocated by waiting list.

A great deal of publicity has been given to the rise in house prices, particularly in London and the South East. On regional policy grounds the effects of the now considerable disincentive to move to the London area may well prove beneficial. Those fortunate enough to have been the possessors of a house in the London area before the surge in prices have made substantial capital gains — but these can be realised only by a move to cheaper accommodation which, for most house owners, involves moving to a different part of the country.

Future policy trends

The most pressing regional-policy problem is the future role, if any, of subsidies which reduce operating costs. The basic argument for such measures is that Britain's regional problems cannot be explained entirely in terms of industrial structure. Although the traditional declining industries in the assisted areas now account for a much smaller proportion of employment there than twenty years ago, problems of fundamental regional imbalance remain: 'If a region suffers from major locational disadvantages then encouraging new industry to establish there may well be ineffective, wasteful and possibly counter-productive.' (CBI 1972) A much more appropriate policy instrument would be a subsidy which reduced industrial costs, such as a wage subsidy or a regionally differentiated value-added tax. As a result of the investigations of the Trade and Industry Sub-Committee of the House of Commons Expenditure Committee, evidence has been made public on the additional costs borne by particular firms from setting up in the assisted areas rather than in a preferred location. Lord Stokes has given the total quantifiable cost to the British Leyland Motor Corporation as a minimum of £70 million over ten years. In addition to higher transport costs and lower labour efficiency, Lord Stokes stated:

> The third cost is the greatest but cannot be precisely defined. Clearly excess costs of the size I have mentioned cannot all be absorbed by the Corporation and a substantial element must be passed on. This blunts our competitive edge, particularly overseas. There is no doubt that when a vehicle costs more than it should, fewer are going to be sold. This erodes the benefits of scale so vital to our industry and in the last analysis results in lower employment (House of Commons, 1971).

The total picture unfortunately is not so clear. There are many firms which have not suffered increased costs from moving to an assisted area and many whose operating costs are lower. Yet the doubt remains that assistance to operating costs may prove to be a more cost-effective approach than increased expenditure on investment aid and environmental improvement.

It is not the purpose of this paper to discuss the European Community's regional policy but in view of its great importance for the future it is valuable to finish with two brief and general comments on its objectives. First, the Community's efforts to harmonise the incentives given by member states have received considerable criticism in the UK, although in the event their application in detail to Britain's regions has been widely regarded as satisfactory. The Community's general objectives of making regional incentives measurable on a common basis and reducing the level of such incentives in non-member states are both desirable. A major difficulty is to ensure transparency for the many incentives given in a number of the member states by institutions other than the central government, such as municipalities and the German Länder. We in Britain, with our relatively clear and centralised system of regional incentives, must ensure that everyone plays by the rules.

Secondly, there has been some confusion surrounding the relationship between the proposed Regional Development Fund and other Community policies. It is widely hoped that the new fund will enable the UK to claw back much of what is contributed to the Common Agricultural Policy. It has always seemed unrealistic to expect this compensation objective to be accepted by those who would have to pay for its implementation. Given that we shall be contributing up to 25 per cent of the fund, and the other demands on it, advanced mathematics are hardly required to conclude that, unless the fund reaches huge proportions, a substantial net gain is most unlikely. More fundamentally, an effective Community regional policy must be designed in its own right and not be seen as an indirect method of correcting the unfortunate consequences of other policies.

Progress towards economic and monetary union may create disequilibria which will require the Community to move resources across frontiers in order to compensate. An effective Community-wide regional policy is therefore a necessary prerequisite for EMU. But except within the long-term context of full economic union, it can never be a substitute for flexible exchange rates. The potential harm to British industry and the economy as a whole from participation in the kind of monetary integration currently aimed at by the Community is on a completely different scale and time-span from the benefits of expenditure under their Regional Development Fund.

References

Commission of the European Communities, *Report on the Regional Problems in the Enlarged Community*, Brussels (1973).

Confederation of British Industry, *Reshaping Regional Policy* (1972).

Expenditure Committee (House of Commons), *Minutes of evidence for 16 June 1971 to the trade and industry sub-committee*, HMSO (1971).

Expenditure Committee (House of Commons), *Sixth report: public money in the private sector*, HMSO (1972).

Rhodes J. and Kan A., *Office Dispersal and Regional Policy*, Cambridge University, Department of Applied Economics, Occasional Paper 30, Cambridge (1971).

West E. G., ' "Pure" versus "operational" economics in regional policy' *Regional Policy For Ever?*, G. Hallett, P. Randall and E. G. West, International Economics Association (1973).

13 Regional Policy and Planning: Future Research Priorities

P. M. Townroe

A constrained view of research

Those involved in any broad area of enquiry into the structure and activity of human or natural systems, be it for intrinsic interest or for some more particular objective of policy or welfare, will always have a personal view of the immediate research priority within that area. That this view will be idiosyncratic, constrained by expertise and experience, goes without saying. We all have our hobby-horses, not only for our own speciality, but also for advances in other areas of our background discipline or professional application. Indeed, there may well be a point of optimum partial ignorance specifying the highest propensity to suggest new avenues of research. If we know nothing, be it in astrophysics, gerontology or sixteenth-century Russian literature, we will not suggest new research projects. Where we are expert, we are so fully aware of the difficulties, both conceptual and operational, that research proposals tend to be made cautiously and incrementally, with strong caveats as to the benefits which will flow from the work. Only where we know enough to be knowledgeable, but not enough to be cautious, will we be suitably cavalier with our suggestions for research for others to undertake.

We also have our own ideas as to what constitutes 'research'. The term may apply to thought processes covering any of the following: observation, analysis, induction, deduction, speculation, prediction, invention and evaluation. Together, in the field of regional analysis and planning, these activities constitute the desirable technical inputs into the process of generating policy alternatives. Within these activities will lie all the usual sub-divisions of research into 'pure' and 'applied', 'theoretical' and 'empirical', 'specific' and 'general', etc.; as well as (in the context of this volume) the usual divisions of planning studies, problem-oriented research and pure or abstract research (Bayliss, 1968).

In considering this wide compass of activity, directed towards regional planning and policy, many disciplines and institutions will be involved. Within these disciplines and institutions there will be those trying to form an overview of the present priorities in research activity, working from a much stronger base than that of a single academic with his one-eyed view of the world. Therefore this paper does no more than point to some of the pressures which generate research activity within this field, highlighting some key areas which require further investigation and also briefly discussing one or two organisational issues of special relevance to research in regional analysis and planning.

The origins of demands for research activity

In any area of intellectual endeavour, research will move forward in response both to external demands made upon the research workers and to new lines of enquiry initiated by those workers themselves. Either way, research will be seen to be needed, typically only incrementally, because of a number of different situations and pressures. In regional policy and planning, we might categorise these pressures as follows:

1   There is the pressure, normally from within the appropriate academic discipline, generated by an advance in theorising; or, more specifically, a new line of theory which cannot be judged as an advance until it has been tested empirically. Usually this research will take the form of testing a model (for example, the testing by Warntz (1959) of his spatial price-variation model) but it may involve a less quantitative approach, testing a theory by its compatibility with empirical facts, the logic of the theory and the implications of its conclusions not being contradicted by observation – for example, Greenhut's theory of industrial location which used a wide range of supporting empirical material (Greenhut, 1956).

2   A similar pressure arises from advances in techniques of analysis. These may be techniques borrowed and adapted from elsewhere in the disciplines usually associated with regional analysis (e.g. input/output analysis) or from other disciplines (e.g. entropy models). Or they may be statistical techniques developed elsewhere (e.g. factor analysis, cluster analysis). Or they may be techniques specifically within the context of regional analysis (e.g. industrial-complex analysis). Of course, no technique is theory-free, in the sense that limiting assumptions are always demanded, but it is the interpretation of the results of using one of these techniques which leads to theoretical explanations of behaviour.

3   From within both of the previous groups of pressures there may come, at any one time, pressure for research work which, although long regarded as desirable, has not been undertaken in the past due to lack of personnel, funds or data. Personnel of the relevant experience and expertise will be

important when access to data is otherwise precluded. For example, an analysis of industrial development certificate refusals can only be undertaken in detail within the Department of Trade and Industry of the British government, the danger being that there is no-one made available for such an analysis or that the analysis is weakened by lack of the appropriate skills. The lack of funds and relevant data are familiar problems and are reasons why some of the important but difficult research questions do not get tackled. Questions such as the multiplier effects of differing forms of public infrastructure or the general social costs of urban congestion would require very large data collection resources to be tackled adequately and even then there would remain great uncertainty as to whether the correct or relevant information had been collected.

New data sources do, of course, themselves generate research activity. In fields such as regional analysis, where research workers have been overly dependent upon limited data sources, any new data source is eagerly fallen upon. For example, the collection of information, for the first time, about the movement of offices in London by the Location of Offices Bureau, has occasioned a number of research papers, some very sensibly sponsored by LOB itself. Another example is the boost given to migration research in Britain by the migration questions asked for the first time in the 1961 Census of Population. One may envisage the availability of the results of the 1971 Census of Population, on a grid-square basis, similarly developing new lines of enquiry and analysis. Of course, data sources are sometimes used only with great difficulty and do not match up to expectations, or do so only as a result of a new line of approach (as, for example, the establishment data from the Factory Inspectorate used initially in the West Midlands but now being used much more carefully in the Clydeside conurbation). Some data sources, just like some of the multivariate statistical techniques, will also not generate new research until there is easy access to large enough computers for storage and manipulation. The development of on-line and interactive modes of computer operation, as well as the wide dissemination of easy-to-use statistical analysis package programmes must (or should) make research more cost effective.

4 If new data sources, like new theories and techniques of analysis, generate research, so, quite clearly, do new policies, political pressures and political institutions. New policies pose new questions and provide new statistical series (e.g. the regional employment premium, introduced in the United Kingdom in 1967); we may hope that new political pressures will generate research activity before a policy is decided upon — as, for example, with the Royal Commission on Local Government (Cmnd 4040, 1969). New institutions, such as regional economic planning councils or

the Highlands and Islands Development Board in Scotland, generate research, both as sponsors and as focal points for interest, as do new political situations, such as membership of the European Economic Community or the troubles in Northern Ireland. However, in many of these examples of pressure, research findings are not used in the classic policy-formulation sequence and regional research often seems to follow on as an afterthought to the pursuit of a national policy objective. The sponsorship of three large aluminium smelters in the United Kingdom in the late 1960s is an example, and the current haste to exploit the resources of North Sea oil may be another. And there is always a converse danger: that research can be used to procrastinate when a difficult political choice has to be made, a charge that has been levelled at the work on the siting of the third London airport (Roskill, 1971).

5   Related to political pressure is the rather wider, but more diffuse, pressure which results from changing views of the importance of particular situations, problems or variables. In the United Kingdom, we often seem to be the victims (or the beneficiaries) of a demonstration effect from the United States, which changes the conventional wisdom of the way in which attributes of situations are classified. Recent examples are the concerns of pollution and resource depletion or the attempts to assess environmental quality. These changing views may be the result of changing circumstances (e.g. the role of rising real income in the provision of leisure facilities) or they may signify a more fundamental change of opinion about the way in which social life is organised or valued (e.g. the rights of an employee in a redundancy situation or the social obligations of industrial concerns in the prevention of pollution).

6   Disagreement between research workers, as to the policy implications of both past work and as yet untested or inadequately tested concepts and theories, may also be expected to generate new activity. The current disagreement about the role and importance of agglomeration economies in regional economic growth — as seen in the recent books by Brown (1972) and Richardson (1972) — may well be an encouragement for the investment of more resources in a very difficult research area. The quality of past work may also be in dispute and will be an encouragement for further study (for example, in the heavy reliance on *post hoc* questionnaire methods in the study of industrial location).

7   Planning studies, at the regional and sub-regional levels, develop in their methodology, often demanding research into the plan-making process or into the core techniques of analysis which may be a land-use model or a regional econometric simulation model. There is the need to assess whether particular approaches or planning sequences produce better re-

sults than others, in whichever region they are applied, and likewise whether the form of a given model is capable of universal application. An example is the work by the Centre for Environmental Studies to develop a general structure planning model with the Cheshire County Council (Cordey-Hayes *et al.*, 1971).

8   Planning studies also generate generalised research demands, both of techniques (current examples might be in the use of Delphi panels and of social surveys for arriving at weights for objectives) and of required inputs of information general to all regions (for example, the timing and incidence of the benefit of infrastructure investment or the changing trade-off between migration and commuting).

9   There is also an indirect pressure for research at the regional level from those with particular interests seeking to use the region as a 'test-bed'. This may be for the testing of theories (e.g. the determinants of industrial investment) or for the increased understanding of general, social and economic change in society, perhaps related to changes in value patterns or to urbanisation or to changes in the workplace.

All of the above categories overlap, and, of course, they are neither exclusive nor comprehensive. Whatever might be decided upon in an ideal listing of future research priorities, the research which actually gets undertaken will be in response to the above pressures. However, there is a danger in viewing research as generated solely in these various ways. That would place research work only in a reactive capacity and rarely in a pre-emptive capacity. Some overview needs to be continuously undertaken to avoid gaping holes in the spectrum of effort. More contract research from central government may encourage a wider assessment within relevant departments — but even there the job may be given to a single person, with his limited view of overall requirements. In the field of regional policy and planning there must also inevitably be a certain amount of suspicion about the constraint of the 'London view', a syndrome which looks as if it may well get a good deal worse when it is the 'Brussels view'.

Some current priorities

What are the current priorities for research work in the fields of regional analysis and regional planning when seen in a United Kingdom context? The original draft of this paper identified sixty-eight areas seeming to require attention, or more intensive investigation. Here we may point to a few of the more important, under seven sub-headings:

1   The economic structure of regions: We still know far too little about the differences in industrial efficiency between regions; about the related differences in technical progress and innovation; and about the returns to social infrastructure investments. Much work remains to be undertaken on regional production functions. The susceptibility of regions to trade-cycle swings or to changes in the terms of international trade is recognised but not well documented; and, looking ahead, we should perhaps be thinking about the regional element in the more general implications of selective resource depletion, tighter pollution controls and higher transportation fuel costs.

2   The social and cultural structure of regions: Inter-area comparisons in living standards, whether of countries or of regions, are always difficult. Not only do the supply of statistics and the statistical conventions differ from area to area but the public service and intangible elements vary tremendously in only an indirectly quantifiable way. However, both assisted area policies and more general regional planning exercises require the study of the spatial implications of rising real incomes and changes in expenditure patterns. There remains much to be gained from international comparisons of life-styles. The study of living standards will relate to work on geographical and occupational mobility and on the cultural differences and influences on entrepreneurship and managerial innovation. And in turn this points to the need for more work on inter-regional differences in work practices and attitudes, related to labour productivity, flexibility, journey to work patterns etc. The inter-area comparison of age-specific birth rates may also be an area of study where research has yet to adequately tackle the influence of local culture and social structure.

3   Regional economic growth: The uncertainty surrounding the role of agglomeration economies and linkages in local economic growth has already been referred to. The role of urbanisation in regional economic growth, and the importance of distance in economies of scale for both industrial and public-sector investments, are also areas of uncertainty and point to the need for further research into the relevance of the growth centre concept in a developed economy with a high population density. Growth centre thinking has hitherto tended to revolve around manufacturing industry as the basic sector but the categories of industry growing most strongly in employment terms in the future will be in the service sector. We know very little about the role of the service sector in regional economic growth, either as propulsive industries or as necessary conditions or accompaniment to growth in manufacturing. It may be that the internal and external patterns of information flows in large service sector organisations will become an increasingly important element in the choice

of locations for new investments. This points to the need for a continuing appraisal of the efficiency and growth criteria for public subsidies to new investment. The old debate as to the relative merits of capital-intensive and labour-intensive industry, and of immigrant and indigenous industry, should continue.

4   The regional labour market: Work attitudes have already been referred to and in this context there is a need for research into the way in which inter-regional differences in these attitudes relate to differences in industrial relations and to the process of the diffusion of job skills. The problem of measuring the level and nature of job skills in a given regional population has worried many a regional planner and relates to an important area of necessary research into the procedures and methods of industrial training as they relate to programmes of area development. The degrees of transferability of different occupations may be very important for the recruitment and training policies of relocating companies, as well as for public policies for redundancy situations.

5   Factor movements: The majority of studies into labour mobility rely upon census statistics or material from cross-sectional social surveys. As a consequence we know too little about the longer-term experience of mobile workers (mobile both occupationally and geographically), about non-job-change geographic mobility and about the economic effects of labour mobility. We also know little about the information used and the search patterns established in geographical mobility from one labour market to another. Also, in the migration area, the economic and social implications of retirement migration are only slowly coming to be understood. In considering the inter-regional migration of capital, there are also a number of areas suitable for future research work: the opportunity costs involved in diverting flows of private capital; the role and manner of assessment of the non-pecuniary factors in industrial location decisions; the longer-term economic experience of mobile plants; the causes, patterns and remedies of plant closures in mobile (and non-mobile) industry; the interactive impact of road, rail and telecommunications investment on the location of new industry. We also know little about the locational discretion available for new investment in the multi-plant and multi-national companies.

6   The assessment of regional economic policies: The need to review continuously the subsidies available to new investment has been referred to in (3) above. Further aspects of these subsidies to consider will include the multiplier effects of differing forms of subsidy (and of public investment) and the important discretionary elements in the subsidies. Research is also required into the impact of regional policies on the non-assisted

areas of the country as well as into the impact of the policies on real incomes within the assisted regions. In the longer term, the assessment of policy measures will clearly be aided by larger and more sensitive dynamic inter-regional planning and programming models.

7   Regional planning processes: The continuing development of both programming and simulation models, both partial and comprehensive, will clearly also be important for better regional planning. But recently, increasing attention has been paid to the problems of the inputs into these models. Goal-setting and the criteria for weighting objectives require the development of social survey techniques, and greater use will be made of Delphi panels in the forecasting of particular inputs. The temporal sequence of plans and studies of a region also requires more monitoring of performances in terms of the projections made. Various aspects of life and public policy in each region can be highlighted as requiring future background research activity. These include: the inter-relationships of urban welfare policies and regional development programmes; the problems of equity and efficiency in the provision of transport in rural areas; the implications of increased leisure time and the growth of tourist demands for regional development; and the relationship of housing needs to both the ability and tendency to migrate and to housing stocks and prices. As regards politics, it would be both interesting and relevant to know more about decision-making at the local and regional level and about the interlocking of representation on regional and local bodies.

The list is not complete, and anyway it would be a brave man who could claim to specify criteria for the completeness of a list such as this. Clearly some of the research areas suggested will be more tractable than others, given current technology and the current supply of statistics. Any movement towards regional and sub-regional income, expenditure and output (or value-added) accounts would be welcomed with all that that implies in the way of better statistics. It is important also to remember that a defence is required for the regional statistics we already have, to prevent changes in administrative procedures ending useful statistical series. However, better statistics is not the only requirement for good research work. In this field there are institutional problems also, both within and among the academic disciplines contributing and in the funding and organisation of research.

242

Research in regional policy and planning

Research in the areas of regional policy and planning, as well as in the wider area of regional analysis, comes from a tradition of strong policy orientation. This welfare concern has tended to lead to a concentration of research into the policy problems of the day (e.g. unemployment in British regions, poverty in American regions), rather than into underlying causal mechanisms of regional activity and development. As a young and evolving area of study within the various disciplines concerned, regional analysis is only slowly growing into academic respectability, perhaps because of the eclectic nature of its use of theories and techniques from elsewhere and perhaps because of its applied concerns. We have not seen much home-grown theorising in this field so far, although many have tried to borrow and bend theories from other disciplines, as well as from other areas of their own subjects. We have, however, seen a very considerable development in the last few years in the techniques available for analysis, techniques which have far outrun the availability of suitable data to service them. The misapplication of sophisticated techniques is now a central danger. As in so much social science, there is a continual need to return to fundamentals and to re-examine assumptions.

The inter-disciplinary nature of research into regional policy and planning is both a strength and a weakness. There is the danger that any member of an inter-disciplinary team, or any one man using an inter-disciplinary approach, will have insufficient grounding in at least one major discipline to be able to assess fully the potential contribution of that discipline to the problem in hand. The difficulties of teamwork, of harmonising differing research strategies and of familiarity with two or more streams of literature are perhaps more obvious and well-known. And yet the nature of the problems and the issues in regional policy and planning seem to demand inter-disciplinary working. The region forms the level of aggregation where the interdependence of the social, the economic and the physical requires the co-ordinated approach of a full range of relevant skills and knowledge. However, at the level of research studies, rather than at the level of operational regional plan-making, it is an open question as to whether there really is a need for several disciplines to combine in work on a single problem or whether benefit is maximised by the close proximity of a number of disciplines tackling a number of problems in the way they know best, hoping for spin-off only at the technical and social interfaces.

If true inter-disciplinary working is so difficult (as experience seems to indicate), one may ask if the establishment of multi-disciplinary research centres with interests in a number of aspects of regional (and usually urban) analysis is as productive as the concentration of funds on to more narrowly focused groups of research workers. The wider approach can only work with a strong positive effort to overcome disciplinary barriers, combined with very sensitive leadership and clear objectives to guide the work. Perhaps these conditions are only approximately found in regional and sub-regional planning teams and are unlikely to be present in university departments or in government-sponsored research centres. This may be one reason why university departments and centres tend to end up with particular strengths and specialisms within the wider area of study.

The potential role of the individual academic, working on his own but who hopes to contribute to greater effectiveness in regional policy and planning through his research work, is weakened both by his role and his career structure within the university system and by the applied nature of the subject area. Much academic work is one-off, individualistic, short-term and ill-defined in terms of policy application. The limited resources available to the individual scholar, particularly early in his career, can lead him (or her) to unstructured speculation or to the delimitation of research problems in self-defined terms of his own ability to emerge with credit. Peer-group esteem does not come from asking unanswerable, and hence wrong, questions. The rise in staff—student ratios and the increasing feelings of obligation to be aware of alternative teaching methods (and the monitoring of their success and failure), combined with a career structure which is only partially dependent upon research activity and certainly not dependent upon policy-relevant research, tends to lead the British academic towards a model of the research project which is one-off and abstracted from a wider context. This leads to considerable misunderstanding with those involved in policy formulation and in regional plan-making.

Perhaps the key to this institutional problem of the relationships between university-based research workers and those employed within government (as to other undiscussed relationships between research workers within government departments or within government research institutes and the policy-makers or between firms of consultants and their clients) is to recognise that there must rightly be many levels of research activity with varying degrees of immediate policy relevance, and that different types of problem need to be tackled in different types of places. Within this diversity, however, there may be a requirement for research work undertaken outside the government machine, to be financed on a much longer-term basis than hitherto in centres with more clearly defined objectives. This would allow such centres to be less concerned with survival and to develop a coherent programme of inter-related activities. The exception here would be those necessary short-term studies of specific problems which require rapid examination, applying the fruits of a range of past research work. These studies will be best left to the commercial consultants or, exceptionally, to those academics with expertise in a particular field.

The applied nature of the subject area under discussion, requiring as it does considerable co-operation between public agencies and research workers, will inevitably lead to a degree of tension, particularly if the researchers are academics maintaining (rightly) a stance of openness of comment and freedom to publish results. Political sensitivity, as well as problems of possible disclosure of information relating to individuals or to organisations, and the restrictions of a tight brief demanded by the research contractor will always involve a divergence of opinion. Any involvement of individual 'freelance' academics will also be made difficult by the typical scale of projects in this area, involving as they do a degree of teamwork; and, additionally, by the difficulties within the university system of short-term research appointments at other than the most junior level. Within many universities, there is also little financial assistance available for the presubmission development (prior to an approach to a grant-giving agency) of research proposals. Development of the contractor—client relationship or of longer-term funding of chosen centres will help to minimise these problems.

Overall, it can also be argued that, at the end of the day, the system of sponsoring and financing research activity must back people. Recognition of this should therefore involve more careful attention being paid to the early career development of those people, the project team leaders of ten years hence. Good people will find the right or relevant areas for research and will find the means to undertake the work. But this requires a level of judgement only acquired through a number of years of involvement of research activity in the field.

Conclusion

In conclusion, three specific points and one general hope for the development of research in regional policy and planning.

First, a note of caution. The experience of the past ten years or so has shown that we need to be particularly careful in the formulation of researchable questions. Research proposals sometimes tend to be framed in a way which implies patterns of behaviour waiting to be discovered, which are both sufficiently consistent and precisely forecastable for the fruits of the research to be applied to each and every situation. Some proposals also imply a precision of response of public policy which just does not exist. In most areas of regional policy and planning, we do not have either good optimising or forecasting models. Nor do we have sufficiently interventionist policies to implement the output of such models.

Monitoring is a theme which surfaces from time to time in connection with regional planning and yet we are still rather unclear as to what is required from it. Clearly, operational monitoring is required within regions for the years between regional-planning exercises; but there is also room for more monitoring as a research input. Only those research studies using available statistical series consider longitudinal change. Much more continuous assessment is needed of such variables as travel-demand elasticities or response to migration pressures. There is also a monitoring requirement of changes in life-style and associated policy responses in other countries — particularly in those European countries which now have higher levels of personal disposable real incomes than ourselves.

The plea for more statistics which was made earlier is perhaps so familiar that it is immediately discounted. Everyone is aware that the assessment of the cost-effectiveness of the collection of additional statistical information is always very difficult. However, the research-generation role of new statistics has been referred to and the returns to particular figures may be very high in some cases (e.g. statistics which allowed a detailed evaluation of the regional employment premium). Perhaps more important than the collection of additional statistics is the need to make those we have more widely available. The Statistics of Trade Act is overly restrictive for work in the United Kingdom (for example, a research worker in Glasgow recently contacted over 1,500 companies by telephone and only four refused to answer his question about the number of employees, information he had been refused by a government department). And insufficient use is made of material either especially collected by government departments or more routinely collected, but not available to research workers even with the strongest guarantees about non-revelation of individual cases (e.g. IDC applications or files on investment grants). Of course, guarantees of confidentiality are a prime consideration for a government department, both for the protection of civil servants and for the continuing encouragement of honesty in making statistical returns, as well as for safeguarding the interests of individuals and companies; but we do seem to be much more restrictive in this country than is the case with many of our neighbours and competitors.

Research for regional policy and planning is young and it would be difficult to argue that there has not been a considerable social welfare benefit from the work undertaken so far. However, we are now moving into a changing situation in the United Kingdom. From April 1974 we will have a smaller group of larger and more powerful local authorities which may be expected to undertake, generate and sponsor more research. The Kilbrandon Commission argued for greater regional devolution of political power, again generating a new form of research requirement. And the prospects of policies from Brussels must widen the horizons of British research activity. These changes, combined with the development of post-Rothschild contractor—client links between Whitehall and research bodies, have implications for all those involved in research work in this area, whether in local or central government, in the universities and poly-technics or in firms of commercial consultants. One may only hope that a greater volume of activity, overlaid by demands for relevance, will not mean any decline in quality.

References

Bayliss D., *Some Changing Characteristics of Research in Environmental Studies*, Centre for Environmental Studies, London, Working Paper No. 8 (1968).

Brown A. J., 'The Framework of Regional Economics in the United Kingdom', *Economic and Social Studies*, 27, NIESR, Cambridge (1972).

Cmnd 4040, *Report of the Royal Commission on Local Government in England and Wales*, HMSO (1969).

Cmnd 5460, *Royal Commission on the Constitution*, HMSO (1973).

Cordey-Hayes M. *et al., An Operational Urban Development Model of Cheshire*, Centre for Environmental Studies, London, Working Paper No. 64 (1971).

Greenhut M. L., *Plant Location in Theory and Practice*, Chapel Hill, North Carolina (1956).

Richardson H. W., *Regional Economic Growth* (1973).

Roskill, *Commission on the Third London Airport: Report*, HMSO (1971).

Warntz W., *Towards a Geography of Price*, Philadelphia (1959).

247

14 Discussion and Epilogue

Morgan Sant

Introduction

The purpose of seminars is to provide an opportunity for informed discussion in response to carefully prepared papers. Often this discussion is as important as the papers themselves. It can indicate the effect of new ideas upon a varied audience; it can raise new issues beyond those contained in the papers; and it can illuminate areas of basic disagreement (or agreement) between participants.

But the publication of discussions can carry undesirable risks. In an unexpurgated form a transcript tends to be cumbersome, repetitive and rather unstructured. What follows, therefore, is an edited version in which verbatim statements have been interspersed with reported accounts of discussions and, where appropriate, some additions by the editor.

Rather than follow a format in which each paper is accompanied by the discussion specific to it, the approach here has been to seek themes. Some of these can be easily related to the papers; others are more broadly based. For example, the problems of administrative articulation and of selectivity in regional planning were mentioned in several of the papers and reappeared through the discussions. But statements about them have been grouped under individual headings.

Finally, the participants in the discussions have been identified, along with their affiliations. Apart from removing the possibility that readers may come to believe that the editor holds a multitude of conflicting opinions this has at least one interesting feature. Central government policy-makers, local government planners and academic researchers tend to have different views. Notwithstanding within-group variations, it is possible to seek broad disparities in the way in which they approach questions and in the answers which they give. It is, of course, right that this should be the case, for there is nothing that so stultifies progress as total agreement.

Regionalism and regional policy

The seminar took place about one month before the publication of the

Report of the Kilbrandon Commission on the Constitution. There was, therefore, an air of expectancy in the seminar. *Donnison*'s paper contains a point of view not markedly different from that of the majority report of the Commission. Challenging the proponents of regionalism to prove their case he makes two major assertions. First, while fully accepting the case for regional planning and policy, he propounds that, taking the country as a whole, the politics of regionalism are simply non-feasible. Effective regional politics have been, and could continue to be, conducted in Scotland, Northern Ireland and, perhaps, Wales, but this does not form a sound basis for a wholesale devolution of powers to elected regional bodies. One reason is that regional and national objectives can differ radically, leading to divided loyalties. Another is that the movements of population and the changes in urban structure currently occurring are creating a pattern of life that does not fit at all well with traditional ideas of regional economics. A third, and this applies especially to Scotland, Wales and Northern Ireland, is that although regionalism is politically viable, democratic institutions would frequently be ill-equipped to carry forward policies that will be needed to produce real economic growth.

The second of Donnison's assertions is that if there is to be a meaningful regionalism for administration and planning, it is necessary to list the issues which could be resolved at the regional level, *and only there*. Issues, that is, which are too big for the large municipal authority and which are capable of solution without recourse to central government. Donnison considers that such issues are very few.

Without objecting to the rationality of Donnison's arguments, *White* (DOE) recognised a source of ambiguity which tends to arise in practice. A civil servant, made responsible for a regional area, tends to identify himself with the problems and to look at the region as an integrated whole. On the other hand, if there is a popular regional consciousness it tends to follow quite different boundaries from those of administrative regions. Indeed, the issues which promote genuine public participation are local, at a scale where communities possess a natural geographical cohesion. *Rhodes* (Cambridge) followed this reasoning but added a cynical view, which nonetheless has strong political relevance. This is, that if Whitehall is seen to be solving problems then a strong regional consciousness may not develop: political regionalism varies inversely with the success of central government. The last assertion implies that regional consciousness exists, but generally in a latent form, a point made by *Powell* (DOE), especially in regard to employment opportunities. *Gay* (Rouen) was sceptical of the manner in which regions are delimited and proposed

250

the need for greater attention to the mental and social space of the population.

Allen (Glasgow) widened the context to a European one. Noting that membership of the enlarged EEC had led some commentators to expect regionalism to be superseded by internationalism, he found it ironic that in fact the movement towards regionalism had, if anything, become stronger. Devolution of political and economic power is not a sufficient or necessary condition for regional development, however. Nevertheless, we can apply Rhodes's argument again. With economic and monetary union (EMU) scheduled to start in 1980 it is essential that the EEC finds the institutions to satisfy the aspirations of the least advantaged regions. Otherwise EMU will leave these open to even stronger competition and without the protection of rational currencies, leading to dissatisfaction which would endanger the existence of the EEC.

Donnison's second challenge, on decisions appropriate at the regional level, was taken up by *Bird* (DOE). Pointing out that Donnison's examples were mainly of *ad hoc* decisions for which the Whitehall machinery was adequate, Bird identified strategic planning, where the complexity and inter-relatedness of decisions, the need to co-ordinate the work of different government departments and the long time-span of research and implementation, all make it necessary to work on a regional basis. Referring to the problem of the physical restructuring of cities, Bird criticised the past tendency to ignore the opportunities afforded by urban growth to change the regional distribution of transport or employment infrastructure. Support for this view was given by *Gaskin* (Aberdeen), who added that a regional focus provides an important educative function, especially for local government, by bringing the thoughts of local politicians to bear on questions (such as regional development) of which their understanding is frequently deficient or to which they give imperfect attention.

Lastly, *Boudeville* (Paris) considered that it is necessary to approach the discussion of regionalism in two different ways: either from the point of view of national economic policy, or on the basis of a consensus of the local population in regard to common objectives. But, even if the former course was taken, and if the regions had a degree of internal interdependence, it would be possible for common interests to be built up. This was occurring in France (via the *régionalisation du plan*) where such interests were becoming focused on regional infrastructure and town and country planning. Moreover, current trends appeared to be reinforcing the economic interdependence and social interconnections between regions, through integration poles (e.g. Pau–Lourdes–Tarbes and Mulhouse–Belfort–

Montbéliard) and also within regions containing constellations of large and medium-sized towns (e.g. urban regions of northern and eastern France).

Administrative articulation

Between an idea and its implementation there lies a stony path of consultation and negotiation. Rarely do regional policies convey benefits to all regions and all people (though Rhodes and Moore would have it otherwise). Even if there were ubiquitous benefits, this would not stop some parties to an act trying to increase their own share at the expense of others. Such is the political process found to operate not only within countries but also among, for example, the members of the EEC.

But, while democracy insists on this process as a means of safeguarding people's interests, there is an inevitable danger that the idea and the implemented act bear little relation to each other. *Allen* (Glasgow), in responding to Stabenow's paper and, more broadly, to the work of the EEC Regional Policy Directorate General, was disturbed by what had been described as 'horse-trading' between the different departments and members of the Community. The danger was that although a regional policy might be secured, it would be much less than ideal and might only be gained at the expense of something else, leading ultimately to the question of whether a Community regional policy was worthwhile.

This provided a lively exchange of views, of which a short extract is reprinted below:

Allen: If Dr Stabenow is very keen on regional development being pushed forward, what would he be happy to exchange for its implementation?
Stabenow (EEC): Well, for example, there is a German interest in economic stability and anti-inflation policy. In Germany there is a strong feeling that they especially will be contributing to regional policy, and to some extent that is true. What they are asking before agreeing to the size of the fund is for some precise measure in the field of anti-inflation policy. The French are saying that there is a connection with progress in the monetary field.
Allen: If the Germans are keen on anti-inflation policies, that might mean that they are very keen on pegging the British £ before seeing money spent on regional development purposes. What say do the British have in that? Would not this be very expensive, if we were to take a decision on strengthening regional policy?
Howard (DTI): If only we could sell the Rhodes and Moore thesis to the

252

Germans, they would realise that they would be better off by enlarging the regional development fund.

(Laughter)

Rhodes (Cambridge): ... only if monetary union was in existence. But, an adequate regional policy is a precondition for that. If EMU comes before regional policy, the Common Market is likely to break its back.

Allen: Regional policy is no substitute for a flexible exchange rate.

Stabenow: It is not my brief to develop the case of individual governments; I am concerned only with the Community case. But, while the German and Dutch governments would agree to the establishing of a regional fund even if there was no passage to the second stage of EMU (in contradiction to the Paris summit mandate) they are still asking for some commitments for the future in order to know in which direction they are going. This is more important from the French point of view. The main problem is that the Community makes commitments on timing, rather than on specific actions.

Considering Stabenow's last statement on the crucial nature of timing, it is instructive to look briefly at the machinery of decision-making in the EEC. Research (for example on regional policy) is carried out in the Directorate General which then presents a document containing proposals to the Commissioner responsible, who then decides whether to proceed. If the answer is positive, the Directorate General then prepares a draft directive for the Commission to put before the Council of Ministers. If accepted there, the directive then goes to the national parliaments for ratification. Meanwhile, the other Directorates General and their Commissioners work on their own draft directives which may have direct or indirect relevance for regional policy. This process may appear cumbersome, but a proposal that parliaments should consider the draft directive before the Council of Ministers would make matters even more protracted.

The problems of administrative articulation are no less severe within the UK, as the paper by *Jay* indicates. Over recent years there has been enacted a hierarchy of policy and planning activities: national, regional (strategic planning), sub-regional (structure planning), and local (development control). To these can be added *ad hoc* decisions about major investments. But the hierarchy is little more than a myth, for there is little integration between the stages, despite its desirability.

Powell (DOE) pointed out that strategic plans have no statutory force. The South East plan was produced as a document for discussion and, ultimately, when the Secretary of State for the Environment accepted it, for guidance. In this it is different from structure plans which are part of the statutory process. These are intended to reflect the broader framework of the strategic plan but so far have tended to be produced too spasmodically and in insufficient numbers to adequately test this objective. Indeed, *Saunders* (DOE) criticised structure plans for tending, in aggregate, to overbid the resources available to a region and to over-estimate regional growth.

Denton (DOE) saw the same problem arising with strategic plans, linking his fears with arguments against further devolution of power to regional bodies. All regions aspire to a share of resources, and in order to ensure it they seek problems that do not exist or exaggerate minor deficiencies. However, *McEnery* (DTI) did not regard the issue as a major one. In the end the central government has to allocate the priorities in response to the pressures from the various regions. For the long term it is a matter for the democratic process. In the short term, however, destructive competition is avoided by a set of ground rules which are heavily biased in favour of the less advantaged regions. Thus, the financial capacity of Yorkshire and Humberside to compete for resources with Scotland is severely limited.

Demand management

There is now a consensus that the basic underlying regional problem is the relative lack of demand for labour in the development areas and that one major reason for this is to be found in inter-regional differences in the structure of industry. *Rhodes and Moore* carry this argument through by asserting that a meaningful evaluation of the effects of regional policy must be carried out in the context of its impact on overall demand-management policy for the national economy. Thus, when an active regional policy diverts demand to development areas, they assume that the government acts so as to maintain the pressure of demand in other areas where it would have been in the absence of regional policy. In this way additional resources are brought into use to make any general expansion more easily sustainable. Moreover, they argue that the real costs, unlike the Exchequer costs, of regional policy are negative, because regional policy instruments in effect increase labour-supply by more than they pre-empt labour resources, thus making possible some reduction in general taxation. The estimated outcome was that regional policy in the 1960s had made possible an increase in GDP of about 1 per cent.

This is a bold extension to recent thinking on the costs and benefits of regional policy and has not been without criticism. *Shaw* (Norfolk CC) believed the argument to hold inconsistencies about the advantages that accrue to the South East and Midlands as a result of diversion of demand. If it is true that diversion, in terms of jobs, is very limited in *any one year*, the consequence of allowing those jobs to have remained in the South East and Midlands would not have been so inflationary as to require a dampening-down of demand by higher taxation, as Rhodes and Moore assert. The critical issue is the rate of diversion, which seemed to be sufficiently slow for adjustments to be made simply through population change.

McEnery (DTI) added that the argument also ignored the prospects of increased productivity as a result of increased capital investment in the South East and Midlands in response to labour shortages. Although this point is valid, *Cameron* (Glasgow) distinguished between a *net* gain in output, which would be the outcome of raising productivity within the pressured regions, and a *gross* gain in output arising from a diversion of jobs to take people out of unemployment in development areas. The alternative, to take unemployed people from development areas to the pressured regions (i.e. using national financial resources to encourage more out-migration) is neither politically nor economically desirable.

Crum (UEA) was concerned that the Rhodes and Moore case hinged on the argument that the Treasury runs the national economy so that the fully employed regions are at a certain level of demand. This is not the way the Treasury acts and none of the official advice given to the government on how to run the economy is couched in terms of fully employed areas and regions. Rather, it speaks of national averages and these would not be affected if the objective is simply to remove demand in the fully-employed regions and give it to the development areas. Moreover, resources are not always fully employed in the South East and the Midlands. In reply, Rhodes was careful to state that there was no assumption of full employment in these regions in his paper. But there was an assumption, which it was important to stress, that the government aims for the *same* pressure of demand in non-development areas, whether or not there is an active regional policy.

As an evaluative exercise based on well-conceived assumptions there is little to fault in the Rhodes and Moore argument. However, it can be questioned whether it goes far enough, on two accounts. First, the diversion of jobs to development areas does require inducements and there is some evidence to suggest that increasing marginal Exchequer costs are involved. Even when inducements were almost nil, in the 1950s, there was still a flow of jobs to the peripheral regions and the massive increase in expenditure through the 1960s did not bring a proportionate increase in industrial movement. The question, therefore, which must be raised is: At what point do the real resource costs outweigh the benefits? Secondly, anticipating the issue which arises again in the next section, we may presume that the real costs of diverting the same job would differ among the various development areas. From this we would ask whether the case might not be extended to greater selectivity among and within development areas.

The heterogeneity of regions

The treatment of development areas as a single group, as for example in Rhodes and Moore's paper, was criticised by *Keeble* (Cambridge). To regard all such areas as though they were uniform, with uniform problems and potentialities, was misleading. Suggesting that location relative to the central core of the Midlands and South East was crucial in the ability of assisted areas to attract new activities, Keeble drew a distinction between the apparent success of Yorkshire and Humberside and its less accessible competitors, such as Scotland.

However, *Goddard* (LSE) noted that the importance of distance, in a conventional sense, appeared to be important only when firms were viewed in aggregate. Surveys of individual firms indicated that the effect of distance on distribution costs was relatively unimportant. To Goddard this paradox suggested that it was not physical distance which was critical, but distance in the sense of separation from sources of knowledge and expertise. These are heavily concentrated in London and the South East but there are also variations between the conurbations of development areas and the remainder of their territory.

Regional entrepreneurship and promotion

From time to time there have been changes in the emphasis given to different instruments of regional policy. At the outset, in 1928, the choice lay with the encouragement of labour movement out of the depressed regions, through the setting up of the Industrial Transference Board. That was superseded in 1934 by the Special Areas Act whose objective was to promote economic development and social improvement in the problem regions but with very limited powers and resources. Post-war emphasis has lain with industrial movement guided to development areas by a varying set of controls and inducements. Yet after more than four decades, in which well over half a million manufacturing jobs have 'moved' to the peripheral regions and excess labour supply has been partially met by migration, there still remains a strong dissatisfaction with the rate of progress. Not surprisingly, therefore, there has been a continued search for methods which will improve conditions still further.

A view, partly embodied in the 1972 Industry Act, and still being pursued, is that much greater attention should be given to the indigenous entreprencurship found within the problem regions. The point was given some impetus by *Donnison* (CES) who asserted that there was a need for regional development agencies capable of finding and backing enterprise and managerial talent and raising productivity in various sectors and at various levels. Such agencies should be opportunistic and discriminating and be innovative rather than defensive. *Goddard* (LSE) suggested an extension to this role, by having the agencies play a positive part in building up the inter-industrial linkages within regions. Arguing that medium-sized firms which do not operate on a national scale are crucially dependent on the nature of their local or regional contract environment, a purpose of a development agency would be to improve that environment.

However, *McEnery* (DTI) insisted that this had become precisely the job of the regional offices of the Department of Trade and Industry since the 1972 Act. Referring to his role in Yorkshire and Humberside, he suggested that the new strength of the region had come by following arguments such as those put forward by Donnison and Goddard. Local entrepreneurs and management were being backed and there was close co-operation with the merchant and clearing banks, increasing the amount of commercial, rather than government, money going into industrial projects. Further, priority was given to firms providing high-productivity jobs rather than a mere quantity of jobs.

This did not fully allay *Gaskin*'s (Aberdeen) scepticism. Although Scotland has a number of well-established merchant banks, the problems of development remained unsolved. Also there were doubts that the DTI regional offices might not in fact create a self-sustained entrepreneurial consciousness. The spirit of enterprise might go little further than the DTI itself.

On a different level an increased role was proposed by *Roudeville* (Paris) for local authority promotion, especially when several authorities were able to combine their efforts in order to present a composite picture of their locational advantages. An example had occurred in a study prepared by the towns with over 100,000 inhabitants in the Parisian Basin. *Stewart* (CBI) had doubts about current practice whereby there was duplication of activity at different levels of government and non-productive competition by neigbouring local authorities.

Selective assistance and the branch plant syndrome

One of the sources of discontent with the effects of post-war industrial movement has been in the preponderance of branch plants moving to development areas. However ill-informed this criticism, the feeling at its most extreme has been that such industrial units add little to a regional economy in the form of higher skills, managerial talent or entrepreneurship and that by remitting profits to head offices elsewhere they form a novel kind of colonialism. Hence some of the arguments, such as those in the preceding section, in favour of measures to promote enterprise among the indigenous industries of the problem regions.

In fact there are two issues involved here, neither of them irreconcilable. *Feinstein* (DTI) pointed out that while it might be desirable to foster certain types of industry (e.g. services and firms employing top management) in development areas, it was not practical politics to exclude others which did not fit into this category. *Howard* (DTI) went further, stating that if a region had a chance of attracting a viable project it was bound to take it. Moreover, whatever the contribution to regional development of lock, stock and barrel moves, the opening of new branches remained a cornerstone of the government's distribution of industry policy and the development areas could not manage without them.

Nevertheless, as *Keeble* (Cambridge) indicated, there are regional variations in branch plants. Although difficult to measure, the differences appear to lie between those tending to employ female and semi-skilled workers and to be concerned with the production of standardised products, and those which employ higher skills and may even have a research base. The former are disproportionately located in the development areas, where doubtless they play an essential role, but one likely to be less valuable for long-term economic growth than that of branch plants in non-assisted areas. *Gaskin* (Aberdeen) saw the issue in a slightly different light. Experience of American branches in Scotland showed there to be a very high quality of management, but there was a tendency for decision-making, marketing and financial functions to be absent. On the other hand, a beneficial side effect of branch plants is their ability to withstand recessions – possibly because of the protection afforded by being part of a larger corporation.

However, *McEnery* (DTI), while agreeing with all the above statements, insisted that in their most basic form branch plants were useful only in treating the symptoms of problem regions. They did not necessarily attack the disease at the roots by building up the self-generating capabilities of a region. The key issue was whether or not industrial units were 'profits centres'; that is, whether or not they were autonomous. If they were, it made no difference in the regional context who owned them or where the ownership was located.

One way of fostering such profits centres is through the use of the selective-assistance provisions of the 1972 Industry Act. This is complementary to standard incentives and can be given to companies in both manufacturing and services in the assisted areas, as well as to incoming projects from outside the assisted areas. The assistance can take the form of grants or loans in support of viable projects. The criterion is that there should be some benefit to employment, either by creating more jobs or safeguarding existing jobs. Applications are made through the regional industrial development boards set up under the 1972 Act. These also have power to deal entirely with applications for £500,000 or less; larger applications are referred to the Industrial Development Executive in London. Hence the new machinery involves a significant element of devolution for the purpose of promoting industrial expansion and can be used for stimulating 'centres of growth'.

McEnery (DTI) describing the early operations of selective assistance in Yorkshire and Humberside, stated that discrimination had favoured firms with a high potential gain in productivity and establishments with a high component of top management. In particular they were trying to attract headquarters as well as operative processes. It was claimed that £5 million of government selective assistance had attracted £50 million of investment, although it was not clear, as *Cameron* (Glasgow) pointed out, how much of this would have occurred without selective assistance.

Finally, despite all the virtues of selective assistance, Cameron believed it necessary to guard against sweeping generalisations about branch plants. In particular, it was not possible, at this stage, to characterise with any real understanding the nature of decision-making inside branch plants. Research had shown that management varied widely within development areas. Over a ten-year period some branches had remained unchanged; others had changed dramatically, from being simple processing units to becoming innovative, decision-making establishments. So, although selective assistance could be used to attract the latter type, it was also important to understand how plants could evolve over time and perhaps to use inducements to bring about changes in the desired direction.

Spatial selectivity and planning for decline

Notwithstanding the provisions for selective assistance and the encouragement of 'centres of growth' in the 1972 Act, British regional policy and planning have tended to steer away from the problems of discrimination on a sub-regional scale. The planned depopulation of stranded areas has been confined to a few cases, notably in the Durham coalfield, and the designation of areas for assistance has taken on a broad-brush approach. On the other hand, the areas for which the largest inducements are available to attract industry (the special development areas) are among those with the smallest prospects of self-sustaining growth.

To *Moseley* (UEA), this situation was anomalous. He suggested that a link exists between the process of regional development and the need to plan for decline. It seemed rational to put forward the hypothesis that the pattern and extent of urbanisation within regions had a significant influence on their growth potential. It was instructive, for example, that the Hardman Report on the location of civil service departments had advised, as possible destinations for offices dispersed from the South East, cities having − or planned to have − populations of more than 200,000; there was only one exception, Norwich, and this had other advantages which offset its slight shortfall in size. He was led to question, therefore, whether there should not be a shift from blanket policies towards a policy based on an urban strategy, which would require a redrawing of areas for assistance based on their growth potential.

This, of course, would still leave the thorny problem of how to deal with areas of decline. *Allen* (Glasgow) insisted that the word 'decline' would not be politically acceptable, and preferred the Swedish use of 'balanced contraction'. The required policy for such areas was a humanitarian one. Planned decline imposes costs on the people remaining in an area, through a fall in the level and quality of services. There could be ways of compensating these people without incurring the real resource cost of putting in new or replacement services.

Thus, if the areas discriminated against could be adequately compensated (which may appear nonsensical but is not, because discrimination and compensation would involve different resources and methods of complementation), the arguments for spatial selectivity become strong. *Boudeville* (Paris) believed it was necessary for Europeans to think of themselves as developing countries if they wanted to make progress towards long-term modifications in their structure. In Europe he saw good planning of region based on objective analysis of public infrastructure but rather weak spatial—national planning in relation to industrial productivity. There was a lack of coordination between these two aspects of planning. In France the first is linked mostly with the Plan and the second with DATAR.

However, spatial selectivity, whether or not based on growth centres and planned decline, would be surrounded by difficulties. An obvious one is the unwillingness of areas to be discriminated against, a problem which *Goddard* (LSE) suggested could be surmounted by preserving blanket assistance but having a hierarchy of objectives associated with each region, based on the growth potential of its different parts. But, while such an honest approach might have attractions its very openness would make it unworkable. *Feinstein* (DTI) pointed to the difficulties of administering such plans and ensuring not only that the resources are available for their fulfilment but also that such resources go to the right places at the right time. In addition local authorities had a role to play and they might choose to follow a path which counteracted the grand strategy.

Environmental issues

In a small country where past development has left many poor urban landscapes and where modern development often means an obtrusion of steel and machinery into areas of natural beauty, the management of environmental resources must take on a special significance. The question is whether this issue has any major importance for regional policy, or whether it should be treated separately, perhaps as a series of *ad hoc* decisions to be taken when large projects are proposed, such as the third London airport, motorways across the Chilterns, mining in Snowdonia, or oil bases in northern Scotland.

There is, of course, one policy instrument relating to environmental improvement, in the form of assistance for the clearance of derelict land, some of which has been used to provide valuable recreation space in urban areas. This led *McEnery* (DTI) to point out that in industrial regions the conflict between environmental quality and industrial growth was increasingly more apparent than real because of technological progress. Thus the government's £15 million scheme for the wool textile industry, which included aid for anti-pollution equipment, the destruction of outworn industrial premises, the building of new ones, and the use of technology, would bring great improvements in what had been a blighted environment in parts of Yorkshire.

However, *Clayton* (UEA) noted a dichotomy in the treatment of urban and rural areas. People concerned with urban areas were looking ahead to the future and seeing what they could create that would be effective and workable. But the tendency of bodies with rural interests — such as the Nature Conservancy and the Countryside Commission — was to look back to a past which, in any case, was a historical accident, and talk about retention of values. Discussing the relationship between regional planning and attitudes to regional environments Clayton criticised the parochial attitudes which appear to predominate. Things are preserved in one area which tend to be common elsewhere. Hence there was a need for a national plan and national designation. Parenthetically, he also observed that the process could be usefully applied on an international scale. At the regional level there were other matters that could be appropriately dealt with, such as recreation planning, the designation of country parks and the reclamation of industrial landscapes.

Despite the elegance of this formula, *Lord Zuckerman* (UEA) sustained the argument that in some cases industrial and environmental objectives are irreconcilable and force a difficult choice. But the options had to be defined, as did the people upon whom the onus of choice lay. Experience had so far shown no way of giving a proper weight to environmental factors and there was no definitive answer to whether one should internalise or externalise their costs. Quoting the case of the enquiry concerning mining in Snowdonia, of which he had been chairman, he repeated that about £200 million of investment had been kept out of a part of Wales where social and economic conditions were bad and there was no likelihood of any other source of such capital. But the minerals could not be moved away, to be mined elsewhere. The implications, therefore, are quite serious. If a part of a development area has a chance to raise its standard of living (albeit by affecting the environment) ought that opportunity to be denied?

The coherence of policies and objectives

Planning and policy-making are fluid processes. As conditions change, so do the goals of society. The converse also applies: new goals can demand changed conditions. Hence the need for continuous review and adaptation of policies and plans. But it is not just a question of the obsolescence of old plans and their entire replacement. New ideas need to be placed in an existing framework of policies, plans and institutions. Innovations have to be handled carefully, therefore, in order not to lose the overall coherence, or more positively, to improve what has already been achieved. This raises three major issues. First, there is a need for objectives to be well specified and quantifiable. Secondly, there is a need for policies and policy instruments which do, in fact, lead to objectives being achieved; if these cannot be devised it may become necessary to revise objectives. Thirdly, there is a need for proper integration of policies, plans and objectives at the different levels — national, regional and local.

The first of these has attracted increasing attention. As *Diamond* (LSE) outlined in his paper at least half-a-dozen regional objectives have been put forward and *Cameron* showed that, to be met, these could require the creation of a million new jobs in the development areas over a very short period. The magnitude of the tasks, and the difficulty of finding the resources to achieve them must cast doubts on whether the objectives should not be reviewed. However, successive governments have preferred to pursue the second issue, devising new policy instruments and increasing the level of assistance for industrial development.

The third issue was seen to provide a greater challenge, involving a dialogue between different government departments as well as between government and the regions. *Boudeville* (Paris) described the French situation as being one where there were regional policies with regional objectives. However, he considered that this would be easier to achieve in France than in Britain, owing to the differences in administrative and executive powers at the regional level. *McEnery* (DTI) found this difficult to accept. The regional strategies produced in Britain were coherent documents which were only promulgated after they had been to the Department of the Environment and other relevant departments had been consulted. More precise objectives were then worked out within the region.

But *Diamond* (LSE) regarded this as only half the problem. He did not deny that there was a good and evolving dialogue within regions and between an individual region and government, but the process was piecemeal, taking one region at a time. *Crum* (UEA) supported this, stating that there was no way of knowing whether the populations forecast by plans in aggregate would exceed the total actually occurring and whether they implied resources greater than could be provided. Similarly, there was a plan for motorway networks but it was not known whether it was linked to ideas on the location of airports.

White (DOE) was concerned to take a balanced view, tracing the evolution of integrated planning and policy-making. Local planning after 1947 had been based on individual units — the boroughs and counties — but within a decade it had been realised that proposals in any one development plan often vitiated the benefits which would arise from the implementation of a neighbouring plan. With this there had been a move from the local to the regional level, attempting to secure coordination and harmonisation. In one sense a similar development had occurred in the treatment of assisted areas, which now covered entire standard regions instead of a dispersed set of small areas. Regional planning was a child of the 1960s and the stage had been reached at which all the relevant aspects of a region were put into a single coherent document laying out the broad strategy for its development. There was now evidence of a new stage, that of inter-regional competition for scarce resources. So the point had been reached, in regional planning, at which we had been over a decade ago in local planning. The challenge to government was to achieve a similar integration at this enlarged scale, in the form of a national plan for urban and regional development.

Policy-oriented research

Conceivably, changes in policies could be made on the whims of politicians and there have indeed been cases when promises have been made which required validation later. But usually the process of change is a careful one. based on what can be broadly described as research. In his paper, *Townroe* (UEA) described the various origins of research activity and some of its relationships with policy, sounding a note of caution about the formulation of researchable questions and listing what he considered to be some current priorities. While research was not always necessary to identify broad problems it was needed to delineate and quantify them more exactly. Researchability was an operational problem as well as a conceptual one, often dependent on data of the right type and quantity. Townroe cited as an example the problem of congestion in south east England. It is commonly considered that the costs to the nation of letting the South East expand without constraint would outweigh the benefits. But there was no proof that this would be so. To get the proof would require massive resources and, even if the manpower and the funds were available, there was no certainty that the right answer would be forthcoming.

Bird (DOE) suggested that the gap between research and policy formulation arose partly because of their different time dimensions. Research was concerned with present conditions and what had led up to them; policy was concerned with the future. Thus policy was surrounded by uncertainties of a kind which researchers rarely experience. Other problems also existed. Often in the research of social scientists there were assumptions and implicit value judgements which had to be identified and evaluated by policy-makers before the conclusions could be adopted. A similar constraint was imposed by the tendency for research to be carried out within limited boundaries. It was necessary to look at the sectoral and spatial repercussions of a proposal.

Boudeville (Paris) interposed that it was possible to carry out research on both structures and value systems. The first research could try to link factorial structure analysis with di-graph structure; the second, objective structure analysis of PRDE and OREAM with the two previous ones. The urban and regional study group of the University of Paris (Sorbonne) was working on this subject.

Keeble (Cambridge) raised a practical issue arising from the conduct of research in universities. Traditionally much of this work was stimulated from grass-roots level by research students and academics; very little was commissioned by government bodies or other institutions. One possibility to change this might lie with more directed supervision, to encourage research students to give more attention to policy-oriented questions. Also, the subject committee of the Social Science Research Council might impose a more selective approach to the award of research grants.

Donnison (CES) was sceptical about anxieties to steer research in any particular direction within the universities. There had been remarkably little evaluation of the contribution of research to policy-making. His own findings were that research early in a career was a crucial part of an academic education but the topics studied were not of critical importance. By the time an academic could be influential the problems had changed. Nor should there be too much concern for interdisciplinary research. His impression was that the best research had come from individuals firmly based in their own disciplines who recognised that no one discipline could solve all problems, were willing to learn from others and also exposed their work to the criticism of professional colleagues in their own specialism.

Research is an international activity. With few exceptions there is little to prevent ideas in one country being transmitted to another, although linguistic barriers may slow the diffusion. A suggestion in Townroe's paper was taken up by *Goddard* (LSE), namely that British research on regional structures and development ought to forge more links with European than with North American research. The difference which characterised the approaches on these two continents was the extent to which research had a specific policy orientation. In North America emphasis had lain on explaining the existing situation. This led to a danger of planning based on trends, whereas there was a need for more emphasis on understanding the consequences of current processes with respect to social goals which, to a greater extent, had been the European approach. However, *Allen* (Glasgow), relating these comments to Britain's membership of the EEC, warned against being over-excited by the prospect of being able to learn from the policies and research carried out in the Community. Studies in any one country were coloured by the conditions in that country and their conclusions were not necessarily transferable to another.

Goddard (LSE) continued to argue for a normative approach to research, particularly with respect to technological change and its regional impact. In the field of telecommunications it was known that innovations tended to go first to areas of greatest demand and then to filter down the system. This was a basis for inertia in regional disparities. If it were possible to forecast technological change and apply this to regional policy, it might be possible to change the pattern of development. *Diamond* (LSE) preferred to go a step further, stating that a truly civilised society would ask what sort of technological change it wanted and choose one which gave rates and patterns of change which were desirable.

Epilogue

That there is a need for regional policy now goes without saying. The latest in a long line of justifications came when Britain joined the European Economic Community. It requires little imagination to see that organisation failing in its long-term aspirations unless it develops realistic policies to be implemented at the regional level.

What is equally clear, from the foregoing papers and discussion, is that even after four decades the possibilities for policy-making and implementation are far from exhausted. Partly this is because, as Allen states in his paper, regional problems, like the poor, will always be with us: no sooner is one problem 'solved' than another raises its head. But there is also growing awareness that the conventional approach, via industrial redistribution, only provides limited success, not only in Britain but also in other EEC countries. Thus a strong case can be made for at least investigating other policies to augment (rather than to replace) what presently exists. One such possibility, discounted in the past in the UK because it was supported by crude arguments, lies in studying the roles of migration and occupational change in regional development.

It has been stated elsewhere in this volume that businessmen welcome stability in regional policy. That may be so but we should beware of using this as an argument against research and innovation in order to improve upon the existing situation. Indeed, until we have policies which are generally satisfactory (which may be never) anything else can only be regarded as transitional.

List of Contributors

Lord Zuckerman, Professor at Large, University of East Anglia

Kevin Allen, Department of Social and Economic Research, University of Glasgow

Professor J. R. Boudeville, Department of Economic Sciences, University of Paris, 1

Professor G. C. Cameron, Department of Social and Economic Research, University of Glasgow

Dr Derek Diamond, Department of Geography, London School of Economics and Political Science

Professor David Donnison, Centre for Environmental Studies, London

Professor Maxwell Gaskin, Department of Political Economy, University of Aberdeen

Dr J. B. Goddard, Department of Geography, London School of Economics and Political Science

L. S. Jay, County Planning Officer, East Sussex County Council

A. G. Powell, Director, Strategic Plan for the North West, Department of the Environment

John Rhodes, Department of Applied Economics, University of Cambridge

J. Allan Stewart, Deputy Director (Economics), Confederation of British Industry

Dr Wolfgang Stabenow, Principal Adviser, Regional Policy Directorate General, Commission of the European Communities, Brussels

P. M. Townroe, School of Social Studies, University of East Anglia

Dr Morgan Sant, Director, Centre of East Anglian Studies, University of East Anglia

List of Discussants

R.A. Bird, Director, East Anglian Strategic Planning Team, Department of the Environment

Professor K. M. Clayton, School of Environmental Sciences, University of East Anglia

R. Crum, School of Social Studies, University of East Anglia

J. A. Denton, Department of the Environment

B. Feinstein, Department of Trade and Industry

Professor F. J. Gay, Centre for Research in Regional Development and Planning, University of Rouen

R. S. Howard, Department of Trade and Industry

Dr D. E. Keeble, Department of Geography, University of Cambridge

J. H. McEnery, Department of Trade and Industry

Dr M. J. Moseley, School of Environmental Sciences, University of East Anglia

D. Saunders, Department of the Environment

M. J. Shaw, Planning Office, Norfolk County Council

R. T. White, Department of the Environment